SHAKESPEARE IN AMERICA

THE MACMILLAN COMPANY
NEW YORK · BOSTON · CHICAGO
DALLAS · ATLANTA · SAN FRANCISCO

MACMILLAN AND CO., LIMITED
LONDON · BOMBAY · CALCUTTA
MADRAS · MELBOURNE

THE MACMILLAN COMPANY
OF CANADA, LIMITED
TORONTO

SHAKESPEARE IN AMERICA

by

Esther Cloudman Dunn

It is to be regretted that some means cannot be discovered whereby the impression which the player makes by his acting could be Daguerreotyped, so that his pictures may be handed down to posterity, that those who follow after us may know what manner of man he was. LIFE AND RECOLLECTIONS OF YANKEE HILL

WILLIAM KNIGHT NORTHALL

The Macmillan Company

New York

1939

PRINTED IN THE UNITED STATES OF AMERICA
AMERICAN BOOK—STRATFORD PRESS, INC., NEW YORK

To the Memory of My Father

CHARLES DUNN, Jr.

Preface

This book is not an exhaustive and complete history of Shakespeare in America since our beginnings. But it is an honest effort to discover truly and accurately how Shakespeare took the emphasis and accent of each succeeding era and of each geographical extension as our country developed from the early seventeenth century down to our own time.

It is written for the general reader. While the author can cite 'chapter and verse' for every statement and fact, these citations have remained in the margins of the manuscript instead of being transferred to footnotes.

The author gratefully acknowledges obligations to books, articles, unpublished theses, to Foundations and Historical Societies, and to the courtesy of a large number of individuals, who have shared their expert knowledge on specific points.

It is impossible to list here all those who have contributed to the body of material behind this book. But to a few, I must render my special thanks: to G. C. Odell's *Annals of the New York Stage*, N. Y., 1927 seq., and O. S. Coad and E. Mims, Jr.'s *The American Stage*, New Haven, 1929; to R. L. Rusk, both for *The Letters of Ralph Waldo Emerson*, N. Y., 1939 and for *The Literature of the Middle Western Frontier*, N. Y., 1925; to S. E. Morison both for *Harvard College in the Seventeenth Century*, Cambridge, 1936, and for *The Puritan Pronaos*, N. Y., 1936; to T. G. Wright's *Literary Culture in Early New*

England, New Haven, 1920; to W. C. Ford's *The Boston Book Market*, Boston, 1917; to P. A. Bruce's *Institutional History of Virginia in the Seventeenth Century*, N. Y., 1910; to R. G. Thwaite's *Early Western Travels*, Cleveland, 1904; to W. H. Venables' *Beginnings of Literary Culture in the Ohio Valley*, Cincinnati, 1891; to Eola Willis's *Charleston Stage in the Eighteenth Century*, Columbia, S. C., 1924; to Dorothy Dondore's *The Prairie and the Making of Middle America*, 1926; to Odell Shepard's *Peddlar's Progress*, Boston, 1937; to Newton Arvin's *Whitman*, N. Y., 1937; to R. W. Babcock's *The Genesis of Shakespeare Idolatry*, Chapel Hill, 1931; to Hazelton Spencer's *Shakespeare Improved*, Cambridge, 1927.

For interpretation of American cultural history, all workers in the field are immeasurably indebted to V. L. Parrington's three magnificent volumes on *Main Currents in American Thought*, N. Y., 1927. Constance M. Rourke's three volumes of sprightly and sensitive interpretation, *Trumpets of Jubilee*, N. Y., 1927, *Troupers of the Gold Coast*, N. Y., 1928, and *American Humour*, N. Y., 1931, have been a constant stimulation. The author's thanks are also due to C. A. and M. R. Beard's *The Rise of American Civilization*, N. Y., 1927, to Van Wyck Brooks's *The Flowering of New England*, N. Y., 1936 and to Lewis Mumford's *The Golden Day*, N. Y., 1926.

For the history of Shakespeare in American education, L. F. Snow's *College Curriculum in the U. S.*, N. Y., 1907, and particularly H. W. Simon's *The Reading of Shakespeare in American Schools and Colleges*, N. Y., 1932 are the key books.

For the history of newspapers and magazines, E. C. Cook's *Literary Influence of Colonial Newspapers*, N. Y.,

1912 was useful. F. L. Mott's three volumes of *A History of American Magazines*, N. Y., 1930 and Cambridge, 1939, and L. N. Richardson's *History of Early American Magazines*, N. Y., 1931 furnished valuable material.

The author wishes to make grateful acknowledgment for material in the following theses, some unpublished: T. C. Pollock's *Philadelphia Theatre in the Eighteenth Century*, Phila., 1933; R. D. James' *Old Drury of Philadelphia*, Phila., 1932; Lucile Gifford's *Material Conditions in the Theatre in New Orleans before the Civil War*, Chicago, M. A., 1925 (unpublished); R. H. Land's *The Theatre in Colonial Virginia*, Univ. of Va., M. A., 1936 (unpublished); P. W. Stoddard's *The Place of the Lyceum in American Life*, Columbia, M. A. in Education, 1928 (unpublished).

Articles of particular value were L. B. Wright's 'The Purposeful Reading of Our Colonial Ancestors' in *ELH*, vol. IV, no. 2, June, 1937; L. B. Wright's 'The "Gentleman's Library" in Early Virginia: The Literary Interests of the First Carters' in *The Huntington Library Quarterly*, vol. I, no. 1, October, 1937; E. E. Willoughby's 'The Reading of Shakespeare in Colonial America' in *The Papers of the Bibliographical Society of America*, vol. XXX, Pt. II, 1936; R. C. Harrison's 'Walt Whitman and Shakespeare' in *Publications of the Modern Language Association*, vol. XLIV, no. 4, 1929. More generally the following periodicals have contributed: *Publications of the Colonial Society of Massachusetts, The New England Quarterly, William and Mary College Quarterly Historical Magazine, Pennsylvania Magazine of History and Biography, Journal of English and Germanic Philology, Studies in Philology, Jahrbuch der Deutschen Shakespeare-Gesellschaft, Edda, American Literature.*

Among contemporary records the author is particularly indebted to N. M. Ludlow's *Dramatic Life as I Found It*, St. Louis, 1880; Sol Smith's *Theatrical Journey Work*, Phila., 1854, and *Theatrical Management in the West and South*, N. Y., 1868; F. A. Kemble's *Records of a Girlhood*, N. Y., 1884, and *Journal*, London, 1835; Joseph Jefferson's *Autobiography*, N. Y., 1889–90; James H. Hackett's *Notes and Comments upon Certain Plays and Actors of Shakespeare*, N. Y., 1863.

The author wishes to thank various persons for their courteous response to letters of inquiry: Joseph Q. Adams, Director of the Folger Shakespeare Library; Randolph G. Adams of the Clements Library, University of Michigan; Henrietta C. Bartlett of New Haven; Dorothy Dondore of Iowa City, who has been a lively correspondent on many points; G. T. Goodspeed of Goodspeed's Bookshop in Boston; R. H. Land of the College of William and Mary, Virginia; Christopher Morley; Kenneth B. Murdock of Harvard; Robert M. Smith of Lehigh; Alfred Westfall of Colorado State Agricultural College; Edwin C. Willoughby of the Folger Shakespeare Library; and Louis B. Wright of the Huntington Library. The author is also indebted to the American Antiquarian Society at Worcester, Mass.; the Boston Athenaeum; the Essex Institute, Salem, Mass.; the Massachusetts Historical Society, Boston.

Dr. J. Q. Adams put several items in the author's way during a profitable trip to the Folger Shakespeare Library in Washington.

The subject of 'Shakespeare in America' has been handled in three separate articles prior to the publication of this book: by G. B. Churchill in *Jahrbuch der Deutschen Shakespeare-Gesellschaft*, vol. XLII, Berlin,

1906; by W. B. Cairns in *Edda*, Bd. 6, 1916; by Ashley
Thorndike in the Annual Shakespeare Lecture of the
British Academy, 1927. For Professor Westfall's forth-
coming *Shakespearean Criticism in America* see Chapter
XIV of this book.

The author wishes to express thanks to the Smith College Library, especially to Mr. Grant McColley and Miss
Amelia Tyler, for promptness and accuracy in securing
books from other libraries to facilitate the research.

ESTHER CLOUDMAN DUNN

Smith College
Northampton, Massachusetts

Contents

Illustrations

SHAKESPEARE IN AMERICA

CHAPTER I

Why Shakespeare in America

WITHIN the last twenty-five years our rosy views of the American past have begun to dissolve. The days of eagle-screaming mythology are over. Even though we were supposed to have 'won' the Great War for Europe by the magic of our last-moment appearance in France, the bitter actualities of the last two decades have dispelled the rainbow round our shoulder. Everyone in America from highest to lowest begins to know this. It is time, more than ever before, to scrutinize, with what honesty and skill we have, our past; to see it, glorious and inglorious, as it probably was. Its social predicaments had their inevitable consequences in the making of America as it now is. Recent historical novels, like *Gone With the Wind* and *Northwest Passage*, are read because they are readable as novels. But also they are read by Americans who are glad to have new light on the social history of particular moments in our past.

The story of Shakespeare in America since the beginning of our history is another way of testing our social and cultural growth. Some magic in his pages, either truly felt or taken for granted, has made Shakespeare, along with the Bible, a constant companion of American development. For the first hundred and fifty years he was a symbol of our English 'home'. That symbol was sometimes honored in the breach. The middle-class refugees from England turned their backs on him as a part of all they dis-

liked. But they turned their backs in full consciousness that
he stood there behind them, inalienably a part of their
English inheritance. The colonists, who kept close to England and followed its cultural dictates, found Shakespeare,
both in the library and on the stage, a bond with life at
home. His wisdom enlightened the vicissitudes of their
days. He had appropriate lines for their diaries and letters.
He comforted their new patriotism and enforced their determination to stand against British tyranny. Until after
the American Revolution, Shakespeare in America was a
provincial echo of Shakespeare in England.

Then, in the new American nation the new social values
began slowly to work on Shakespeare. He was still the
symbol of culture. To own a volume of Shakespeare, or to
see Shakespeare in the theatre, to learn how to declaim his
great speeches in the American public schools, was an obligation. The young eagle screamed deferentially in Shakespeare's blank-verse lines. Though severed from Britain
we still claimed him. The way in which his plays, sometimes 'strangely translated', permeated American life in the
nineteenth century is revealing. It shows exactly our national psychology. We were insecure culturally. We had
to protest, and 'too much', that our culture was of the
first water.

The frequent reading, 'orating', quoting, playing and
studying of Shakespeare was an effective way of asserting our culture. School boys and girls, political orators,
preachers, neighborhood clubs, made him their own. He
echoed along the banks of the Ohio and Mississippi as the
flatboats bore settlers and entertainers westward to the new
frontier. He was familiar in mining camps. His effigy on
the fronts of buildings in Pittsburgh and Chicago looked
down to assure the populace that culture was rampant in

their new world. The best minds were equally occupied with him. To the writings of Emerson and Whitman, he is a constant background. Lincoln tided himself over difficult moments with quotations from Shakespeare.

The appreciation was partly 'pseudo' and partly real. Sometimes Shakespeare, as an interpreter of the human situation, spoke directly to this violent new world. Sometimes 'in a social reality ready at hand . . . the unmeted individualism of the characters could dash itself on the emerging crags of the American temperament'. But at other times, any real communion between Shakespeare and his American public was lacking. He was famous and a good basis for 'spouting', but what he was actually saying, they did not understand. After all, the American temperament was still 'emerging'. In this halfway stage of development, the misunderstanding of Shakespeare is just as interesting, just as significant for the story of our culture, as perfect understanding could be.

His prestige penetrated even the maritime history of our new nation. The 'Shakespeare' was launched at Deer Isle, Maine, in 1816. One reads of the 'Romeo' in 1824; and the North Atlantic Packet ships had a whole 'Dramatic Line' in 1836 sailing to Liverpool. The 'Siddons', the 'Shakespeare' and the 'Garrick' were among their ships. Sometimes, in the great sailing days, Shakespeare had more than the honour of naming a ship. 'Books in whose titles and pages the wind blows where it lists are popular at sea as well as on land', and Shakespeare's plays meet this description. Frank T. Bullen sixty years ago, out of New Bedford on a three-year whaling voyage, records that the only books aboard were 'a Bible, a copy of Shakespeare and a couple of cheap copies of *David Copperfield* and *Bleak House*'.

Lincoln Colcord, who 'was born at sea, the son of a shipmaster and spent the first fifteen years of my life in the cabin and on the quarter deck', writes that a 'complete Shakespeare was always in my parents' library on board ship. . . . I read Shakespeare as a boy on board ship in the China trade and I recall my father's reading him but not aloud. . . . I'd be willing to guarantee that half the shipmasters out of New England carried Shakespeare to sea with them'. This is not only a triumph for Shakespeare's prestige. There was something in his mounting periods, in the heroic despairs and triumphs of his characters, which made good reading in the master's cabin during the long tedious months of a voyage. There exists a copy of Shakespeare with annotations at the end of each play, recording the port or the latitude and longitude where the sailor finished the heroic tale.

Richard Henry Dana, of course, was not primarily a sailor. His *Two Years Before the Mast* records a voyage around the Horn to California. It was but an interim in his undergraduate career at Harvard. But when a Harvard sophomore of the early 1830's set out to sea, Shakespeare was at his elbow to express for him his own poignant feelings. Somewhere on the West Coast near San Juan, California, they were throwing down hides from the top of a cliff to be loaded on the ship. To young Dana's mind occurred the passage in *Lear* where Edgar describes to his father how small the figures look at the bottom of the cliffs of Dover. They

> . . . that walk upon the beach
> Appeared like mice.

When Dana's ship returns to port in fine condition, he

recalls the passage from the *Merchant of Venice* describing the very opposite condition,

> With over-weathered ribs and ragged sails.

When the junior partner of his firm greets him with good news he recalls a different sort of welcome in Second *Henry IV*, I, i. Throughout Dana's famous *Two Years Before the Mast*, his only quotations are these three from Shakespeare. The time was the thirties, and the interweaving of Shakespearean lines in all phases of American life was too close for any gale or any foreign port to dislodge them.

Lewis Mumford has said that 'since the break-up of Mediaeval culture' there has been a tendency for men to subordinate 'the imagination to their interest in practical arrangements'. This is probably as true in America as in the history of any part of the world. Yet the Shakespearean accompaniment to the three centuries of our American life does something to balance the scales. His name has been steadily summoned to show that we value cultural intangibles. Sometimes his penetrating thought and feeling have surged up from the pages to feed the American imagination among the wastes of its material struggle. Often Shakespeare has pointed to the 'part that vision must play in bringing all their practical activities to a common focus'.

CHAPTER II

Shakespeare and the First Hundred Years
of American Colonial Life

THE aftermath of glory is interesting to trace. Shakespeare,
so substantial an expression of his own Elizabethan England, so popular and successful a purveyor of entertainment to all classes of people in the London of 1600, has
possessed the imagination of English-speaking people, both
in England and in America, from that day to this. But
there is unreality about remembrance. The general phrases
of praise continue to be echoed; but the magic of flesh-
and-blood characters speaking warmly, movingly, gaily
to Tom, Dick and Harry, as they paid their ticket money
for standing room or a seat on the stage or a place in the
'Lord's Room', ceased when Shakespeare's play-writing
career ceased. Going to see Shakespeare or buying a
printed version of one of his plays was a perfectly natural
thing to do in his own day. One thought no more of it
than one does now of going to a movie. There was nothing 'cultural' about it. It had none of that smug sense of
self-improvement which insults the imperishable works of
art which have survived their own world. They stand,
unfamiliar, shorn of their natural setting, isolated in some
museum for an alien world to gape at.

Great art pays dearly for its survival beyond its own
day. The Parthenon frieze, or a play by Shakespeare, is
one of the most lonely things on earth. It has survived its
own society, its own *milieu*. It is like an octogenarian, try-

8

ing to be reminiscent with a youth who does not comprehend his customs and way of life.

The history of the attitude toward Shakespeare's plays, both in England and in America, in the three and one-third centuries since he ceased his career as a popular and successful playwright, is a history of the overemphases and distortions which are bound to attend the survival of art beyond its own social setting. His plays and the impact of his personality, his magical sureness of touch in re-creating and revealing the meaning of life in all its aspects, trivial and important, have never been entirely forgotten. There have been periods when he was overestimated, admired for the wrong things, played with the wrong emphasis, overlaid with a burden of false adulation which had nothing to do with his art. He has been misquoted, turned orator, asked, through the mouth of this character or that, to pronounce laws of conduct and behaviour. Individuals and different ages have tried to distort this very Elizabethan personality into that of some utterly alien time. He has been roughly handled by the admiring centuries. All the while his essential greatness has remained inviolate and aloof.

The story of Shakespeare in America from the settlements on the James River and in New England at the beginning of the seventeeth century to the present day has yet to be told. The prejudices and enthusiasms of the sequent decades; the ups and downs of his fame with the ups and downs of political and religious influence; the spread of his reputation with the expansion of our frontiers westward; the different emphasis which different sections of our country inevitably gave to his work; the development of America from a string of colonies closely following English fashions in Shakespeare to an independent nation, still playing and reading Shakespeare, but reading him without benefit of British interpretation; the story of his securing and maintaining an honourable if somewhat boring eminence in the American school and college curriculum—these aspects of Shakespeare in America during the more than three centuries of our national growth make a touchstone for the curves and directions of our cultural evolution.

As soon as Shakespeare ceased to be an active figure in the London theatre world, there was much more written about him and his skill. The books of literary gossip and anecdote are full of legends about him. The first collected edition of his works, begun only three years after he died, was brought out in imposing and expensive form in the famous First Folio, seven years after his death. The expensive format (it probably sold for around five dollars), the portrait frontispiece, the eulogistic preliminary verses, the careful preface, all this pompousness about the First Folio presaged ill. Shakespeare had already become almost a classic. He was being taken seriously by critics and editors. They expected a selected group of readers to pay generously for this huge volume and place it reverently on their library shelves. The First Folio was already false to the actual playwright. The greatness of the plays and the magical power of this man, remembered piously now that he was no more, had stepped in between the true sense of his creations and the readers of these great folio pages in double columns. The red-hot speeches, wittily improvised by his urgent pen, with his eye on the company and the theatre public and tomorrow afternoon's show, were already museum pieces, nobly preserved upon noble and impressive printed pages. Gentle Will and his plays were already in danger of becoming 'literature'.

This reverent effort on the part of Shakespeare's fellows to turn him into literature luckily failed. Though there were three more of these handsome Folios during the century, in '32, '63–'64 and '85, the size of the editions was rather small, and perhaps even these small editions did not sell out. There were rumours that 'numerous unsold copies' of the Third Folio had been destroyed in the great London fire of '66. In spite of the imposing folio format, Shakespeare's Collected Plays did not become very valuable or much sought-after books during the seventeenth century.

Shakespeare himself would have been the first to understand this. If he had been consulted, he would never have advised a collected edition in such handsome form. Like the rest of his world, Shakespeare understood perfectly that plays for the popular stage were one thing and literature as such was something quite else. He had made a bid for literary reputation when he was beginning his career in London. He wrote, in 1593 and '94, two poems on classical themes, *Venus and Adonis* and *The Rape of Lucrece*. He had each of them printed by a reputable printer and dedicated them both in careful prefatory letters to the Earl of Southampton, a well-known and munificent patron of the arts. These poems are not great art. At the time they were issued, Shakespeare already had some very good plays to his credit. But it never would have occurred to him to use the plays he was writing for the public theatres in London as a passport to literary reputation. They were as necessary for making money and as transient as the script of a movie today. In the perspective of time there is something ironic about this. There he was, producing plays which are now considered among the finest pieces of English literature. But then, they were simply not considered by him as things which could give him distinction in the literary world.

It was not that plays, as such, were outside the pale of 'literature'. If one imitated a Latin play of Seneca or did an allegorical play for a University festivity or translated a classical play, one might easily claim literary recognition for it. In fact such plays were frequently written at Oxford and Cambridge. They followed the ancient rules, were careful academic exercises, showed learning but not a whit of creative ability in the way of originality or timeliness. But they were 'in the tradition' and could safely be so recognized. Whereas Shakespeare's plays for the London popular stage were so new, so utterly unlike anything in the traditions of the drama, so instinct with life, so gripping to a mixed audience of all classes and all degrees of education that a good Cambridge don would have found his correct rules for criticizing drama quite useless in appraising these new creations. And if they could not be tested by the rules, they could not be literature.

As has been quite usual with universities until this present century, the creators of new tendencies in the arts have had to proceed without the sympathy and understanding of the traditional university taste. Only afterwards, when a new phase in the particular art has been successfully achieved, does the university recognize it. It follows, then, that it was the 'correct' and standard books which people purchased for their libraries. Classics, histories, stage-plays of the ancient world, scientific books, poetry, the Bible. But popular stage-plays, no matter how handsomely printed and bound, or how extravagantly praised by the author's devoted friends in prefatory poems, were not to be taken seriously.

It has been customary to blame the Puritan negations of the early seventeenth century for everything that looks stupid and narrow to our modern eyes. It is not too much to say that whether the Puritan objections to the theatre had been made or not, Shakespeare's plays stood very little chance of being regarded as great literature. That the Puritans were against the public stage for a variety of reasons is true. Their opposition simply strengthened the prejudices against popular play-reading.

The Puritan objections to the theatre were not merely on moral grounds. For years before the death of Elizabeth, the City Government of London had been opposed to the public playhouses. Their opposition was based chiefly on practical difficulties. The public playhouses were likely to give opportunity for public disturbances. Quarrelsome, drunken people attending there were likely to start a riot. Also the spread of disease was fostered by such public audiences. Altogether the theatres bothered the city fathers; they presented an awkward problem in policing. This early prejudice against the theatres, on the practical grounds that they made trouble for the government, was increased in the thirty years after Shakespeare's death. As the cleavage between classes, King's men and Puritans, developed into a political struggle leading to Civil War and the temporary domination of the Puritan party, the theatre became more and more identified with the King's party and hence more and more undesirable to the Puritan party. When this party dominated the government and declared by public edict in 1642 that 'public stage-plays shall cease and be foreborne', the long battle against the stage was temporarily won, and it was won quite as much on political and social as on moral grounds.

The situation in America—in Virginia and Maryland

and in Plymouth and the Massachusetts Bay Colony—is in
its essentials very like the situation in England. To be sure
the people who came over as colonists, came to improve
their condition, to get a better place in this new society
than in the old. Some of them, too, came for cause of conscience. But the best and most recent authorities on
America in the seventeenth century are trying to undo
the false emphasis upon Puritanism with which our modern America has been taught to credit its beginnings. True,
the early journals of leaders in Plymouth, like Bradford,
and leaders in Massachusetts Bay, like Winthrop, are
highly religious in tone. The events of daily life are seen
as direct manifestations of the pleasure or displeasure of
Providence. The leaders, having won this new world for
religious liberty, are likely to be dictatorial about that
liberty, to force upon the people ideas of conduct and
church government.

But all this emphasis upon religion in the colonies is
seen more correctly when one remembers that the mother
country itself was in the throes of a violent religious and
political disturbance which was leading rapidly to Civil
War. Religion, in England or in England's colonies, in the
first half of the seventeenth century, was as burning a personal question to every man, of whatever creed or whatever social status, as fascism, communism and democracy
are burning questions in our world today. It was a period
of flux, of ominous uncertainty. Old standards were giving way; each man was trying to hold his footing and
clarify in his own mind his course from day to day. Our
popular idea of the American Puritans as a humorously
stern set of psalm-singers is entirely wrong. They simply
expressed, a trifle more sharply because they were iso-

lated against a strange, untamed landscape, phases of the religious and political turmoil which was affecting life 'at home'.

Thinking people of all parties were not stocking their libraries with stage-plays. They were not interested in them. The first half of the seventeenth century and the first third of the twentieth century are notably alike in the number of *serious* books on politics, philosophy, science, and religion (or its modern equivalents) which were generally read. A terrible urgency came upon the individual to *find out* what the world was about, to postulate what would be likely to happen, to see, as far as one could, how one's own poor little life could survive in this chaotic period. One is not surprised to find that the only university man in the Plymouth Colony, William Brewster, left, at his death in 1643, substantial books on voyaging, history—both world history and English history—and the Renaissance equivalent to Marx, Machiavelli on the theory of the state. Nor is one in the least surprised *not* to find Shakespeare there. Dramatic pageants for royal entertainment were included, showing that 'literary drama' was perfectly acceptable to a Pilgrim father. But popular stage-plays had no standing and were of no aid in the serious reading which the times provoked.

John Harvard, trained at Emmanuel College, Cambridge, England, came to the Massachusetts Bay Colony in 1637, as a young Puritan divine of thirty years. Harvard's name is of romantic significance in this chapter. Dying in 1638, the very next year after his arrival in America, he bequeathed his library of four hundred books and one-half of his estate to the new college for which the General Court of Massachusetts had already appropriated £400. The authorities decided to name the college after the generous donor, and thus Harvard came by its name and its first considerable collection of books. That collection was practically destroyed in the Harvard Library fire of 1764, but by skillful reconstruction a large number of the titles are known. They were, to be sure, nearly three-quarters theological. After all, Harvard's profession was divinity.

But among the other quarter, one finds most of the outstanding titles of the time on cultural and social problems. The witty and teasing discussions on all sorts of social questions which Erasmus had reproduced in his *Colloquies* are distinctly the reading of an intellectual liberal. These *Colloquies of Erasmus* were in Harvard's library. Camden's historical material on men and history in Britain's past, the *Remaines*, were there, too. The worldly and voluminous correspondence between Roger Ascham and the most famous scholars and statesmen all over Europe was included. The classics include Homer in an English translation (probably by the Elizabethan Chapman whose spacious English rendering so moved Keats a couple of centuries later). The worldly and often slightly salacious Latin comedy writers, Plautus and Terence, were there. The English translation of Greek and Roman history which Shakespeare used for his Roman plays, North's English version of Plutarch, was also in John Harvard's library. There was even a copy of a Cambridge University play, one of those frigid, correct performances written according to the literary rules and thoroughly acceptable to professorial Cambridge, though quite unreadable and unactable, in the lively sense of these words. But of course there was no Shakespeare. Popular stage-plays had not sufficient dignity and standing yet to win admission to a Cambridge divinity student's library, or to most gentlemen's libraries, regardless of their leanings toward divinity.

Yet the closeness of certain places and events in John Harvard's early life in England to William Shakespeare's lends romantic suggestiveness to the coupling of these two names. Of course John Harvard was a much younger man. He was born in Southwark very near Shakespeare's Globe Theatre in 1607, when Shakespeare was at the height of his career. *Lear* was just behind him, and the magnificent *Antony and Cleopatra* was probably in process of writing. There is absolutely no direct evidence of a connection between Shakespeare and the Harvard household in Southwark. But certainly it does set one's imagination building possibilities to know that this baby of 1607, John Harvard, had a mother, born a Rogers, who had grown up in Stratford and been married from Shakespeare's Stratford Church, Holy Trinity, in 1605. The Rogerses were people of importance in Stratford as the Shakespeares were. The father had succeeded well enough as 'a market-man, provision dealer and butcher' to be chosen bailiff and to build himself a handsome house in the High Street. Shakespeare's father, of course, was a bailiff also. Charles Rogers, one of the sons, was about the same age as Shakespeare and would have gone to the same Stratford Grammar School at the same time. The two mothers went to the same church. Nothing is more natural, remembering the strong evidence of Shakespeare's close feeling throughout his London career for himself as a Stratford man, than to suppose that Shakespeare would have known about young Katherine Rogers marrying Robert Harvard. Furthermore she came to settle in

Southwark where Shakespeare's theatre was, and had there her first child, John Harvard, in 1607.

As young John Harvard grew up, this William Shakespeare, old Stratford family friend of his mother's, would have seemed to the young man merely a famous old London entertainer, who had died when Harvard was nine years old, who had had a great popular reputation in the roaring days of Queen Elizabeth, before Harvard was born. But to this young Harvard, as a student at Emmanuel College, earnest and ambitious of learning and influence, forming a library, dreaming of coming out to America for a new and wider range of influence and opportunity, it would never have occurred to invest five dollars in a collected edition of this man's public plays.

How necessary it is to revise our perspective upon Shakespeare, before we pronounce judgment upon the seventeenth century libraries of America for not having copies of his works. Our idea of him was not theirs and could not be theirs for a thousand reasons. Time alone can bring perspective and can establish the permanence, the intrinsic value in things which under the pressure of momentary circumstances and prejudices are temporarily obscured. It is, I believe, wrong to say of Harvard's library that 'English literature and history find scant place' there. The fact is true; but the implication that Harvard's narrowness, his Puritanical bigotry are responsible for it, is not true. In a library of cultural and improving books, Shakespeare's collected plays were not likely, in that period, to have a place.

Yet how contradictory and uncertain all conclusions from this scanty evidence are bound to be. It is unwise to be too sure of anything when three centuries have rolled between the America we are trying to reconstruct and the present day. In the first place it was a colonial world, separated by weeks of rough sea-voyaging from the centre of civilization, somewhat constricted in material goods, somewhat too occupied, perforce, with settling and developing and evolving towns and roads and buildings. Altogether it was a world not old enough to have earned the right to leisure, nor in a mood to want it. For every colonial enterprise is undertaken by energetic people, doers, strugglers for position, security. This condition brought about a strict regard for those books that were most useful. Also there was a much greater chance for destruction, in the movings and comings and goings of this new-world life. What is most misleading of all is the fact that the articulate people, those who have left a record of their libraries and their taste, were likely to be not entirely representative. In New England they were the theocrats, the religious and political leaders whose pronouncements for public consumption were likely to show only those parts of themselves which were consistent with their avowed social standards. It is probable, therefore, that any conjectures one draws from the accidental and scanty evidence will be well 'off centre'. But let us, with these precautions, attempt the impossible.

Contrary to one's expectation, Shakespeare appears among the records of the Cottons. John Cotton (the first of that great New England dynasty) 'though he was bred in Elizabethan days', says Parrington, 'and entered college when Shakespeare's *Henry IV* and Jonson's *Every Man in His Humour* first appeared on the stage' . . . [shows] 'no touch of Renaissance splendour in his crabbed style and ascetic reasoning'. One reads this, at this distance, and says to oneself inwardly: 'Well, a Cotton was a Cotton. There's your bedrock of Puritan New England!' Yet how falsely simple to make one man's austerities cover his whole family or make him typical of his world. While John Cotton was on voyage to America a son was born and appropriately named Seaborn Cotton. He grew up in this Puritan New England and graduated from Harvard in 1651. The book in which, as an undergraduate, he copied passages that he liked has survived. As S. E. Morison has shown, it contains some two hundred closely written pages of *flores* from contemporary poets and prose writers. Herrick, Spenser, Sidney and passages of 'downright Elizabethan bawdry are what catch the eye of these sons of Puritan parsons'. For instance, Seaborn Cotton copied out the lovely lyric from Shakespeare's *Measure for Measure*, which begins,

Take, O, take those lips away.

To be sure he gets it from an anthology published in London in 1641. But he gets it, copies it, reads it over. This business of what one reads, clearly comes down to the individual and what he can lay hands on. Whether the world three hundred years later knows that he read it is entirely a matter of chance.

Shakespeare turns up, also, in the commonplace book of another Harvard student in this century. Elnathan Chauncy quotes an ingenious figure of speech from Shakespeare's *Venus and Adonis*, though he quotes it from an anthology. These poor little undergraduate notebooks of Cotton and Chauncy have assumed an importance out of all proportion to their intrinsic worth. The reason is that time and change have spared them to us. They are fossilized bits of that everyday world three centuries away, which modern scholars stubbornly and with almost inevitable defeat attempt to re-create. Yet because John Cotton's library titles are known and his son Seaborn Cotton's commonplace book is known, and because the literary taste in the two is widely divergent, we have a warning against making easy assumptions about Shakespeare in early seventeenth century New England. If he was disregarded by Cotton *père*, his amorous lines were worth copying and preserving to Cotton *fils*.

Another pair of opposites confronts us. Increase Mather made a list of the books in his library in 1664. It contains all the expected titles: Milton, Herbert, Bacon, Fuller, author of the *Holy and Profane State*, and a good larding of the classics including Latin and Greek stage-plays, which were safely remote from the popular Elizabethan stage-plays of one William Shakespeare. This list runs true to form and presents just about what we should expect. But in the very next year, according to T. G. Wright, a certain Thos. Grocer, 'a London trader who had dealt with Barbadoes', had bought 'as a venture' a library. It is probably just as 'typical' as Increase Mather's. But it offers an entirely different sort of titles. It includes three of the most famous Elizabethan novels, as well as Montaigne, Burton's *Anatomy of Melancholy* and '9 paper bookes of Manuscripts', the contents of which were more probably 'profane' than 'holy'.

Writers on the seventeenth century in New England differentiate the spirit of the two halves: the first was liberal; the second constricted and narrow. True, the Restoration of Charles II to the throne in England in 1660 probably did mark the end, in the mother country, of liberal and ennobling aspects of Puritanism. New England must have felt the change bitterly. The home government which had been growing increasingly sympathetic, at least in principle, since 1620, was now definitely ended. A

new royal set, definitely French and worldly in point of
view, was in power. This probably made New England
draw in upon itself and hold more tenaciously and un-
bendingly to the restrictions and limitations of the Puritan
idea. Parrington calls the period between 1660 and 1720
'the twilight of the oligarchy' and notes that 'with the
passing of the emigrant generation, a narrow provincialism settled upon the Commonwealth of Massachusetts
Bay'. 'The horizons of life', he says, 'were contracting to
a narrow round of chores and sermons.'

This is probably a fair general statement. Yet no general
statement will exactly cover the situation. The number of
books imported into New England in the last part of the
century increased. John Dunton, the London bookseller,
who visited Boston in '86, records the frivolous taste of a
lady customer who called for 'Plays and Romances which
to set off the better, she would ask for books of gallantry'.
The actual invoices of books to Boston bear out this fact.
Usher, the Boston bookseller, received 'on sale' from London in '82 an invoice with some titles of light reading,
including Deloney's citizen novels and the Arcadian romances of Sidney and others.

This same Usher's connections with publishers and
importations of books are interesting. One of the chief
London publishers, says W. C. Ford, from whom Usher
imported was Richard Chiswell. To be sure, Chiswell was
chiefly interested in theology and was, therefore, the natural book advisor to Increase Mather who bought many
theological books. The largest number of titles Usher imported from him were theological. Yet this same Chiswell
in 1685 was one of the four who issued the Fourth Folio
edition of Shakespeare. The last surviving itemized list

of books sent out from Chiswell to Usher is for April, 1685, 'by the *Elizabeth*, Peter Bolles, Master'. There is no Shakespeare in this list. But one is tempted to argue for the possibility of a Fourth Folio being sent later, either to Usher or directly to some private buyer. The grounds of supposition are interesting. Chiswell's connections with Boston were strong. The religious books, which he dealt in and which he imported, do not argue that his activities excluded other literature. Theology was simply the best seller. The fact that a publisher of theological books took on Shakespeare's Fourth Folio, in 1685, shows that the century is getting old. Shakespeare as 'literature' now stands some chance of emerging, bereft of his unsavory 'stage' connections. Usher might easily, therefore, have imported a copy of Chiswell's new publishing venture, Shakespeare's Fourth Folio.

In any case, the world and its pomps were not eschewed by either Usher or Chiswell. When Usher was in London in 1677 or '78 he arranged through Chiswell to buy an imposing coach and harness to be sent over from London for resplendent use in Boston. W. C. Ford has discovered the letter which Chiswell wrote Usher regarding the shipment (from London, May 4, 1675). It will bear quoting.

We have at last shipt off your coach but could not get it into the hold of any, but a mast ship, and therefore by Mr. John Ives' advice it was put on board the Black Cock, Captain Cook, Master.

It was an impressive affair with 'two pairs of harnesses and toppings and odd glass for the door and case for the coach'. A man with such a taste for the appurtenances of his private life may well have carried in stock the latest elegant venture in publishing by his London publisher-friend in 1685. That would have been Shakespeare's Fourth Folio.

One may say that all this is idle supposition. If Shakespeare as a title is not present in the book lists that survive from the New England of the late seventeenth century, then Shakespeare was not read. But such a conclusion is not necessarily true. There are too many chances of titles and book-owner's lists which have not survived; there are too many records of books not itemized by title; there are too many casual hints of lighter reading. Certainly the reading of Shakespeare was not common. His thought did not permeate the age as it has done succeeding ages. But to say this is simply to say what was already true in England, though to a lesser extent. Shakespeare's work in the century after he died enjoyed no such general reputation as the later centuries have gradually heaped upon it.

S. E. Morison makes an interesting test of the generality of books among all classes in New England. 'A tabulation of the inventories of estates in the probate records of Middlesex and Essex counties, by Dr. Shipton, shows a surprisingly large proportion of the population owning books. The Essex estates include many of which the inventories have disappeared and a considerable number of estates in both counties were left by fishermen, servants and poor widows.'

This general study of the book world in New England in the late seventeenth century furnishes a background for the famous problem of Cotton Mather and his possible ownership of a First Folio of Shakespeare. The tradition is persistent. Only in 1937, the First Folio in question changed hands again and is, at this present writing, believed to be in the possession of Mr. A. S. W. Rosenbach. The history of the tradition is worth pausing over. It was known as early as 1874 when Mr. Justin Winsor, Librarian of Harvard, recorded this copy in a census of First Folios of Shakespeare. Again in 1902, Sir Sidney Lee, reaffirmed the tradition. The copy was at that time in the possession of Amos Prescott Baker, Esq., of Boston. This Amos Prescott Baker, by ins and outs of family connection, stemmed from Mather. Lee's account of the connection is as follows: 'While in the possession of a female descendant of Mather, a child tore five leaves from the volume. This owner presented it to her son-in-law, whose adopted daughter gave it in 1864 to her nephew, the present owner' [that is, Baker]. In spite of a good deal of skirmishing, new authority for this tradition has not been secured. But if Mather owned a copy of Shakespeare, it would not be surprising. For, as E. E. Willoughby has pointed out, 'Shakespeare was gradually being regarded primarily as a poet'. The evil aura of the 'stage' was growing fainter. Or, as Willoughby again suggests, 'Mather's concern with Shakespeare may have been merely controversial'. In any case the picture of Cotton Mather poring over the pages of Shakespeare's First Folio is too good to lose, especially since it hangs upon a persistent tradition lasting right up to the present moment.

In writing about our American past, it used to be the fashion to ascribe to New England and Virginia absolutely different cultures. New England was settled, it used to be said, by Puritan people, mostly middle-class (whatever that nebulous word was supposed to mean); whereas Virginia was settled by royalists, by gentlemen of the Church of England with generous ideas of living for themselves, a chivalrous code of behaviour, a sophisticated eye for the elegant externals of existence.

If this were true it would follow that Shakespeare would stand somewhat more chance in seventeenth century Virginia libraries than in those of Boston. But recent authorities on the cultural history of America have shown that so far as the first hundred and fifty years of American life is concerned, this supposed cleavage in class and taste between New England and the South is largely a myth. By the middle of the eighteenth century, twenty-five years before the Revolution, the development of the plantation way of life and the code of manners and standard of culture that went with it certainly did differentiate the South from the North. But for the first hundred and fifty years over here, the cultural situation in New England and Virginia was somewhat the same.

To be sure, the colonists in Virginia were, so far as religion went, likely to be supporters of the Church of England, so that certain religious accents of Puritan New England were not paralleled in the South. But the enormous upheaval in religious belief which had finally severed England from a thousand years of thinking along Catholic ways was only sixty or seventy years back of the colonization of America. Such a violent wrench, after so long a conformity to one set of beliefs about man in relation to eternity, was bound to be felt for many decades. Both believers and non-believers, in England and in the English colonies, thought much and talked much about religion throughout the seventeenth century. It touched their personal safety and welfare; the confusion caused by a break with religious tradition made it necessary to think things out afresh. That is why there is such a wealth of books dealing with religion and why both New England and Virginia, though differing in particular church allegiance, read these religious books avidly.

Economically and socially the two groups had many points in common. While the early settlers in Virginia expected to improve their economic condition and then, perhaps, return to England, the New Englanders had turned their backs upon England and meant to carve out life newly for themselves in the new world. But both groups socially belonged to that section of English society which must strive for itself, which sought to better the very modest or even distressing economic and social circumstances which life in England offered. The great Cavaliers and the great Puritans of social importance and fortune were naturally not the ones to emigrate into a new and hard existence. Money making, therefore, or its equivalent, and the bettering of one's modest lot were prime motives both North and South. What this meant and always means is a relatively small amount of time, energy and interest for cultural subjects. There were few cultural libraries, and a very slender chance for the expensive folios of Mr. William Shakespeare. Yet Shakespeare's ghost hovers on the fringes of the seventeenth century South.

One must keep in mind the enormous element of chance that works both for and against anything like a fair estimate, at this long distance, of the Shakespearean situation. So very few carefully itemized lists of books were likely to have been made; and of these few, it is the merest chance that any survive. How many grandchildren of present twentieth century Americans who own books will be likely to know whether grandmother possessed and, still more problematical, read a copy of Shakespeare? And if this is true in our age which so nauseatingly records itself with the aid of every kind of mechanical contrivance, what of Virginia in the 1600's?

By a careful study of wills and bequests, deposited in

the county records of Virginia in the seventeenth century, Philip A. Bruce has found plenty of evidence that the Virginians owned books and thought enough of them to bequeath them. He says: 'I have gleaned from the records that have come down . . . sufficient evidence at least to show that there were many owners of books in each county: and that the whole number of books to be found in the Colony amounted to many thousand volumes'. Following this suggestion I have gone through several seventeenth century wills which contain bequests of books. I have found entries, general in nature, unspecified in title, in some of which it is not too fantastic to imagine a Shakespeare.

For instance, in the will of Col. Ralph Wormeley, born in England, 1650, matriculated at Oxford in 1665, coming to Virginia as a member of the Virginia Council and Secretary of the Colony and dying there in 1701, there are the following items:

Books
In Madam Wormeley's closet, books inventoried not valued . . . fifty comedies and tragedies in folio.

One of these folios, containing thirty-six comedies and tragedies, might well have been a folio of Shakespeare's collected plays.

Among the books in Esq. Wormeley's closet, inventoried not valued, were, according to the entry, 'six new plays'. These, being 'new', were likely to be Restoration plays which the Colonel had perhaps witnessed in England. But the entry, in itself, shows no discrimination against plays as suitable for his library. The inventory of books

belonging to Mr. Samuel Ball, taken March, 1690–91, is
also suggestive. It reads:

19 books, some quarto, some octavo, all old . . . 2 English
books in folio; 30 small Latin books some in folio, some
in quarto, all old . . . 29 books in quarto unbound.

Though we know nothing of Mr. Ball and his tastes, there
is a chance that one of these folios or one of these 'quartos
unbound' might be Shakespeare. In the inventory of William Colston who died in 1701, there is an item reading:
'in the closet by the chimney in the Hall, one hundred
books of all sorts'. One surely can let his fancy roam under
the stimulus of this item. I present these specimens not
as serious arguments for the presence of Shakespeare in
these particular seventeenth century Virginia collections.
Yet they are an indication of how tantalizing, in specific
detail, and how reassuring, on general grounds, the documents are for the presence of books in considerable number and variety in our American seventeenth century
South.

In fact, while reading just such documents, I came upon
one which did contain Shakespeare. It was the inventory
of one Capt. Arthur Spicer, made in 1699. The name
Macbeth (with no further specifications) is sandwiched
in between 'A Dictionary Hollyoke' and 'History of ye
Holy Warr'. The juxtaposition is interesting. This Captain
Spicer was a 'lawyer, justice of the peace and burgess' who
'desires that his son be sent to England for his education'.
One sees here a Virginian closely in sympathy with life
at home, reflecting liberal interest in books both holy
and profane. E. E. Willoughby of the Folger Library, in

an article which came to the author's attention after the above discovery, calls this Spicer *Macbeth* 'the only copy of a Shakespearean play apparently recorded in America in the seventeenth century'. Dr. Willoughby arguing from the fact that the first separate *Macbeth* was published in 1673, postulates that Spicer's copy may be this edition or may be Sir Wm. Davenant's adaptation from Shakespeare, first published in 1674. Thus even Spicer's *Macbeth* may not be Shakespeare 'undefiled'.*

In the library of three generations of Virginia Carters, sprung from 'apparently a distressed royalist who came to Virginia about 1649', Dr. L. B. Wright has found no Shakespeare. Medicine, religion, farming and country life, war and troops, architecture—these are the subjects which predominate. Even in the third generation 'King Carter', who was rich and powerful and lived on into the century, dying in 1732, had in his library very few belletristic books and no Shakespeare. But this, as Wright points out, was the result of the environment and needs. Books on medicine, on government, on law were of practical value in a frontier world where the owner of the great house was called 'King Carter' and, perforce, took on many royal functions in the control of his employees. 'If they knew anything of the works of Chaucer, Spenser, Shakespeare or Milton', says Wright, 'their inventories do not disclose it. . . . Entertainment was clearly not the objective that prompted the accumulation of these books. On the con-

---

* The 'Shakespeare's Works' in the will of Edmund Berkeley, Esq., 1719, may have been a seventeenth century copy. But the title 'Shakespeare's Works' sounds to this author as if it referred to Rowe's edition of 1709 which is distinctly eighteenth century and marks a new era in Shakespearean editorship and reading. See *Wm. and Mary Quarterly Hist. Papers*, Vol. II, Williamsburg, 1893–94, p. 250; and E. E. Willoughby, 'The Reading of Shakespeare in Colonial America', in *Papers of the Bibliographical Society of America*, Vol. XXX, Pt. II, 1936, p. 48.

trary, the Carters' libraries, like most other colonial collections, show a consistent purposiveness.'

While Wright's statement is surely generally true, yet it may possibly be overemphasized. The people who put their books on record were likely to be the more serious people, the people who cheerfully undertook the positions of responsibility and who, therefore, stood as representatives. There is, too, such a strong individual taste reflected in a private library. Right in Virginia, for instance, in the library of a contemporary family of somewhat the same social position as the Carters, namely the Byrds, one finds a greater proportion of *belles lettres*, and a folio of Shakespeare.

The catalogue of books printed at the time of the sale of the Byrd library is dated, to be sure, well toward the end of the eighteenth century, in 1777. In this catalogue under the head 'Entertainment, Poetry, Translations', in 'double presses of black walnut', there are some significant entries. In the 'Eighth Case', there is a lowest shelf, constructed to take books of folio size; then in the 'second shelf' (and also for folio-sized books) there were, among others, three Folios side by side, 'Beaumont and Fletcher's Works, Shakespeare's Works, Ben Jonson's Works'. There is, of course, no absolute proof that these folios of the Elizabethan dramatists existed in the Byrd library before the eighteenth century. But knowing the tastes and lives of the three Byrds, authorities agree on a strong probability that this Shakespeare Folio belonged to the second William Byrd.

He was the second generation of Byrds in Virginia, born there in 1674. He lived, as a young man in the late seventeenth century, much in England, and was a member of the Middle Temple and a Fellow of the Royal Society, where according to his epitaph 'he made a happy proficiency in polite and varied learning'. This Byrd was obviously a different sort of individual from his contemporary Virginians, the Carters. His closeness to England was evident in his set of values. The son of a Cavalier mother, he was sent to England at ten to be brought up among her people. He went back frequently throughout his life. Writing to a friend in London in his later years, he is a trifle nostalgic about living as a colonial, away from the centre of culture. 'We that are banished,' he says, 'from these polite pleasures are forced to take up with rural entertainments. A library, a garden, a grove and a purling stream are the innocent scenes that divert our leisure.' In the library of such a man, surely, would belong a Folio of Shakespeare. It was probably the Fourth of 1685, purchased in London and brought over seas as a 'polite pleasure' to spice his 'rural entertainment'.

Thus Byrd and the Carters seem to cancel, as far as evidence for the reading of Shakespeare in seventeenth century Virginia goes. Probably Byrd was unusual, and the Carters were more typical. But the danger of generalizing too conclusively in one direction or the other is clearly seen by juxtaposing the libraries of these two families.

In this relatively 'Shakespeareless' century, then, actual evidences of the presence and reading of Shakespeare's plays are scarce. But the evidences are there. Attention to Shakespeare was not considerable, as measured by later standards, even in England. The English-speaking world both there and here was, for obvious reasons, interested in a different sort of thing. What the evidence shows, so far as it goes, is a rugged, busy world in which libraries were not common. Yet in those recorded, vaguely or specifically, Shakespeare has a fair chance of being present. The chance is not as good as it was in England, but Puritan restrictions and the austerities of pioneer life have not excluded him. The adulation had not begun, nor the criticism. But granted colonial stringencies, provincialisms, and physical remoteness from the centre, Shakespeare's ghost is as stalwart in seventeenth century America as we could reasonably expect.

CHAPTER III

The Attitude Toward Shakespeare on the Stage in the Eighteenth Century up to the Revolution

THE history of Shakespeare on the American stage in the seventy-five years between the opening of the eighteenth century and the American Revolution is full of details which stimulate the imagination. The productions were crude, the buildings in which they were performed were often improvised halls and lofts, the quality of the acting was stiff and oratorical. But the circumstances which surrounded the performances, the things featured in playbills and newspaper advertisements to catch the public's attention, the picturesque quality of a colonial society 'playing at' belonging to the '*haut monde*' and imitating afar off, amidst mud and the physical clumsiness of provincial life, the 'polite' London of Steele and Fielding, all these things make the reconstruction of Shakespeare on the colonial stage both amusing and touching.

Perhaps the dominant emphasis is the 'class' emphasis. It accounts for the phrasing of playbills, the wording of legislation touching the stage, and the etiquette of play-going. With the turn of the century, something new had taken possession of America. Instead of its being a world of refugees for religious independence from the mother country, it had become something quite different. The old religious oligarchy of the Sewalls and the Mathers was no longer the dominant force. Something more frankly worldly had submerged their religious domination. The world and life here and now were again in the saddle. And as is always true in such eras, there were two ways of reaching for this goodness of the worldly present. One was by way of property. If the individual could build up for himself financial security, and perhaps a surplus of property, he and other individuals who had the same ideals could run the world for their own good. They could either spread charity among the rest of society or 'sweat' it, as they felt inclined. Thus emerged the merchant group whose power was based on property and whose outlook, politically and socially, was determined by the advantages which one action or another would have. Running along with the ideals of this group and fundamentally opposed to them was the ideal of 'free-hold, democratic natural rights' for the nameless, propertyless, hard-working people who made up the other half of the social picture.

This group was steadily increasing. There was more immigration in the first half of the eighteenth century, not only from England but from other countries. German, Scotch-Irish, Huguenot French, as well as English 'nondescript', came in and made the new American frontier. The chance for free land was what brought them, combined with the absence of economic future in the countries from which they came. With the possession of acres, even though they were reluctant and yielded return only after the most back-breaking labour, came an increased sense of personal dignity and individual rights. All the bitterness and venom against the privileged classes in the countries they had left were turned into a positive and savage conception of rights for themselves and democratic freedom for all, in this new world. The indigent men with trades who sold themselves into a term of slavery in order to get out here were an extreme instance of the way in which 'fighting' democratic ideas were fostered. Rousseau was born in 1712. His *Social Contract* and *Emile* were printed in 1761 and '62. Though these stalwart back-woodsmen and their children, too, were and would be innocent of the cogent doctrines set down in Rousseau's pages, they were unwittingly in sympathy with him. Of course they were at the moment inarticulate. Both the rugged terms of daily toil and the lack of education and of access to the literature of democracy made them un-aware of the social struggle and their place in it. But as Parrington wisely points out, their attitude was 'the origin of the coonskin democracy of Old Hickory that was to bring eventual disaster to the plans of gentlemen'.

These people were parodied occasionally in accounts of the theatre audiences, but their positive share in Shake-speare on the American stage before the Revolution is, of course, *nil*. They served, however, silently, negatively, and all unconsciously, to emphasize in the other social class its sense of 'politeness', of belonging to the elegant world of English gentlemen, albeit transplanted to the crudities and makeshifts of a colonial setting. A feeling in the air that this world of merchant-gentlemen was being threat-ened by a subterranean growth of social power in a strongly antagonistic group, heightened the affectations of culture and class-consciousness. It is reflected amusingly in the records of Shakespearean productions in Virginia or Philadelphia or New York or further south in Charles-ton.

All those ways in which Shakespeare can penetrate a social culture—by reading, owning of his works, and by seeing him played—are reflected only among the 'Tory' group in the first seventy-five years of the eighteenth cen-tury. The truer, larger and more essential America of the future, busy then on the farms and the frontiers, had no time and no tradition for Shakespeare. Their own appropriation of him was to come later and in different form. The playing of Shakespeare in America then was bound to be a fashionable gesture, clinging as well as it could to the methods of presentation used in London.

The strongest proof that Shakespeare and the stage in general were 'fashionable' and belonged to the élite, is the opposition to the theatre which was raised by soberer, less sympathetic, civic and religious authorities to these folderols and their fashionable followers.

The moral prohibition, which dogged Shakespeare's plays from his own day right down across the next two centuries, was stronger in some parts of colonial America than in others. Boston, as one would expect, was stony ground for Shakespearean or any other stage productions. The moral opposition existed, of course, in other parts of the colonies: sporadically in New York, quite steadily in Philadelphia. It all but disappeared in Virginia and Charleston. Yet the moral attack upon Shakespeare was at all times and in all places imminent. It continued to be talking ground, *pro* and *con*, throughout the century. Perhaps in no way are the old and new world more interestingly linked than in this persistent raising of the question of Shakespeare's moral virtue. The quarrel is a curious human phenomenon and its real origin is hard to determine. Perhaps it lay in the strange potency of the theatre to transport men and bemuse them; to present a world more fascinating and in some ways more immediate and real than the world of common daylight, so that the actual world became fearful and jealous of the theatre's power and persecuted it.

It will not do to place upon the shoulders of the American colonies alone, and more specifically upon New England Puritans and Pennsylvania Quakers, the whole burden of the moral opposition to the stage in general and Shakespeare in particular. The new world opposition is exactly like the opposition that Shakespeare faced in his own lifetime. This opposition reared its head at intervals in the most elegant English society. This point needs to be emphasized. The Mathers and the Sewalls were not the only offenders. In Shakespeare's own day the public theatres had to be built outside the city limits because the city government of London, composed of hard-headed merchants, simply would not have these places of entertainment within their jurisdiction. It was too difficult to police the possible riots, to control the drunkenness and immorality which were likely to manifest themselves near a theatre. The London government must have felt toward the theatres, as selectmen of small towns feel about giving licenses to travelling circuses. The trouble involved and the responsibility involved were too great. The easiest thing was to withhold the permit.

This practical reason for governmental opposition to theatres is, perhaps, the strongest element in the war against the stage. To it were added other probable sources of nuisance. The Elizabethan actor was likely to live dangerously. He was, *ipso facto*, suspect and catalogued in the laws of the realm among 'rogues and vagabonds'. He was, potentially at least, an undesirable citizen. His way of working for his living was quite incomprehensible to acquisitive merchants who lived regular and rewarding days in their counting houses. It became easy to regard him and all his works as a source of evil influence in the community.

When, therefore, some thirty years after Shakespeare's death the public theatres were officially closed under the

Puritan régime, this action was nothing sudden or new. A factor in public life which had long bothered the government was officially removed. The stage and all that had to do with it were of the devil and should be eschewed by honest folk. A whole section of London society felt this way. Only two years before Charles II's restoration, as Hazelton Spencer points out, a lady in high circles prophesied the end of the Opera because 'the godly party are so much discontented with it'. As late as 1672, when the King's Playhouse burned, the Earl of Anglesey saw this burning 'as an evidence' of God's judgement against the sin of theatrical performances.

With this background of opposition in the mother country, one ought not to be surprised at the legislation against theatres in colonial Boston. Increase Mather, in his preface to a book published in London in 1687, laments that 'there is much discourse of beginning stage-plays in New England'. But the threat was not carried out for one hundred and fifty years. Even in the new American post-Revolutionary world of 1792, the sheriff appeared uninvited upon the stage and closed Boston's first theatrical season which at long last had produced Shakespeare's *Hamlet* and *Richard III*.

The geographical section which came next after Boston in civic opposition to the theatre was Philadelphia. In Philadelphia, however, the aristocratic party, buttressed by support from the royal government at home, contrived to develop a very active stage, in spite of the opposition of the Quakers, Lutherans and the municipal government. The records of performance in the first half of the century are difficult to come by. The press, which under normal circumstances would print playbills, announce dates of coming performances and sometimes find space for a new pro-

logue produced by a gentleman of local repute, was closed
to theatrical news in Philadelphia. It was largely controlled
by Quakers. In 1700 the Assembly of Pennsylvania passed
a law prohibiting 'stage-plays, masks and revels', which it
classed among 'rude and riotous sports'. This last phrase
touches the heart of the difficulty. Theatres invited rough
behaviour which might endanger the public peace. It was
the same old opposition which had dominated Elizabethan
London government in Shakespeare's lifetime a century
earlier. In 1705, 1709, and 1713, Pennsylvania legislation
against the theatre was passed. But it was immediately re-
voked by higher authority from England.

When a new theatre was contemplated in 1759, to be
built by Douglass, a successful troupe manager of some
reputation and experience, the same kind of opposition
arose. A petition to prevent this building was sent to the
Pennsylvania Assembly from Quakers, Presbyterians,
Lutherans and Baptists. The Governor and his Council
were obviously of the aristocratic English party. They
really wanted the theatre. But the necessity of placating
the large section of public opinion represented in this petition kept them from refusing it outright. The Governor
dodged the issue. Actually, he allowed the building of the
theatre by sending the petition back granted, but with
legislation which could not take effect till January of the
next year. This gave Douglass six months' leeway. He took
it and built his theatre. When the prohibiting law was
finally passed it was repealed by the King and Council. So
much for the clever political straddling of the fence which
divided the middle-class Pennsylvanians from the gentlemen and ladies who wanted to be driven to Douglass's
theatre on Society Hill (significant locality) and attend

performances and imagine that they were breathing the fashionable air of the London night at Drury Lane.

A phrase in Douglass's building permit recalls startlingly to the student of the Elizabethan theatre, the persistence of the old struggle between City and Court. Douglass was to 'act without the bounds of the city'. So William Shakespeare's Globe and all the other public theatres of Elizabeth's day were consigned either to the fields north of London or to the southern bank of the Thames. The fact that one had to add a boatfare to the price of a ticket in Shakespeare's day did not prevent his theatre from successful seasons. No more did the removal from city limits curtail the attendance at Douglass's Society Hill House in the Philadelphia of the mid-eighteenth century.

With such a feeling of opposition abroad, it is no wonder that Francis Hopkinson, prominent Philadelphian, wrote a prologue for the opening night in which he emphasizes the moral effect of stage shows upon the public. It is the same line of argument, directed at a particular opposition group, which a hundred and fifty years earlier was responsible for so much cant, in the otherwise lovely *apologia* for poetry written by Sir Philip Sidney. One inevitably overstressed the moral value of art in order to quiet the Philistine. Thus Hopkinson's prologue for the opening night on Society Hill in June of 1759 maintains the purpose of the theatre is:

> To bid reviving virtue raise her head
> And far abroad her heavenly influence shed;
> The soul by bright example to inspire,
> And kindle in each breast celestial fire.

And he concludes with this pious wish:

So may each scene some useful moral show;
From each performance sweet instruction flow.

This is wishful thinking, to say the least. But the confusion
and insincerity of purpose behind it were in answer to the
confusion of thinking which had always lain behind religious and civic opposition to the stage.

There were other and more tangible ways of assuaging
opposition. The last performance of this 1759 season was
a benefit of *Hamlet*, the proceeds to go to the Pennsylvania
Hospital. The managers accepted the money but they pro-
tected themselves from criticism for this act by maintaining that the play had been given 'without the consent of
the said managers'. Yet even within the managerial board
were some who obviously favored the theatre, for two
members of the board sold tickets. Strange predicaments
the melancholy Dane has found himself in, ever since he
was created as a precious microcosm of the exultations and
despairs of man's life. Here, in a mid-eighteenth century
English colony, he was being served up to fashionable
Philadelphia and earning his way with the general public
by turning over the few pounds in box-office receipts to
the sufferers in the Pennsylvania Hospital. He was still
functioning as a solace to the human spirit, though the
particular method in this case was material and external.

In 1766, this same Douglass, returning with his troupe
from engagements in the West Indies, built another theatre
in Philadelphia. About this building there seems to have
been less violent opposition. But this theatre, too, was
'built just outside the city limits' and was called, in memory
of the Elizabethan theatre section in London, the 'Southwark'. The very next year a clergyman from England
lent the support of the cloth to dramatic enterprises in

Pennsylvania. In 'Remarks on the Theatre Addressed to a Young Lady in Pennsylvania', in 1767, he writes:

I am ashamed to combat superstition; but must Shakespeare, the immortal Shakespeare, be destroyed—shall Molière be burn't—; shall Plautus, Terence, Euripides—be involved in the horrid 'conflagration'?

Thus Shakespeare at last is championed by the clergy and placed in the sacred category with the classics. But one must remember the date. The eighteenth century is more than two-thirds over, and the romantic movement, which was to smother Shakespeare by too much idolatry, was just below the horizon.

The history of the theatre in New York up to the Revolution is full of colour and engaging incidents. The opposition to the stage was less organized and less effective than in Philadelphia. Yet it occurred at intervals and was urbanely met by the producers themselves, usually in the pages of the *New York Mercury*. As early as 1699–1702 a petition to the Governor and Commander-in-chief of the Province of New York for 'acting plays in this city' was granted. That there were plays in New York in the first half of the century and playhouses for them as early as 1740, is certain. The first record of opposition on moral grounds does not come till the beginning of the second half of the century. Exactly what the attack was, we do not know. An answer by Hallam, who had brought his well-known troupe to New York from Virginia in the spring of 1753, shows how urbanely a London theatre manager can meet opposition. In the *New York Mercury* of July 2, 1753, he printed an article with the following caption:

The Case of the London Company of Comedians, lately arrived from Virginia, humbly submitted to the Consideration of the Publick; whose Servants they are and whose Protection they entreat.

Surely the battle with New York 'society' must have been half won by this tactful and ingratiating caption.

The notes Hallam harps upon are ones calculated to stir in colonial breasts the echoes of their beloved London world. New York, says Hallam, is 'to all appearance so polite'. Here is 'polite' in the precise connotation used by Addison and Steele in the London of Queen Anne. It means urbane, elegant, finished, accomplishing that most difficult and desirable of all tasks—to be civilized—and set apart thereby from the rough and tumble of mere existence. He argues further for the 'instruction' that lurks in the performances of 'the immortal Shakespeare' and 'other great geniuses' of England. He maintains that the 'dignity' of the stage is by his company supported 'with proper decorum and regularity'. The very words 'decorum' and 'regularity' utter the *sine qua non* of the London world. He plays further upon this class snobbishness by assuring them that he and his troupe have only left Virginia and travelled up to New York because they were 'persuaded . . . by several gentlemen' whose names he could give but withholds from print out of a sense of propriety. These 'gentlemen' have assured him of a 'genteel . . . reception' and have emphasized the fondness of New York for 'rational' diversions. This, surely, would disarm the most stubborn opposition.

In December of that year, after Douglass's company had been playing, among others, *Hamlet*, there was criticism of the plays and also of the character and manners of

the actors. That old Elizabethan criticism, which placed
actors on the statute books as 'rogues and vagabonds' and
made them liable to arrest at any moment, was not dead.
After more than a hundred and fifty years Douglass refers
to it in his answer to the attacks. He assures the New
York public, through the pages of the *New York Mercury*
for December 28, 1761, that the plays he has been offering
have in England been 'read and admired by the . . . most vir-
tuous'. As for the social standing of his company, Mr. Douglass 'is of a good family and has a genteel and liberal education'. In fact, growing smoothly venomous, he suggests that
Mr. Douglass is much worthier of the title 'gentleman' than
his attacker, one 'who', says Douglass sarcastically, 'so politely and generously lavishes the appellation of vagrant
and stroller on him'. It is this phrase 'vagrant and stroller',
echoing the 'rogue and vagabond' of the Elizabethan statute books, which has lacerated his feelings. Surely the urbanity with which the charge is met should have stirred
remorse in the bosom of the attacker.

But Douglass did not trust to urbanity alone. Two
months later the proceeds of a performance of *Othello*
went for the benefit of 'such poor families as are not provided for by the public' and the sums involved were publicly printed. There was another 'benefit' of *Hamlet* in
April, and the *Mercury* for May 3, 1762, comments on
the effectiveness of these gestures in assuaging public criticism:

This is the second Play the company have given this
season to public uses; which, with their unblamable conduct during their residence here and the entertainment the
Town [word full of London echoes] has received from
their performance, has greatly increased the number of

their friends and considerably obviated many objections hitherto made against theatrical representations in this City.

Thus on the grounds of fashion, gentility and morality the New York stage up to the American Revolution won prestige and established itself.

In Virginia and the South generally, the opposition to the theatre was less vocal. As early as 1716, William Levingston and Charles and Mary Stagg drew up an interesting agreement for future coöperation in a theatre. It is a document newly discovered* and shows their substantial plans and high standards for acting in the best London tradition. They contemplated, apparently without expecting opposition, securing a license from the Governor 'for the sole privilege' of acting 'Comedies, Drolls or other kinds of stage plays'. This plan, as preserved in the York County, Virginia Orders, is known well. But the actual success of this venture or any details about it are lacking. The significant thing, however, is that in Virginia as early as 1716 such a careful plan for a theatre of good standards should be drawn up with the expectation of its being approved by the government. The next considerable theatrical record in Virginia is in 1751. Thither a New York troupe, which had suffered a falling off in receipts, came, built a theatre and gave a season of plays without encountering vocal or recorded opposition. The next year the Hallam Company came out from London directly to Virginia. Their playing was at first opposed by the Governor and Council, but the action was soon rescinded. The resulting series of seasons and selection of plays made theatrical history in the New World.

* For interesting material, I am indebted to an unpublished Master's thesis, Univ. of Va., 1936, by R. H. Land on *Theatre in Colonial Virginia*.

Virginia seems to have prided itself on a toleration of the stage. In the *Virginia Gazette* for May 14, 1767, occurred a poem on 'Dance and Drama'. It was provoked by the news of a Pennsylvanian who had criticized unfavorably a clergyman for attending 'Balls and Spectacles'. The Virginian rises to the defense of the stage as an opportunity for literary genius. The company which Shakespeare keeps in this gentleman's quatrain is noble; for he writes

> Twixt Sophocles and grand Corneille,
> Twixt Shakespeare and DeVego [sic]
> Twixt Molière's and Menander's style,
> Decide who will, non ego.

Clearly these lines hold more of the gentleman's knowledge of famous playwrights than of penetrating comment. But the fact of value is that in 1767 in Virginia, Shakespeare is listed among the great playwrights of all time. The gentleman proceeds with his argument in defense of the stage. He shows that such impeccable authors as Milton and Addison wrote plays. If they did, then surely no opprobrium can possibly attach to the playwriting art:

> These serve to prove, the stage, at root,
> Must needs be very blameless.

Thus Virginia bears witness to its liberal appreciation of the theatre and reproves its neighbour to the north, Pennsylvania, for prudish opposition to 'spectacles'.

But it could not be the eighteenth century either in England or in America without a certain section of society putting art to the acid test of morality. Thus as late as 1772, some commentator of restless conscience in Virginia

comments in the pages of the *Virginia Gazette* for April
2 of that year:

If the comic writers . . . would present us only with
moral plays the stage would become a school of politeness
and virtue.

That virtue necessarily consorts with politeness is a curious
assumption. He admits that 'most of the new plays . . .
have had a moral tendency', but regrets that 'there is not
enough of them to support the theatre'. Thus even in Virginia on the eve of the Revolution the old battle ground
of art versus morality is still frequented.

The Charleston theatre was, as Eola Willis points out,
exclusively the 'aristocratic haunt of the rice growers and
plantation dwellers and merchants that surrounded the
town'. Of the urbanity of the newly reconstructed Plant-
er's Theatre there is corroborative evidence. Yet even here
in 1774 the stamp of moral approval had to be set upon
the performance. At the 'Close of the Charles-town Season', as recorded in the *South Carolina Gazette* for May
30, 1774, the season is reviewed. The choice of plays has
been 'very judicious', representing 'the most approved
English poets'. Their effect is commended, for 'while they
entertain, [they] improve the Mind by conveying the
most useful lessons of Morality and Virtue'.

Thus that unresolved confusion of thinking and judging,
which dogged the appraisal of the theatre, from the beginning of the Renaissance down to our own century, was
reflected in colonial America right up to the Revolution.
It was a part of the theatre from the time of Rome. Rome's
late, debased theatre had been justly suspected and re-
pressed by the Christian world. Crying down acting and

the theatre as such, yet using it for the promulgation of Bible history and ethical teaching, went on through a thousand years of the Middle Ages. When that period in man's history, in turn, gave way to the Renaissance, the contradiction still remained. Great Renaissance dramatists, who were the glory of the civilization which produced them, were persecuted on moral grounds. The war went on, full of humorous instances, right across the seventeenth and eighteenth centuries. Each period added its own shadings and reflected arguments drawn from its own peculiar standards. Our colonial stage presents 'in little' and with even sharper highlights, because of its smallness and of the self-conscious nature of its protest, the same dilemma. When Horace in the height of Rome's greatness had written that literary art should mix the useful with the sweet, he asked for an impossible blend of incongruities. His formula still poisoned the wits of America's colonial censors, magistrates and critics.

CHAPTER IV

The Aping of London Fashions in Shakespeare on the Colonial Stage

THE business of conjuring the past, making it deliver it-self up, 'in its habit as it lived', is, as everybody knows, mostly a failing business. The accents of everydayness, the long littleness that makes up living for the myriad human beings who possess this small planet in a particular moment of its history, are so evanescent that after the drift of cen-turies it is no wonder that they are practically irrecover-able. Yet the game of reconstructing the past will always go on because it has an irresistible fascination. In fact, the past seems more friendly to exploration than the future. But even though the past is reconstructed with skill, the resulting picture is likely to be distorted. One can never be sure that the light falls properly or that the composition of elements is correct. With this warning one may pro-ceed with the reconstruction of Shakespeare on the stage of the American Colonies.

The chief places where one finds the material are in playbills and newspaper advertisements. Luckily the files of weekly news-sheets in New York, Philadelphia, Vir-ginia (at Williamsburg), Maryland, and Charleston have been worked through with meticulous scholarship and in-formed imagination by students of the American past. They have, thereby, put us much in their debt. In New England the absence of theatrical entertainment is evi-denced by the lack of press comment, except the record from time to time of preventive measures whenever the spectre of such diversion raised its frivolous head. In Rhode Island, at Newport, in June, probably in the early 1760's, an intrepid London actor and his company put on in the Public Rooms of the King's Arms Tavern, a distorted show of *Othello*. It was designed to make stage and pulpit seem interchangeable to the pious Rhode Islanders who read the playbill. Except for the chance survival of a copy of this old playbill and the advertisement of another show (not Shakespeare) in Providence at about the same time, New England yields nothing prior to the Revolution. In other colonial centres, however, the Shakespeare hunting is good.

But one must not look for theatre anywhere until the eighteenth century was half over. In the first fifty years, the active life of a strenuous colonial world dominated the scene. The farmers and frontiersmen were, of course, consumed with the physical struggle from morning till night. They had no leisure and therefore no need of diversion. Even among the merchants, who were building up their class upon the foundations of property and trade, there \ was very little leisure. But by the middle of the century financial and social security began to give to their leisure stability. They began to look about for fashionable diversions. Although in New York, petitions for permission to act had been granted at the opening of the century, yet no real theatrical activity emerged. One glimpses an occasional amateur production, as the performance of *Romeo and Juliet* in New York in 1730. There was a regular building for plays there in 1746. Yet before 1749–50, the New York theatre as a regular and recurring source of amusement simply did not exist. Clearly this was not because of opposition but because of lack of interest or, to put it another way, because of absorption in another and more urgent interest. Then a change came, and the theatre intermittently, with Shakespeare well represented in the plays offered, was a dominant feature of colonial New York until the Revolution.

The same thing was true in Virginia. As early as 1715–16 a troupe in Williamsburg drew up a prospectus for a substantial and enlightened theatre in that town. The agreement filed in the York County, Virginia Orders, Wills, etc., has only recently been rediscovered. The company contemplated governmental sanction, a substantial building exclusively for a theatre, a school 'to influence others in the manner and way of acting'. They considered 'clothes, music and other necessaries'. Most significant of all, one of them 'hath at his own proper cost and charge sent to England for actors and musicians for the better performance of said plays'. But whatever their intentions, the project did not come into being. The public was still too busy to support a theatre. There were plenty of separate individuals who owned and read Shakespeare. But this is quite different from having a public large enough to support plays. The next theatrical news in Virginia, after this abortive attempt of 1716, was made in 1751. Thereafter for the next twenty-five years, the theatre was a permanent feature of Williamsburg. Among the offerings, the plays of Shakespeare had a considerable place.

In Philadelphia in the first half of the century, the active opposition of the Quakers who controlled the printing of news and who steadily opposed the royal supervision of affairs and fashionable taste is recorded again and again. But even if the Quaker prohibition had been lifted, it is improbable that the 'Tory group' in Philadelphia could have summoned a large and steady enough audience to support a regular theatrical season. But by the middle of the century, this theatre became a part of social life in Philadelphia. In fact, Philadelphia, between 1749 and 1774, presented one of the most active theatres in the New World. In these activities the plays of Shakespeare had a very considerable part.

The history of Shakespeare on the American stage, then, practically began in 1750. What sort of Shakespeare was it? Before one answers that, it is important to know what sorts of buildings housed it.

A building constructed exclusively for theatrical productions was envisaged in Virginia as early as 1716, but was not realized. Actually the performances up to 1751 were in places built for quite other purposes and improvised for occasional theatrical use. The two seasons of Murray and Kean in New York in the winters of '49–'50 and '50–'51, for example, were set in 'one of the buildings lately belonging to Hon. Rip Van Dam, Esq.'. These improvised rooms were pretentiously advertised as 'the theatre in Nassau St.', though the original announcement frankly admitted that the 'company of comedians . . . have taken a convenient room for their purpose'. The actual room, Odell pictures as *'sans* ventilation, *sans* space, *sans* everything'. Yet here *Richard III* in the Cibber version, which David Garrick had made famous in London eight winters earlier, opened the New York season of 1750. It was played twice more in that first winter, and again in the following year.

How one wishes that the fashion of reviewing first nights by a dramatic critic had existed in these years before the Revolution. Then some atmosphere of the occasion would linger to fuse the cold facts into a living picture. But dramatic reviews were only just beginning when the

Revolution broke out. One has to fall back, instead, upon the advertisement in the paper or the playbill itself. Sometimes a new prologue or epilogue written for the occasion by a well-known gentleman of the town became local news for the next week's press. If something unusual or violent occurred at a performance, it got into the press. An obliging traveller, with all unconscious kindness toward posterity, might record in a letter his attendance at the play. Such sources of knowledge are sparse and only to be regarded as largesse by the eager reconstructor of our American past.

That there were 'clothes, scenes, etc. belonging to the Playhouse' (magniloquent word for the late Van Dam's Rooms), we know from the advertisement for Kean's benefit at the end of the second New York season. But details about the structure of the stage, lighting and costuming are quite lacking. Exactly what local carpentering did to a bare room to create the semblance of 'pitt and gallery' as advertised, one cannot imagine. Yet they appear in the advertisements with the varying price of tickets according to the place of the seats.

The next autumn Murray and Kean were in Virginia at Williamsburg. They carried an advertisement in the *Virginia Gazette* for October 17, announcing the famous Cibber version of *Richard III* 'at the New Theatre in Williamsburg'. What sort of building this was we do not know. To be sure it had 'Box, pit and gallery', which suggests that the ranks of Williamsburg society were carefully considered. But the boxes were probably nothing but roped-off sections of seats on the main floor or 'pit'. Their distinction was in their occupants and not in any architectural differentiation. The building must have had some good features, since Murray and Kean had been in Virginia since August raising money for it.

Hither came in the early summer of 1752, a troupe of London actors well sponsored at home. Their connections wove their lives into the whole theatrical history of London in the heyday of Garrick. They performed in the 'New Theatre' built by Murray and Kean in the preceding year. Somehow they contrived to make it an adequate setting for their pretentiously advertised opening performance of the *Merchant of Venice* on the night of September 15, 1752. The interior arrangements for seating sound elaborate. In addition to the divisions into boxes, pit and gallery, the pit is again subdivided into 'Pit and Balconies' at five shillings and ninepence. Exactly what the difference is between a 'balcony' and a 'gallery', especially in such a simple interior, is hard to imagine. Yet the distinction spoke loudly to one's pocket; for a ticket in the balcony cost nearly twice as much as one in the gallery. Whether the stage was large enough to accommodate the settings which they had brought with them from London in the hold of the *Charming Sally*, we shall never know. These included scenes 'painted by the best hands in London' and decorations 'extremely rich and furnished in the best taste'. The audience was promised 'as polite a manner as at the theatres in London'.

In these details one sees two underlying emphases which fit well into the general picture of colonial culture. Theatre audiences were aping London. That a scene had been painted in London or a play produced there commended it. The frequent use of the word 'polite' and the arrangement of seating in three distinct groups, according to social differences, show what valiant Englishmen at heart these

colonials were. The frontiersmen and farmers further in-
land, out of whom the independent America of the next
century was to emerge, were completely 'underground'
at this moment. Snobbery, pathetic but sharp, was triumphant.

The *Virginia Gazette* of August 21, 1752, carried a
news item on the intended opening of the *Merchant of
Venice*. 'The Ladies', it read, 'are desired to give timely
notice to Mr. Hallam at Mr. Fisher's, for their places in
the boxes and on the Day of Performance to send their
servants early to keep them in order and prevent trouble
and disappointment.' In this audience for the opening
night, George Washington may have been sitting, for he
was a frequent attendant 'at the play'. There is such a
'build-up' of elegance for this *Merchant of Venice* and
such a 'polite' report afterward in the press that one has
to correct one's elaborate mental picture of the occasion
by recalling that the 'New Theatre' must have been bare
and crude.

Yet the audience and the reporters pretended that the
whole affair would have been worthy of Garrick and
Drury Lane. At the top of the playbill it was announced
that the 'Honorable Robert Dinwiddie Esq., His Majesty's
Lieutenant Governor and Commander-in-Chief of the
Colony and Dominion of Virginia' lent his august permission. The royal Latinity, *Vivat Rex*, concluded the bill in
the lower right-hand corner. A prologue written especially
for the opening night gave Hallam's troupe a mandate
from the Muse and assured them of 'polite' reception:

> Haste to Virginia's plains, my Sons repair,
> The Goddess said. Go, confident to find
> An audience sensible, polite and kind.

The expectation was apparently met, for we read afterward that a 'numerous and polite Audience' greeted the performance 'with great applause'.

After a winter in Virginia the Hallam Company moved to New York. There they found the old 'Nassau Street Theatre' just as it was left by Murray and Kean when they departed from New York in the summer of 1751. In the meantime, Shakespeare had been played there by a certain Robert Upton who had been sent out by the Hallam troupe from London. He had presented *Othello* in the winter of '51–'52 on three different occasions, and the inevitable *Richard III* once.

This Upton apparently understood the necessity of catering to 'society', for he inserts in the pages of the *New York Mercury*, in January, 1752, a notice exclusively for them. 'As Mr. Upton', the notice reads, 'is an absolute stranger, if, in his application he should have omitted any gentleman or lady's house or lodging, he humbly hopes they'll impute it to want of information, not respect.' One pictures the rascally English actor, cruising about the snowy streets of the small town of New York (it had fewer than two thousand houses) in midwinter, calling at doors and soliciting the purchase of tickets. It shows the provinciality and amateurishness of the whole enterprise. It hung upon the individual patronage of the mere handful of New York 'society' for whom probably a chance to be gathered together in a 'theatre' of an evening was as much of an attraction as the name of Shakespeare upon the playbill.

Upton and his season were completely overshadowed by the arrival of the Hallams from Virginia with their London and Virginia laurels rustling about their ears. They needed every ounce of prestige they could summon in order to overcome opposition. Whether Upton had left a bad taste in the mouths of the New York authorities or what had come over their liberality, we shall now never know. A tactful press campaign and the support of 'several gentlemen' finally won for them a full and successful season. They tore down the old Van Dam building in Nassau Street and built a new one on the same site. For their opening performance they offered a 'fine, large and commodious theatre in the place where the old one stood'. This was called on the playbills 'the New Theatre in Nassau Street' and was ready by mid-September.

This 'New Theatre' was to see several Shakespearean performances during this winter. There survives a rare description of it in a letter by Philip Schuyler. He had come from Albany to New York, intending before he left home 'that if the players should be here, I should see them, for a player is a new thing under the sun in our good province'. Either the performances of the troupes prior to Hallam's had carried no prestige, or Schuyler himself was a provincial in these matters. Anyway he felt a thrill of wickedness in attending the theatre for he felt compelled to say to his correspondent that he might have improved his time at the Club where he might have heard 'many wise sayings'. One regrets that the performance on the night of Schuyler's attendance was not Shakespeare. Instead it was Steele's *Conscious Lovers*.

What impressed Schuyler was the occasion itself; the looks of the theatre, the mechanics of curtain-raising, the diversions, and whom he saw in the audience that he knew. In fact, if Schuyler's account is at all typical, it proves that going to the theatre in mid-eighteenth century America was chiefly a social occasion. It was a chance to see and be seen by one's little world.

Schuyler's letter might as well have been an account of

a fashionable reception. After five o'clock tea, they pro-
ceeded to Nassau Street and were in the theatre 'before
sundown'—it was September—'for the players commenced
at six'. The next item of interest is the audience. 'Among
the company were your cousin Tom and Kitty Livings-
ton.' A small enough auditorium, mark you, even in this
new theatre, to make the personnel of the assembly at once
evident. The 'large green curtain' was 'hung before the
players until they were ready to begin' and 'was raised
[not parted, notice] on the blast of a whistle'. What the
opening scene was, how effective, or from what play, is
not Schuyler's concern. He merely comments that 'some
of them [the actors] appeared and commenced acting'.

Schuyler clearly was not transported into the play but
sat solidly and consciously at a playhouse in New York
in a 'company' of which friends and acquaintances made
part. He records the names of the actors but not their
parts. The only theatrical feature he notes is a divertissement by 'a sprightly young man named Hewlett', who
'played the violin and danced merrily'. To be fair to
Schuyler one must add that he would have liked 'to tell
you about the play'. But his only chance of getting the
letter back to Albany was by boat which 'sails this afternoon'.

How many things about the 'New Theatre in Nassau
Street' Schuyler omits. What of lighting? What was the
size? What was the construction of box, pit and gallery?
What was the music? What size was the stage? Was it
raised? How were exits arranged? What sort of scenery?
Presumably the scenes 'painted in London' which the
Hallams had brought to Virginia the preceding year were
still doing duty. All these questions will never be answered. Yet we are grateful for knowing that 'the large

green curtain' was raised at 'the blast of a whistle' and that the 'town' was well represented in the audience.

In the spring after this long and successful winter, the Hallams played for two months in Philadelphia. There the performances were given in a warehouse. One wonders whether it seemed cramped after Nassau Street.

When the Hallam Company again turned up, under Douglass's management, in New York, the authorities were very severe. To meet their objections he promised a 'Histrionic Academy' for 'dissertations on subjects, Moral, Instructive and Entertaining'. But this did not conceal his intention to play Shakespeare and other *bona fide* plays. No drama was allowed in the 'new' theatre till after the New Year, when *Othello* was produced. Douglass kept his colours flying in spite of the official opposition. Through the pages of the *Mercury* he made 'thankful acknowledge-ment to the town for the generous encouragement'. There had, he boasted, been 'crowded houses since we began to perform'.

Douglass was a man of determination. When he took his troupe south to Philadelphia in April, 1759, after this chilling New York reception, he apparently determined to make a strong fight. He built a new theatre on Society Hill. What one would give for some specific details of the interior which was to be the setting of a six-month season with over eighty plays and a generous proportion of Shakespearean titles. But no architectural details survive. Only the name, 'Society Hill', and the fact that the build-ing permit specified acting 'without the bounds of the city' survive. But they are enough to show the importance of the season and to place Shakespeare among the lively imaginary presences in Philadelphia in that winter of 1759.

When Douglass took his troupe on tour he put on his

shows, apparently without great curtailment, once in the
Public Room of a tavern and once in 'the new School
House'. This was during a tour of Rhode Island in the
towns of Newport and Providence. The theatre world
was still on sufferance, not expecting a permanent physical
place yet in the community.

In New York, whither Douglass came again in 1761, he
opened a theatre in Chapel Street. Here he played a vigorous season which included several Shakespearean plays.
No actual description, either in words or by illustration,
survives of the playhouse. Yet an advertisement of the
building to be let, two years later, shows that it would be
'very convenient for a store, being upwards of 90 feet
in length, nigh 40 feet wide'. No wonder the management
in order to put on Juliet's funeral procession in a building
of this size had to solicit 'the gentlemen to give us the entire use of the stage'. Yet in spite of the size, the illusion of
a regular theatre interior with boxes and gallery was preserved. Toward the end of the season someone 'was so
very rude to throw eggs from the gallery upon the stage'.
The boxes must have been very close to the stage for 'the
clothes of some ladies and gentlemen in the boxes were
spoiled'.

A sidelight on the way in which the theatre became
more and more identified with England, the oppressor,
as the Revolution drew near, is shown concretely in the
history of this Chapel Street Theatre. A group of rabid,
hundred-per-cent Americans, as we should say today, had
organized themselves under the name of the Sons of Liberty and used their prerogative, then as now, for many
deeds of violence. The theatre was the particular object
of their fury as being the incarnation of all that was British and detestable. They burned playbills publicly with as

much venom as they burned the hated stamps of the Stamp Tax. It was probably this group that broke up a performance at the Chapel Street Theatre in the spring of 1766, routed the audience, wrecked the building and set fire to it. This was, the press records, 'to the satisfaction of many at this distressed time, and to the great grievance of those less inclined for the public good'. Thus the lines were drawn between the growing American public who would have none of England and its fashionable diversions and that small aristocratic group who aped London and modelled their lives and pleasures as closely as they could upon it.

The prejudice against England was growing. Douglass in 1776 renamed his troupe the American Company. He probably hoped by this means to avoid the growing feeling against the theatre as the work of Britain and the devil. In Philadelphia with his 'American Company' he built the New Theatre in Southwark. It was a section 'just outside the city limits'. Thither the theatre-loving world came, just as in the heyday of Shakespeare they had crossed the Thames to the southern side for their shows. Douglass tried to lessen the discomfort of his patrons on their way thither. 'A foot-path is made across the common to the corner of Pine Street, in Fourth Street, on which those ladies who are not provided with carriages may come to the house without dirtying their feet.'

For this theatre, at last, there is a description of the interior. The 'stage was lighted by plain oil lamps without glasses. The view from the boxes was intercepted by large square wooden pillars supporting the upper tiers and roof'. Probably the mention of the lack of glasses for the lamps bespeaks a smoky and dingy interior. There is no knowledge of the exact size of the stage and the seating

JOHN ST. THEATRE opened by Douglass in New York 1767.

capacity. Yet the New Theatre, built expressly for theatrical performances and used as a playhouse for fifty years
until the early nineteenth century, is a landmark in the
conquest of America by the stage. It outrode the storms of
the Revolution. And in it were played, in this first season
of '66-'67, one hundred nights of performance which included a generous number of Shakespearean productions.

The companion piece of the New Theatre in Philadelphia was built in New York the very next year. It was
the famous John Street Theatre opened by Douglass in
December of 1767. A drawing of this interior survives.
It seems a tiny, provincial affair. Yet there are chandeliers
over the audience, footlights at the edge of the stage,
proscenium arch and scenery. Dunlap records that 'two
rows of boxes with a pit and gallery could accommodate
all the play-going people of the time'. And he was probably correct, for New York at this time, according to Odell,
had 'fewer than 20,000 inhabitants'.

The building sat back about sixty feet from the street
and had a 'covered way of rough wooden material from
the pavement to the doors'. This entrance was made famous by being described in a contemporary play where
a country boy, Jonathan, gives a vivid account of his bewildered and delighted attendance at the theatre. The
first thing is the 'great crowd' at 'the long entry that had
lanthorns over the door'. He was shown 'clean up to the
garret [as it seemed to his country mind] just like a meeting house gallery'. No doubt the comparison of a theatre
gallery to a meeting-house gallery provoked roars of
laughter. As he looked down from his vantage point he
saw 'a power of topping folks'. They were 'sitting around
in little cabins, just like father's corn cribs'. There were
fiddles and 'a tarnal blaze with the lights', and when 'they

lifted up a great green cloth', the naïve Jonathan, looking
at the stage, thought he was looking 'right into the next
neighbor's house'. So Partridge in Fielding's *Tom Jones*
had thought he was witnessing real life when he saw Hamlet 'at the play'. But in spite of the dazzled eyes of young
Jonathan from the country, the John Street Theatre in
New York was a very small affair indeed.

Yet to it a press of people came on the opening night.
According to the advance playbill, 'Ladies will please to
send their servants to keep their places at 4 o'clock'. There
was congestion of traffic before the performance. 'To prevent accidents by carriages meeting, it is requested that
those coming to the house may enter John Street from the
Broad-way, and returning drive from thence down John
Street.' Possibly the performance of Shakespeare's *Richard III* three nights before, combined with the spectacular
audience on that occasion (it had included ten Cherokee
chieftains and was a request performance), had precipi-
tated a 'traffic jam'. Shakespeare was well represented in
the performances of this first winter in John Street. There
were, according to Odell, ten plays by the Bard, four of
which had not been played in New York before.

The long story of these first seventy-five years of the
eighteenth century is one of pitiful makeshifts. Theatre
interiors were improvised from warehouses and stores,
from crude wooden structures put up rapidly by an en-
terprising manager for the temporary housing of his
troupe. When they toured, the public rooms of an inn did
excellent service. Yet ladies, in carriages, attended and sent
their servants at four o'clock to possess the boxes. Finally
in the very teeth of the war two real theatres were built
and maintained, and were hospitable to many Shakespearean plays.

CHAPTER V

The Quality of Colonial Performances: Shakespeare with 'Added Attractions'; Shakespeare for Cherokees

THE plays of Shakespeare hold their own on the eighteenth century American stage. They occur in about the same proportion and with the same range of titles that one would find in London. The acting and production over here were certainly inferior to the London standard, yet they belonged in the same great tradition. Shakespeare then, on the London stage, was very unlike our Shakespeare of the 1930's. Our approach to Shakespeare is as to an unquestioned source of wisdom and beauty. We invite the core of essential comment on life which is in his amazing plays. We do not apologize for him; on the contrary, perhaps we approach him too solemnly. His greatness is unquestioned. Furthermore we play him with fewer and fewer trappings. Gone are the days when producers like Sir Herbert Beerbohm Tree created an elaborate stage reproduction of a corner in Westminster Abbey in order to set off a Shakespearean scene. The boards are left bare. Without benefit of costume, the actors speak the lines as holding in themselves both the form and the content of life, as it was, is and ever shall be. But in the eighteenth century, Shakespeare's case stood in a quite different position.

Since his death much water had flowed under the bridge of the years. The stage producers, critics and actors had somehow lost the key to his greatness. In a world of new decorums, of Frenchified manners and critical ideals, the ability to read and act Shakespeare in his entirety, as he timelessly was, became impossible. Furthermore an entirely alien art, the opera, was so bedevilling men's ideas of entertainment all over Europe that legitimate playwriting was somewhat overshadowed. Songs, dances and elaborate mechanical stage effects began to creep into productions of the regular stage. That these were utterly foreign to the spirit of Shakespeare, to the artistically single crescendo of his plays, to their true meaning, no one seemed to remember. D'Avenant's reworked version of *Macbeth*, for instance, was enlivened by the introduction of new songs and dances. The performances of the witches on slack wires and trapezes delighted the spasmodic powers of attention in these new and different audiences. It was as if Shakespeare had been transported to another planet. His prestige still lingered. One *must* produce him; one *must* go to see him. It was a mystical compulsion. But to make his text palatable, to keep oneself awake and diverted, he must be generously buttered with new enchantments. To produce him was, of course, correct. But to keep the audience from yawning, he must be served up with some utterly new and alien sauces.

Thus Shakespeare 'adapted'—which means unbelievably mangled, rewritten, 'combined', furnished with divertissements—had been played for a bemused and befuddled theatre audience for nearly ninety years before our colonial Shakespeare began. Much of the text as he wrote it had to be cut out to make room for these 'improvements'. The acting, of course, reflected the change in the script. It became merely the occasion for speeches in oratorical style. How could one play Beatrice or Viola as Shakespeare and life itself conceived them, if one had, at a certain point, to interrupt the subtle build-up of one's characterization in order to take part in a quartet beginning 'Our Ruler has got the Vertigo of State'? This is near to Gilbert and Sullivan; yet the material is completely unadaptable to the cheerful and superficial wit of such light operetta.

This process of adaptation continued right through the last half of the seventeenth and into the eighteenth century. Colley Cibber, as manager of Drury Lane from 1710 onward, had butchered Shakespeare to suit the 'polite' taste of the 'town'. Garrick had followed in Cibber's footsteps with new versions 'fixed up' with added attractions; music between the acts, funeral processions, songs, dances. Under Garrick's hand, the *Taming of the Shrew* was altered into a play called *Katherine and Petruchio*. The peculiarly beautiful proportions of the *Winter's Tale* were destroyed by reworking it into a sugared entertainment entitled *Florizel and Perdita and the Sheep Shearing*. Speeches like Jaques' in *As You Like It*, on the periods of man's life, were taken out of their setting and made set-pieces with new titles, such as *The Seven Ages* with musical accompaniment. Speeches from Shakespeare, Milton and James Thompson occurred together on a single programme and were set off by music. Havoc was wrought upon the beauties of the *Tempest* by the vulgarities of its alterations. All these fashionable atrocities from London were reproduced in the Shakespeare of eighteenth century America.

The double bill, in which the Shakespeare play was followed by an after-piece, usually a farce, was another London fashion which the colonial stage adopted. The curse of the double bill is again with us in the 1930's when one good moving picture is likely to be companioned by a piece of offensive vulgarity.

The standards of acting and production were set in England. It is not fair to measure colonial Shakespeare by Forbes-Robertson or Katharine Cornell or John Gielgud or Orson Welles. Rather one must take the best acting of contemporary London and that means, David Garrick. The ghost of theatre nights in Drury Lane haunts every crude provincial show in improvised warehouse, loft or tavern public-room.

David Garrick, who had set out for London from Litchfield, trudging along beside the great Sam Johnson in that endearing vignette of literary and artistic history, had, after vicissitudes, made a great success in Shakespeare's *Richard III* in London, in 1741. How closely the New World was sensitized to English taste is shown by the predominance of this same *Richard III* among the theatrical offerings over here in the middle of the century. It was the most frequent Shakespearean title in America for years. After this success, Garrick had acted at Drury Lane, brilliantly from the point of view of contemporary taste, between 1742 and 1745. His management of Drury Lane from 1747 onward and the important reforms in stage structure and in the standards of acting belong to a different story from ours. Yet his influence upon the colonial stage is perfectly evident.

For one thing, he took a strong stand against the age-old custom of allowing the fashionable and privileged gentlemen to sit on the stage during the performance. It was a custom which, a hundred and fifty years earlier, had driven Shakespeare's great contemporary Ben Jonson, to furious but unsuccessful protest. This reform of Garrick's seems to have been immediately reflected in the American productions. For the recurrence on numbers of colonial playbills of the statement that 'no Person, on any Pre-

tence whatever, can be admitted behind the scenes' is interpreted by authorities like Odell to mean the prohibition
of seats upon the stage. An excuse for this prohibition in
the colonies could be made because of the limitations of
stage space. In a performance, for instance, of Garrick's
own version of *Romeo and Juliet* in New York in the
winter of 1762, the advertisement states that in order that
Juliet's funeral procession may be conducted with 'the
necessary decorum, we must renew our application to the
gentlemen, to give us the entire use of the stage'. Thus
Garrick's Drury Lane innovation echoes over-seas in the
provincial little shows of our New World.

The recurrence of *Richard III*, which is one of Shakespeare's most 'stagey' plays and one of his least subtle
among the earliest offerings over here, suggests many interesting thoughts. The first is the predominance of English influence, for it was *Richard III* in Colley Cibber's
perverted version which had brought David Garrick into
national notice as England's greatest actor when he played
it in 1741. The first recorded *Richard III* in America is
only eight years later, and this title turns up again and
again: at openings in various cities; for benefits, where a
play was selected with the hope of drawing as large houses
as possible; and in the meagre repertory of amateurish
travelling companies.

In advertising *Richard III*, sometimes Shakespeare's
name as the author is included in the playbill or newspaper
advertisement, and sometimes it is not mentioned. The
name of the fashionable adaptor, however, is used as a
drawing card. Sometimes no authors' names are used. But
the blood and violent deeds of the play are described as
the best guarantee to the prospective ticket buyer that an
evening of thrills and rhetoric is before him. If one re-

flects on the fact that nowadays one goes to see 'Shakespeare' and the name of the particular play is almost an after-consideration, one has some small gauge of the difference between the prestige of the man in the mid-eighteenth century and in the twentieth.

The advertisement for the performance in New York in 1749, printed in the *New York Gazette and Weekly Post Boy*, announces *Richard III* as 'wrote originally by Shakespeare and altered by Colley Cibber, Esq.'. What was mere Shakespeare to the great Colley Cibber of Drury Lane fame? In the four-line description of the plot a death, 'the artful acquisition of a crown', a 'murder of the Princes' and a battle are announced. Bloody events were obviously a drawing card. On this occasion there was no after-piece. But a week later, when *Richard III* was played again, the managers did not risk it on its own drawing merits. The bill announced as an added inducement the farce of *The Beau in the Sudds*.

Such a double bill offers something 'heavy' and something 'light'. It caters to a taste none too subtle which asks for excitement tending both toward chills of horror and toward titters of mirth. Under this system, Shakespeare was to find himself with many strange programme-companions. Not only was there likely to be an after-piece, but also there were likely to be interpolated songs and dances and sometimes a masque or pantomime. But this incongruity would not have shocked Shakespeare himself. In his own day there had been many a divertissement in the form of a bout between the audience and a professional joker. The jester Tarlton, for instance, took the stage when the play was over and gave the audience as good as it sent in quips, jests and improvised rhymes. The regular practice of this sort of thing was called the Elizabethan Jig.

Its colonial parallel would not have upset Shakespeare.

During the winter of 1749 in New York—a winter which begins to resemble a theatrical season—*Richard III* turns up three different times: once alone, for the opening night; once with *The Beau in the Sudds;* and once with another farce, *The Mock Doctor.* One is likely to find a record of only about a third of the plays. For the shrewd managers carried advertisements for those plays alone which came out after the weekly newspaper was issued. The other two performances in any week were thus unrecorded. Critical comment in the press on the production and the acting, such as is usual today, was only just beginning when the Revolution set in. Thus knowledge of the way of playing pre-Revolutionary Shakespeare is largely a matter of inference, with an occasional lucky chance auditor's impression when something unusual or diverting occurred at the performance and would rate as news.

These three performances of *Richard III* were the only Shakespearean offerings in New York in this season of '49-'50. The same company played again in New York the next winter. *Richard III* was offered as a benefit night for one of the actresses. This bill was obviously made up to coax money out of the little town of New York's pocket. For it offered a second feature. Also the management threw in 'a favorite dialogue, Jockey and Jenny, to be sung by Mr. Woodman and Mrs. Taylor'. *Richard III* was scheduled again for a benefit in April and announced in the *New York Post Boy.* But it would be no wonder if this frequently repeated morsel was growing a little stale in a town which at this time had less than 2,000 houses! In any case it was not played. In its place was substituted 'a comedy called *The Busy Body*, with the *Virgin Unmasked;* with singing by Mr. Woodman, particularly the celebrated Ode called *Britain's Chart*. One can see at a glance that here was a very attractive programme.

In the winter of 1751–52, when the renegade Upton from the Hallam Company was trying to create a New York season single-handed, he presented *Othello*. His advertisement in the *Post Boy* does not mention Shakespeare as the author. It apparently had no drawing value, but the name of Garrick carried with it the right connotation. The notice announces 'a tragedy called *Othello, Moor of Venice;* to which will be added a Dramatic Entertainment, wrote by the celebrated Mr. Garrick, called *Lethe*'. The same double bill was offered again a week later. This was in December. Late in January, the ubiquitous *Richard III* was again offered 'to which by particular desire, will be added the farce of *Lethe*'. One week later *Othello* was played again, this time in company with *The King and the Miller*.

Clearly Upton's repertoire was meagre, with no time for learning new parts. But the presence of Shakespeare in this chary winter no doubt lent some kind of dignity to his venture. It looked like a real season, if Shakespeare was on the list, though the inability of the audience to take their Shakespeare straight and the inferiority of the companion pieces show again the curious position of Shakespeare in the theatre world. It must be played and witnessed, for it was 'the thing'. But it was violently wrenched out of its norm to suit the public taste and was washed down with draughts of highly inferior entertainment.

In Virginia as well as in New York, the first really organized theatrical season opened with Shakespeare. The old New York company of 1749–51 (Murray and Kean) opened in October, 1751, in Williamsburg with that same favorite, *Richard III*. That Shakespeare was the author was not mentioned, but the after-piece and its author were fully described. 'To which [*Richard III*] will be added a grand Tragic Dance, Composed by Monsier Denoier, called *The Royal Captive*.' This delectation was in the height of the London mode being 'after the Turkish manner, as performed at his Majesty's Opera House in the Hay Market'. The next year in Virginia the famous Hallams from London opened with the *Merchant of Venice*. Clearly Shakespeare was the thing to open with, though if one scans the advertisements in the *Virginia Gazette* for August 28, 1752, one sees that the authorship of the *Merchant of Venice* is explained in a parenthesis in very small type. Shakespeare shared the bill on this occasion with a farce, *The Anatomist: or Sham Doctor*.

Of the quality of the production and acting on this occasion there are no details. But the advertisement has one interesting hint. The part of Lorenzo is advertised as accompanied 'with songs in character'. Shakespeare in his own day often interrupted the progress of the play to put in appropriate songs. A boy with good singing voice in the cast was too good a potential source of entertainment to be omitted. It is, therefore, only the inflexibility of our modern adoration of Shakespeare that makes us criticize the Hallams for utilizing their Mr. Adcock's voice in some freshly inserted songs for the part of Lorenzo. Shakespeare would have done the same thing if it had suited his purpose. Yet one wonders what sorts of songs Lorenzo of the *Merchant of Venice* sang and at what points he interrupted the play to sing them. If they were love songs to Jessica, perhaps they enlivened the lovely scene where he bids her sit and contemplate the 'floor of heaven'. Our feeling that that section of Shakespeare's play as he left it is quite perfect, without Mr. Adcock's intrusive songs, is doubtless a bigoted feeling!

The performance on that famous night was a rather small-town affair, utilizing what forces the British company, newly landed, had. We know this from the reminiscences of Dunlap. Lewis Hallam, a little boy of twelve not accustomed to acting, was pressed into the part of Portia's servant. He 'suffered stage fright and broke in tears from the scene'. Not all the suavity of the special prologue, not the *Virginia Gazette* report of the 'numerous and polite audience' which attended, can gloze the amateurish and makeshift quality of this provincial performance.

The second Shakespearean play of this first season of the Hallams in Virginia was *Othello*. It was played with an added pantomime in November. On this occasion the unusual character of the audience turned the performance into news which was reported in the *Virginia Gazette* of the next week. Some Indians came to town and attended the show. The newspaper account of their visit did all it could to elevate this event into something like a foreign embassy. We read that the 'Emperor of the Cherokee Nation with his Empress', their son and several warriors came to Williamsburg to renew a treaty of friendship. The colonial authorities as a mark of 'civility and friendship' gave them a theatre party to witness *Othello*. During the performance the fighting with naked swords on the stage caused such 'great surprise' that the Empress ordered her attendants to go and prevent the actors from killing one another.

What a marvellous juxtaposition of events; a stage fight in a play by Shakespeare sets the heart of a Red Indian thumping! To present a naïve auditor as thinking that violence on the stage was real is a very old device. Beaumont and Fletcher in Shakespeare's day had resorted to this trick in the *Knight of the Burning Pestle;* Fielding only ten years earlier than these events in Virginia had presented the same sort of incident in his episode in *Tom Jones* of Partridge at the play of *Hamlet.* But here in Virginia in fantastic circumstances, the episode had become real.

The Cherokees were destined to be educated in Shakespeare. In New York in the winter of 1767 after the John Street Theatre was well established, ten Cherokee chieftains came to town on a visit of state. They had come, the advertisement in the *Mercury* announces, from South Carolina. Some of their magnificent names were recorded, such as 'Atta-Kulla-Kulla, or the Little Carpenter'. Hearing that there was a theatre in town 'the chiefs', according to *Holt's Journal,* 'expressed a desire of seeing a play acted'.

In the fifteen years between 1752, when the Cherokee Emperor and his Empress listened to *Othello* in Virginia, and this New York winter of 1767, the colonists had changed their attitude toward the Indians. Now, the 'chiefs' are condescended to and 'managed' by the New York authorities. His Excellency, General Moore, 'thought proper to gratify their curiosity'. The management was playing the ever recurrent *Richard III* that night. After Shakespeare they put on *The Oracle* and by command of Moore adapted their bill still further to these visitors by adding a 'Pantomime Ballet called Harlequin's Vagaries'. The house, reports *Holt's Journal,* was crowded on 'the expectation of seeing the Indian chiefs at the Play'. *Richard III,* they regarded 'with seriousness and attention'.

But 'as it cannot be supposed that they were sufficiently acquainted with the language of the author, their countenances and behaviour were rather expressive of surprise and curiosity than any other passions'. General Moore and the management's guess about the success of the pantomime was apparently a good one. We learn that 'some of them were much surprised and diverted at the tricks of Harlequin'. Incongruous New World, reflecting at one moment the decorum and politeness of London and at the next confronting and meeting the new and often ludicrous situations of pioneering on a primitive continent. That Shakespeare should have presided twice at the juxtaposition of these incongruities is quite appropriate.

When the Hallam Company after its first season in Virginia went to New York in 1753, it opened in September with a play of Steele's. But by November, if not before, the company was playing Shakespeare. It was the old reliable *Richard III*. The playbill for this performance survives and states that this play is being given 'by particular desire'. Shakespeare's name is not mentioned but a bloody description of the plot is printed on the bill. It will include 'the distress and death of King Henry VI', 'the artful acquisition of the crown by crook-backed Richard', with 'murder' and 'battle' in gory emphasis. The prospective audience is addressed as 'Gentlemen and Ladies that choose tickets' and the companion-piece will be a 'ballad Farce, called *The Devil to Pay*'.

In January they offered *Lear* in Nahum Tate's version with the happy ending. This was the version Garrick had played and though far away from Shakespeare's original, it had the *sine qua non* of London approval. The same month saw *Romeo and Juliet*, probably, thinks Odell, in Garrick's adaptation.

Between the Shakespeare and the after-piece, Hulett, whose dancing still was advertised as direct from London, danced 'The Drunken Peasant'. How it consorted with *Romeo and Juliet*, even in Garrick's version, one wonders. But apparently the exquisite poetry of tragic young lovers mixed well with alien divertissements. For in March, *Romeo and Juliet* was played again with 'entertainments' which included a Punch's dance, a 'tamboureen' dance and a hornpipe. There were songs, too, by the young boy, Hallam, who had had such bad stage fright as Portia's servant in the opening of the Virginia season. He sang 'As Chloe Came into the Room' and 'The Reasonable Lover'. After all this came the second piece, *The Stage Coach*. This was full measure for a single evening's entertainment and varied withal.

The spring of 1744 saw Hallam in Philadelphia. The press, under good Quaker control, is chary of its theatre news. There is no recorded Shakespeare, though it was prominent in Hallam's repertoire and no doubt was played.

New York next saw Shakespeare apparently in the winter of 1758–59 under Douglass's management. This was the winter when there was so much opposition to plays in New York on moral grounds and when Douglass only was allowed, after much controversy, to have a few brief weeks in January and February. But even in this brief season he played *Othello* and *Richard III* and was, no doubt, in these particular choices as well as generally 'the Town's most obedient servant', as he declared himself in the pages of the *Mercury*.

The next Douglass season in New York was in 1761, when the offerings included a generous share of Shakespeare. *Hamlet* was played with an accompanying farce. *Henry IV*, Part I was offered for the first time in New

York. One wonders how Falstaff was played, whether it was 'farced' and boisterous or sophisticated and thoughtful as Maurice Evans so brilliantly portrayed him in the 1930's. *Romeo and Juliet* was played at least twice, probably both times in Garrick's arrangement which included the 'Funeral Procession of Juliet to the Monument of the Capulets, in which will be sung a Solemn Dirge'. The Hollywood version of *Romeo and Juliet* in 1936 made the same valuable addition, which was pictorial and effective because of the reality of the scene, the setting of Italian hills, the 'life size' funeral moving majestically against it. But in New York in the winter and spring of 1761–62, in a makeshift theatre, it seems improbable that the procession contributed anything to the atmosphere.

'The gentlemen' were asked to forego their seats on the stage, so that the procession 'may be conducted with the necessary decorum'. But even with this concession, it must have been an awkward affair. Yet it furnished a diversion from plain Shakespeare; it dressed him up with an added attraction and a song. And both these additions had the sanction of Garrick's London usage. In the masquerade scene at the Capulet Ball, in the January performance, there were introduced two 'delicacies', 'a minuet by Mr. A. Hallam and Mrs. Allen' and a 'comic dance by Mr. A. Hallam'. In the second production in March the minuet was not repeated, but the 'comic dance' was again given. Probably comic relief was a more welcome sauce to Shakespeare than the stately minuet.

Othello, billed with *The Lying Varlet*, made a benefit for 'the Poor'. It was always a tactful gesture to spare some of the proceeds of the season for local charity and advertise the fact.

But the theatre public was still a very uncertain quantity. In this year of 1761–62, the cleavage between parties which led to the Revolution was growing deeper. The pressure on the Tory group was heavier. Perhaps they did not have so much leisure or disposition to support the stage. In the *Richard III* programme, as advertised in the *Mercury*, there is a significant note. It would seem that the custom of selling tickets at the doors of patron's houses was becoming a nuisance instead of the compliment it had seemed ten years earlier. The note maintains that 'the ceremony [delicious word for house-to-house peddling] of waiting on Ladies and Gentlemen at their houses with bills has been for some time left off . . . the frequent solicitations . . . having been found rather an inconvenience to the persons so waited on than a compliment'. More taxing times and less leisure are what this change of custom seems to argue.

The New York world was bare of professional performances after this season until the winter of 1767–68, with the opening of the first real theatre building, the John Street Theatre. It stimulated Douglass to new and grander efforts. He put on at least ten Shakespearean plays. To the usual six or seven, Douglass added some unfamiliar ones in this first stimulating winter at the John Street Theatre. Dryden's adaptation of *Antony and Cleopatra* was given its first recorded New York performance this winter. *Cymbeline* 'as altered by Mr. Garrick' was presented twice. *Romeo and Juliet* was played with *Katherine and Petruchio* (Garrick's reconstruction of the *Taming of the Shrew*). Our old *Richard III* was wonderfully embellished with a 'humorous interlude', at the end of Act II, 'between a painter and Lady Pentweazle of Blowbladder St.'. After the third act, the echo song from Milton's *Comus* was sung. This was indeed an embarrassment of riches.

In these productions, that miraculous identification of the man in the audience with the actor on the stage, whereby the auditor suffers and laughs with the actor and lives the play throughout from beginning to end, could not have existed. That psychological union between actor and audience of which Aristotle had written so brilliantly in the heyday of the Athenian drama, only occurs when the play and the acting are first-rate. Besides, the tradition of contemporary London acting must have been practised, if inferiorly, by the Hallams and their successors. It was an oratorical tradition in which the great speeches of a play were isolated. They became opportunities for the leading actor to step forward, out of his part. He cut the bonds which enmeshed him with the rest of the play and showed his audience what he could do in the way of gesture, voice and stature in the art of oratory.

Capt. Alexander Graydon in his *Memoirs* (cleverly utilized by Odell) comments that Douglass was 'rather a decent than a stirring actor'. Of Hallam, he says that 'his declamation was either mouthing or ranting'. He could 'tread the stage with . . . ease'; he had 'all the tricks and finesse of his trade'. But the 'trade' was oratory, not great acting as we now conceive it. When Mrs. Hallam acted 'it was absolutely necessary to forget that to touch the heart of the spectator had any relation to her function'. Wooden, conscientious oratorical acting they must have given. No wonder dances, songs and other divertissements did not offend the audience. There was no psychological unity in the playing which these interruptions would destroy.

Miss Hallam as Imogen in Shakespeare's *Cymbeline* elic-
ited a poetical tribute from an anonymous gentleman in
the Poet's Corner of the *Maryland Gazette* in 1771, which
emphasizes this 'oratorical' acting. The gentleman declares

> From earliest youth; with rapture oft
> I've turned great Shakespeare's page.

Yet only now does he really understand Shakespeare. He
pictures Shakespeare nominating Miss Hallam as the exponent of his poetry in America:

> Long [Shakespeare speaks] have my scenes
>   each British Heart
> With warmest transports filled:
> Now equal praise, by Hallam's Arts,
>   America shall yield.

It was undoubtedly the young lady's declamation of certain speeches and her oratorical skill that provoked such
lines.

It may be a too harsh and merely modern standard of
acting which deplores oratory and calls for psychological
consistency throughout a part. Certainly Shakespeare's
own world of actors was full of oratory. The giants of
Shakespearean interpretation in the nineteenth and early
twentieth centuries still thundered their great speeches
and thereby broke through the gossamer of continuous
and interrelated performance. In fact, when a modern
actor like Gielgud in the 1930's plays *Hamlet* as a whole,
without taking his chances to heighten separate speeches
and present them as poetic oratory, one naïve auditor
caught his breath in fear. As the great soliloquies came

falteringly forth, like the hidden thoughts of the man, in pauses and rushes as he lived them, the auditor, used to the oratorical smoothness of these passages, feared that Gielgud had lost his lines! Whatever the playwright's and critic's conceptions of parts may be, the actor and the public more often than not have regarded Shakespeare's plays as a series of heightened oratorical speeches.

Philadelphia had been the equal if not the superior of New York in Shakespeare productions by the same troupe of actors in this year. There had been the season of 1759, managed by Douglass, with more than one-sixth of the recorded titles from Shakespeare and a final *Hamlet* benefit for the Pennsylvania theatre. The cast was distinguished by a granddaughter of Colley Cibber and a young John Palmer who two years later went back to England as 'one of the best general actors [the London stage] ever had'. One snowy evening in Philadelphia just before Christmas, Palmer took a benefit in the part of Romeo. What one would give for a spectator's report of the show.

The New Southwark Theatre, opening for the first time with Douglass and the American Company in the winter of 1769–70, offered a season rich in Shakespeare—*Julius Caesar*, *Merry Wives*, *The Tempest* (in Shadwell's version). In the winter of '72–'73, they were playing there again, offering among plays new to Philadelphia, *Henry IV*, Part I and *Othello*. Shakespeare, in fact, on the Philadelphia stage before the Revolution, as its historian T. C. Pollock says, 'compares favorably with if it does not surpass the modern professional stage'.

In Virginia in 1768 there were *Henry IV* and the *Merchant of Venice* and *King Lear*, the last played on the same bill with *High Life Below Stairs*. In the spring of 1771, Washington was in Virginia and, as was his usual

custom, attended the play. What play he saw we are not
sure, but it may have been Shakespeare. He certainly saw
Hamlet in New York in May, 1773, where Miss Hallam
as Ophelia 'with her tragic gift and her singing voice' undoubtedly repaid the future father of his country for his
expenditure of eight shillings.

The era of amateur playing, which was to beguile many
a weary hour for army officers on both the British and
Colonial sides after the outbreak of the Revolution, was
already in the air. As early as 1769, in Douglass's season
there, 'the part of Othello' was to be 'attempted by a
gentleman assisted by other gentlemen. . . . From a benev-
olent and generous design of encouraging the Theatre and
relieving the Performers from some embarrassments in
which they are involved'.

In 1773, Douglass's season at the New York Theatre
was full of Shakespeare. The *Tempest* in Dryden's version
was played with 'elegant' machinery. A summer performance of *Romeo and Juliet* had an intermission in which
Miss Hallam sang 'The Soldier Tired of War's Alarm',
accompanied by a band of His Majesty's Regiment. This
song, lurking between the scenes of *Romeo and Juliet*,
presaged a time when the royal party and with it the old
theatre should be engaged in a losing struggle with the
forces of an unknown and upstart America. Douglass and
his company, sensing the oncoming trouble, left New
York in the summer of '73 and did not return for twelve
years.

CHAPTER VI

Shakespeare and Some Revolutionary Leaders: John Adams (and Abigail), Franklin, Jefferson, Washington

IN THE marches and countermarches of opinion which accompanied the development of America across the eighteenth century up to the point where it suddenly 'came of age' and asserted its national independence, much ink was spilled and many sheets of foolscap were covered. The eighteenth century was an age of essays, of leisurely letters on topics which concerned the writer. The almost daily shiftings in the kaleidoscopic patterns of the public scene; the 'rights' of England *versus* the 'rights' of the colonies; the claims of fair play against the stronger instinctive claims of kinship and love of 'home' across the seas; the gradual sinking of sectional jealousies and differences in one united front; all these circumstances forced people to think behind the news or the event of the moment, to its meaning. The doctrine of government, the place of the individual in the state, the conditions which each citizen wanted for 'life, liberty and the pursuit of happiness'; these ideas found their way into essays and letters.

This 'climate of opinion' was inevitable in eighteenth century America if one considers the urgency for the individual of the day-to-day development of public events. But had there not been this external pressure to turn thoughtful Americans into moralizers on the public scene, the cast of their thinking and writing would still have been

the same. They were, after all, a part of the English eighteenth century. The tendency toward neat moral epigram,
toward the delightful game of justifying art in terms of
morality, of dissecting human conduct, both public and
private, and rearranging it in categories of behaviour was
as natural to the Englishman colonized in America as to
the thinkers and writers 'at home'. Add to this, the inherited tendency of these colonists, especially in the
North, toward a belligerent moral approach to life, and
one has a perfect explanation for the didacticism and sen-
tentious emphasis which their writings show.

Into this eighteenth century thinking and writing,
Shakespeare frequently steps. He appears not as a drama-
tist at all. His shade seems guiltless of the glamour of theatrical performance. For all one may gather from the
frequent quotations from him by leaders like Jefferson and
Adams, he is a great moralist who has penetrated the mys-
teries of individual and social values and expounds his dis-
coveries with the air of the prophet. He is a book of
wisdom from which to cull some priceless pearl and place
it at that apex of one's argument, where it may cast its
soft lustre over the stern prose which surrounds it. It is
amusing to select a few of the typical thinkers of middle-
eighteenth century and Revolutionary America and see
how much or little they use Shakespeare and in what
characteristic ways.

John Adams is one of the foremost figures in America's
'coming of age', and his background is typical. He was
the son of a Massachusetts farmer, fourth generation in
descent from a colonist out of Devonshire. After a Harvard education (class of 1755) and admission to the bar,
he became a vigorous leader in the new stand against
'British Imperialism' in the Colonies. His first distinguished

political essays were directed against the Stamp Act. They were printed in the *Boston Gazette* in the summer of 1765 when Adams was just turned thirty. His rhetoric against England is earnest. England is our mother, he declares. 'But, admitting we are children, have not children a right to complain when their parents are attempting to break their limbs—will the mother be pleased when you represent her as deaf to the cries of her children—when you resemble her [and here enters our pearl from Shakespeare's Book of Wisdom] to Lady Macbeth' in Shakespeare? Adams then quotes tellingly from *Macbeth*.

This strange Shakespeare, this author entirely divorced from the man of the stage, when he is quoted in this period, often contains no reference to act, scene or line. The fact that the quotation is an integral part of a particular play seems never to occur to those who use quotations. Shakespeare's plays have become Shakespeare's 'Works' with a vengeance. Their lines can be cut to any pattern the quoter has in mind. They are shorn of the implications which they normally have in the play. In this respect young John Adams is no particular offender. He is simply following the practice of his world. This young, eighteenth century Harvard man knew his Shakespeare. He made telling use of it to point the rhetoric of his controversial pamphlet against England's imposition of the Stamp Act.

One wonders what were the particular circumstances which led Adams, then aged thirty-seven and feeling his growing power in the tense American political world, to head the entry in his diary for a certain Sunday in 1772, with the remark of Mrs. Ford to Mrs. Page from Shakespeare's *Merry Wives*. Falstaff had made highly scandalous personal proposals to each of these Merry Wives of

Windsor in identical letters. Mrs. Ford breaks the news of her letter to Mrs. Page, in this speech,

If I would but go to hell for an eternal moment or so, I could be knighted.

The speech is not delicate. It describes accurately the liaison which the wicked old Sir John has proposed. But young John Adams on this holy day uses this speech (without reference to line or act or scene or to the play in which it occurs) as the text of a noble passage of his diary on 'the struggle which I believe always happens between virtue and ambition, when a man first commences courtier'. Thus the bawdy proposal of Shakespeare's old rascal becomes, to this rising young leader, the moral exhortation to stand firm against seductions which might seem the shortest way to personal power. Falstaff's barefaced proposal becomes a moral proverb. One wonders if Adams knew the *Merry Wives* well and if he knew the precise content of this quotation. Probably he did. But Shakespeare, read in the study, has become a volume of wisdom to ponder on. The bawdiest incident may be symbolically interpreted to point a moral.

How far removed Adams is from any sense of the sweating, boisterous Elizabethan pit and the 'Johanes factotum' who fed its greedy maw with popular entertainment. This is clear from his comment on Shakespeare's language in this speech of Mistress Ford. 'Shakespeare', says Adams, 'that great master of every affection of the heart and every sentiment of the mind, as well as of all the powers of expression, is sometimes fond of a certain pointed oddity of language'. He goes on to call it 'a certain quaintness of style that is an imperfection in his character'. This comment is amazing. Apparently it is Shakespeare's style that is to be regarded as 'an imperfection in his character', not the ribald proposal of Falstaff to the madams of Windsor. One remembers that this was the century of Pope when the criterion of wit was

What oft was thought, but ne'er so well express'd.

One remembers, too, that Adams, in his taste, is simply a provincial replica of eighteenth century Londoners. Yet even on this Sunday morning in 1772, forces were growing which should shape his America, at one sudden blow, into a separate and independent nation with a name and personality distinctly original.

Shakespeare accompanied Adams into his prominence and offered him a moving passage to support his point of view in one of the great crises of his life. When the Revolution was over and the peace negotiated, Adams went as our first Minister to the Court of St. James's. While he was in London, he published *A Defense of the Constitution of the Govt. of the United States*. It contained an argument for degrees in the structure of society. It even suggested that 'the rich, the well-born and the able . . . should be set apart from other men in a senate'. It was this argument, smelling of aristocracy, which provoked American criticism of Adams and reduced the electoral votes for his Vice-Presidency under Washington (1789) to a very small number. Tyranny had just been punished at a high price in America; and many of the electors were still smarting from the costly victory over aristocratic principles. They would not risk their vote on any man who recognized and featured class distinctions.

How Adams must have hugged Shakespeare to his

bosom on this humiliating occasion. For he had found in Shakespeare's *Troilus and Cressida* full confirmation of his belief in 'degrees' within society. He had already enunciated his own doctrine on the structure of a successful society in a *Commentary* on an early seventeenth century Italian historian, Davila. In this book, published in the year of his election as Vice-President, he had used Shakespeare to support his point. Adams argues that the greatness of a leader, lapsing for a moment, uncertain of its prestige, quickly loses power over its followers. Shakespeare, 'the great Master of Nature' and the 'great teacher of morality and politics', supports him. Once in the lead, one must keep it, says Ulysses, in *Troilus and Cressida:*

> For emulation hath a thousand sons
> That one by one pursue.

If class distinctions are lost, then the whole structure of society goes to pieces.

To support his contention, Adams again summons the magnificent speech of Ulysses, in *Troilus and Cressida:*

> Degree being vizarded,
> The unworthiest shows as fairly in the mask.
> The heavens themselves, the planets and this centre
> Observe degree, priority and place.

This amazing speech still confounds modern commentators on Shakespeare, carrying as it does a hint that he had read widely in the political theory of his day. Adams concludes his quotation with the line which calls the lack of class distinctions a dangerous illness to the body politic. It is 'the fever whereof all our power is sick'.

Adams puts this line in italics, representing no doubt an underlining with his pen in the original manuscript. It reflects the conservative views of society for which, with detriment to his personal popularity, John Adams consistently stood. In the new nation they made him a prop of the Federalist group. He and Alexander Hamilton were drawn up against the Democratic-Republican views of Jefferson and his followers. During these years the destiny of American society wavered between these two points of view. Adams never retired one iota from his position. His staunchness is concretely confirmed by a note which he added on these *Troilus and Cressida* passages in a later issue of his book. 'The style of these quotations from Shakespeare', he says, 'has little of the fluency and less of that purity which sometimes appears in his writing; but [and here comes the magnificently consistent re-assertion of his conservative point of view after twenty-five years] the sense is as immortal as human nature.' Today in America, after the twentieth century has already completed its first third, the assertions of both Federalists and Democratic-Republicans, in their modern nomenclature of Republicans and Democrats, are as staunchly held and as sharply opposed. That Shakespeare helped to hold the front line of the conservative forces, is an amusing thought.

In the spring of 1786, the new American nation was represented by the presence of some of its most distinguished citizens in London. John Adams and his gifted wife, Abigail, were occupying the American Embassy. Thomas Jefferson, always personally sympathetic to Adams, though the following years were to see a temporary estrangement, was in London with them. What irritating reticences men develop in their diaries! In Jefferson's, for instance, during these two months in England, we read that he and John Adams spent a day at Stratford-on-Avon seeing Shakespeare's house. But Jefferson's note records none of those comments on Shakespeare and his genius which must have passed between these two great Americans. Adams' knowledge of Shakespeare was ever present and Jefferson's was even more fully reflected in his writings. The meagre little entry, however, says nothing about how this visit affected them. What pride they must have felt in this great English poet who was a part of their heritage still, though they had cleft the political bond which kept them Englishmen and now belonged to that rather uncertain new political *genus*, American. But Jefferson's note only records: 'for seeing house where Shakespeare was born, 1s; seeing his tomb, 1s; entertainment, 4s 2d; servants, 2s'.

Probably both Jefferson and Adams attended Shakespearean performances in London during that spring of 1786; for Mrs. Siddons was playing magnificently. Though there is no record of the presence of these Americans in her audience, we know that Abigail Adams (John's wife) was frequently there. She had been a reader of Shakespeare all her life. Her grandson pays her a handsome compliment. 'The young ladies of Massachusetts', he says, 'in the last century, were certainly readers, even though only self-taught; and their taste was not for the feeble and nerveless sentiment, or the frantic passion, which comes from the novels and romances in the circulating library of our day [his day being 1840] but was derived from the deepest wells of English literature.' That Shakespeare was one of these wells for Abigail Adams is shown by the frequent references to him in her letters.

In the first year of her marriage, while her husband was absent in Boston being inoculated for the smallpox, she began that series of spirited letters with which she continued to regale him during his long absences on official business at home and abroad. These letters preserve the warmth and aroma of her personality. One is delighted to see in the intimate picture of her taste and daily thinking, that Shakespeare comes naturally to her mind as the perfect embodiment of some idea or comparison she is making. In her letters as a bride, in the spring of 1764, Abigail Adams makes love to her husband with Shakespeare at her elbow. She dreams of going to him at night, she says, and in between these glimpses of him, she is 'haunted by half a dozen ugly sprites'. One 'will carry me up a precipice, like that which Edward describes in *Lear*'. One 'will be pouring down my throat stuff worse than the witches' broth in Macbeth'. This is half coquetry and half real torture at his absence. No doubt he was flattered to be wooed with such wit and such knowledge.

In the autumn of 1775, when the war was really under way and Abigail had been married to Adams for twelve years, the letters and the apposite Shakespearean quotations were still going on. 'The time is hastening', she writes, 'when George, like Richard, may cry, "My kingdom for a horse!" and want even that wealth to make the purchase.' The next autumn she is saying that she cannot bear the possibility of 'a state of supineness'. She quotes, as a stirring admonition to action, 'There is a tide in the affairs of men', though without any indication of its source or that it is by Shakespeare. She writes this letter after the Dorchester battle in which 'the rattling of the windows, the jar of the house' had prevented her from sleeping. Again she is citing lines from *Julius Caesar* as she writes Adams about the funeral of a local doctor who 'fell a martyr' to 'the noble cause'. During these months she

frequently signs herself 'Portia'. Her grandson takes this
to be the 'Portia' of *Julius Caesar*. In fact, he feels that
the frequent quotations from *Julius Caesar* by Abigail
Adams during the early years of the Revolution suggest
'the historical precedents to which the mind of the writer
at this time inclined'.

There is something magnificently permanent about this
Shakespeare. Even though misquoted and misunderstood,
his words have been so far-flung in the subsequent history
of the little England for which he wrote. In Abigail
Adams' letters, the words he may have written with some
thought in his mind of the political unrest in Elizabeth's
reign were now sent forth, nearly two centuries later,
from a quiet farmhouse in Massachusetts to strengthen the
resolve of one who helped turn an English colony into a
new nation in the western hemisphere.

When Mrs. Adams found herself in London in the
spring of 1786, as the wife of the new American ambassa-
dor to the Court of St. James's, she went to see Mrs. Siddons in many Shakespearean rôles. Her comments, in a
letter to her sister, are characteristic of all eighteenth century comment of Shakespeare on the stage. Shakespeare as
a dramatic artist and the play as a dramatic whole are not
the things the typical theatregoer considered. Rather, he
was concerned with the performance of the actor, whose
personality, especially if it was fashionable as Garrick's
and Mrs. Siddons' were, and performance surpassed in
importance the playwright whom they produced. Eighteenth century theatregoers were the victims of stardom.
The famous artist in the rôle was the thing they thought
about. Poor old Shakespeare, as the mere vehicle, limped
far behind; except that his name gave a kind of snobbish
'cultural' tone to the whole occasion.

Thus Mrs. Adams, watching Mrs. Siddons as Desdemona in *Othello*, is quite oblivious of the deep poignancy of the play as a whole. She cannot get beyond Mrs. Siddons' person to the love and despair of the Desdemona she played. 'I lost much of the pleasure of the play', says Mrs. Adams, 'from the sooty appearance of the Moor. . . . I could not separate the African colour from the man.' And recalling the elegance of Sir Joshua's portrait of the divine Siddons, we cannot wonder that Abigail was filled with 'disgust and horror . . . every time I saw him [Othello] touch the gentle Desdemona'. So, too, in witnessing *Macbeth*, it was not Lady Macbeth but Mrs. Siddons whom Abigail Adams watched, feeling all the while that such an idol of the fashionable London world is 'too great to be put in so detestable a character'. Shakespeare was a vehicle, indeed, but sometimes too mean a vehicle for so much elegance and beauty.

We have left John Adams and Jefferson at Stratford, seeing 'Shakespeare's house' on a spring day in 1786. The background of the poet's work, which Adams must have recalled on that day, was an intrinsic part of his thinking. Jefferson's approach to Shakespeare was as different as his personality was different from Adams'. Yet, as his writings reveal, Shakespeare had a permanent place in his cultural perspective.

Jefferson's connection with Shakespeare began, no doubt, through his father. Peter Jefferson was third in descent from a British family of no particular prominence. They had been living in Virginia as early as 1677. It was through his marriage with the influential Randolph family that Peter Jefferson gave his own children a prominent position. But in his own right, as a member of a quiet colonial family resident in America for a hundred years, Peter Jefferson had both cultivation and learning. In his library along with the usual eighteenth century books, like Swift's and the *Spectator*, was a copy of Shakespeare. His son, Thomas, inherited this interest.

The fairly recent discovery of a little commonplace book, bound in worn old leather and containing one hundred and nineteen pages into which Jefferson copied passages from his favourite poets, reveals what Jefferson valued in the way of quotations. Many entries were made during his undergraduate days at William and Mary College in Williamsburg, Virginia, in the early 1760's. Some, still showing the same sort of taste, were added later. The proportion of quotations from Shakespeare in comparison to Milton and the great Greek and Roman classics, is notable. The nature of these quotations reveals a serious, chivalrous and high-minded young aristocrat. This Jefferson, who was to fight so valiantly for the rights of the farmer and the small property owner against the concentration of property in the hands of a powerful few, needed, indeed, to buttress his youthful ideals with such inspiriting moral exhortations as he found in the pages of William Shakespeare.

The first six Shakespearean quotations in his notebook, all drawn from *Julius Caesar*, are concerned with the way in which one should value life. In these passages there is much fearless reference to death, that it is more honourable than certain sorts of life. The passages have that simple, heroic statement of moral values which makes *Julius Caesar* a perfect play for the adolescent. Though a reader may return to *Julius Caesar* in later life and find there brilliant comment on compromise and on the cloudier issues of existence as one perceives them in middle life, yet at its surface value, *Julius Caesar* is full of the clear-cut issues and ringing challenges that appeal to youth.

Jefferson copies several fine passages on honour from Part I of *Henry IV*. He includes the famous pronouncement of Falstaff on honour in which Sir John argues that honour is a mere 'word', 'air'. It is too dearly bought if it end in death. He concludes his catechism with the comfortable decision, 'Therefore I'll have none of it'. One would give much to know in what mood the young Jefferson copied out these lines into his little leather-covered book. It is now the fashion in Shakespearean scholarship to rate these lines as the argument of an over-rational, disillusioned worldling, a frequent figure in the court in the last years of Elizabeth's reign. It is quite probable that they were taken in a more literal sense by the young Jefferson, as a stern reminder of the fact that mere logic, if applied to moral values, misleads one into cowardice and shame.

Of four passages from *Coriolanus*, two carry no discussion of great principles, one comments neatly on the fact that 'extremity' is the 'trier of men's souls'. But to the fourth quotation one would give much to know Jefferson's reaction. It is taken from the speech of Coriolanus where he deplores and distrusts the leaders of the mob and the mob itself. He beseeches the Senators not to give away their power to the officers of the people. Jefferson seems to have it by memory and rearranges the order of some of the lines, as if they lived frequently in his thoughts and toppled out in disorder, at the end of his goose-quill pen. The passage is, on its face value, an argument for aristocracy, for ruling the many by the wise few.

Why did Jefferson quote it and when? It fits well with

the Tory policy of the early 1760's. But it contradicts faith in the rule of simple people. It was that faith which made Jefferson, in 1776, insist upon changing the phrases 'life, liberty and the pursuit of property', to 'life, liberty and the pursuit of happiness', before he would set his name to the Declaration. Was this *Coriolanus* passage an example of how not to behave toward popular government? a reminder that one's aristocratic inclinations must be kept down and not given utterance? We shall never know. Perhaps it was merely a good passage for declamation, or perhaps the style of its rhetoric was notable. Speculation is idle, but it is tempting.

The only quotation from Shakespeare which is repeated in another section of the book is from *Henry VI* on purity of heart being the only invulnerable breastplate. It was this kind of moral stiffening which the young Jefferson apparently found most helpful amid the turmoils of his own life. He also quotes from *Troilus and Cressida* a long passage on misfortune and storm being the only 'true proof of Virtue'. Interesting, too, is his quotation from Buckingham's adaptation of *Julius Caesar*. It is a long argument on the right of suicide:

> Thus every bondman in his own hand bears
> The power to cancel his captivity.

The right of suicide has been debated from the days of John Donne and Hamlet right down through the centuries. It is a theme appealing to the high intolerance with life which often besets a valiant and noble youth. That Jefferson, too, thought of it is quite natural.

Thus stands the record of Shakespeare in the youthful mind and notebook of Thomas Jefferson. The Works of

Shakespeare were to him, as they were to his great contemporary, John Adams, a book of wisdom. They were the poetry of moral comment on life, set in noble verses. Jefferson usually quotes act and scene. So far he goes in recognizing that these passages were once part of the dialogue in actable and dramatic shows written for the public stage. But Jefferson's recognition of the acting origin is, I think, merely formal. Throughout his life, Shakespeare permeated Jefferson's thoughts chiefly as a great poetic commentator on the human scene.

Confirmation of this opinion, that, for Jefferson, Shakespeare was a repository of persuasive morality rather than great dramatic literature, is borne out in an amazing letter which he wrote from Monticello in the spring of 1771. A friend had asked him for advice on the purchase of books to the amount of fifty pounds sterling. In suggesting titles, Jefferson of course included Shakespeare. In making this suggestion his idea of the value of Shakespeare is purely moral. 'Everything', he says, 'is useful which contributes to fix in the principles and practices of virtue.' The human being is 'wisely' so 'framed' that fiction which points a moral is as effective as fact. Thus the 'fictitious murder of Duncan by Macbeth' excites 'as great a horror of villainy' as if it were real and *Lear* suggests to any young reader 'a lively and lasting sense of filial duty'. These fictions are more effective than 'all the dry volumes of ethics and divinity that ever were written'.

Alas! that Pharaoh is sold for balsams, and the incomparable greatness of Shakespeare is reduced to the neat illustration of moral conduct! But one must remember that Jefferson belonged to his own century. It was a false argument which justified fiction as a 'pleasing' and useful method of teaching conduct. But it was as old as Horace and was popular right down through the century in which Jefferson lived. One could not expect him to be independent of an idea which had permeated criticism for so long. Yet the complete absorption of the playwright into the moralist, and the idea that Shakespeare was a book for the library rather than a script for the stage, is particularly strong in Jefferson.

He is the very reverse of his fellow Virginian, Washington, whose knowledge of Shakespeare was almost entirely built on seeing him performed in the theatre. Jefferson's anti-British and pro-French accent may have been partly responsible for this difference. For to see Shakespeare on the colonial stage was merely to be as fashionably like London as possible. It was more for the sake of Garrick and Siddons than for the sake of Shakespeare himself. Jefferson did not feel this passion to ape contemporary London. He preferred to take his Shakespeare as a great English classic to be read in the study. *78808*

Of Shakespeare as a great poet, with magical powers over the English language, Jefferson was very conscious. He drew up an engaging 'course of reading for a student of law'. This was to be the liberalizing background to the young student's more technical learning. The schedule was arranged to fit into the suitable hours of the day. 'Lighter' reading was reserved for the evening when the brain was less fresh and less able to wrestle with tough adversaries. In a section headed 'From Dark to Bedtime', titles in *belles-lettres* are prescribed. Among these Shakespeare occupies an important place. His poetry will provide the future lawyer whose eloquence must be moving if he is to win his case, with 'the full powers of the English language'. One imagines the earnest young student pursuing knotty problems all day till dusk. Then the arrival of the candle-stand and the drawing of the curtains would bring Shakespeare and 'the full powers of the English language' till 'bedtime'. This was the scholar's dream of how a day should be divided and employed. Milton had dreamed of it in his *Tractate on Education* and college presidents dream of it now, forgetting the variability in the central element of their neat design, the inclination and ability of the student who is to pursue it. Jefferson himself was only twenty-two when he laid out this rigorous programme. He still adhered to it as a grandfather, when at the age of sixty-one he revised it for his grandson.

In 1825, just a year before he died, Jefferson was writing to England to thank for a gift of books to his new University of Virginia at Charlottesville. He was still praising Shakespeare's marvellous use of English. But he showed more than an admiration. He showed a remarkable grasp of what the scientific study of English dialects might do for restoring the precise meaning of Shakespearean passages. When 'country dialects' and 'local vocabularies' have been 'published and digested', he writes, probably 'not a word in Shakespeare' will be obscure. Thus the 'true sense' of Shakespeare will be restored. Though Jefferson himself was not to live to see it, he rejoices that 'we shall find in him [Shakespeare] new sublimities which we had never tasted before'. Magnificent prophecy in 1825 of the wonders of scientific textual criticism which beginning in the nineteenth and continuing in the first third of our twentieth century, have done so much to reveal Shakespeare 'plain', as he spoke and wrote in his own glorious day.

Yet curiously enough after a long life full of reading Shakespeare himself and recommending the reading of him to others, Jefferson did not think of putting a specific course in the study of Shakespeare into the curriculum of his new University of Virginia. There was in this university a place for the study of literature, a professor whose time was to be partly devoted to its teaching, but Shakespeare was not mentioned. He followed the traditional assumption that a gentleman read in his study, without official courses, those things that belong to culture. Shakespeare was in Jefferson's own library. It is listed in the manuscript catalogue of his library, now in the Massachusetts Historical Society's library. He had the four-volume Steevens edition of the plays in octavo and the Johnson and Steevens edition in twelve volumes in octavo. He also had (and this is interesting, suggesting his method of hunting out passages on specific themes) an octavo *Concordance* to Shakespeare.

Shakespeare was distinctly a part of the furniture of a cultivated man in America in the last half of the eighteenth century. James Otis, who left Harvard in 1743, in the midst of a busy lawyer's life pursued his avocation of classics and modern literature. Shakespeare was a part of that 'literature'. He refers to it in a letter of advice on reading. Contemporary poets, he suggests in the manner of conservatives in every age, are not worth much. 'Read Shakespeare, Milton, Dryden, and Pope,' he admonishes, 'and throw all the rest in the fire.' Yale had the same attitude. A Yale B.A. of 1767, John Trumbull, who stayed on in New Haven till 1770, working for his M.A. and writing essays in the style of Addison and Steele, delivered a spirited commencement address in September, 1770, on the brilliant future of American letters. His highest ambition for American literature was that 'some future Shakespeare' might

charm the rising age
And hold in magic chains the list'ning stage.

Thus did the young graduates of Harvard and Yale, without benefit of 'Shakespeare courses', admire this great Elizabethan and feel his prestige.

In a person like Benjamin Franklin, schooled in the university of hard knocks, it is not surprising to find no reference whatever to Shakespeare. To be sure there was a copy of Shakespeare among the handy reference books in the Boston office of the *New England Courant* where he worked with his brother in 1725. But that he took Shakespeare to his heart as Adams and Jefferson did, there is no evidence. Though he was miraculously gifted in absorbing the atmosphere of his time, it was the new atmosphere of science and theory. Shakespeare, where he existed, was a familiar assumption.

It is not surprising, either, in view of the absence of any formal teaching of Shakespeare at the time, that Franklin did not include him in his 'Idea of the English School, Sketched Out for the Consideration of the Trustees of the Philadelphia Academy'. This scheme was produced in 1750 and was sent to his friend Samuel Johnson (the American of that name) for his comment. Now this Samuel Johnson, who was an exponent of the Church of England in the Colonies, was closely in touch with England. To him, then, Franklin's omission of Shakespeare seemed worthy of comment. 'You might do well', he says, 'to mention Milton . . . with the works of Shakespeare, Addison and Pope and Swift . . . as the best English classics.' Whether Franklin accepted the Englishman's suggestion is not sure.

An important Revolutionary figure like John Dickinson

certainly knew Shakespeare. Born on the eastern shore of
Maryland, in a household with a famous library and sent
to England for study at the Middle Temple in 1753 when
he was twenty-one, he of course possessed Shakespeare as
he possessed manners. A 'Committee of Correspondence'
in Barbados in 1766 had written their agent in London,
protesting that it was unfair that Barbados trade should
be discriminated against because colonial trade was in dis-
favour. John Dickinson wrote a public letter to the 'Committee of Correspondence in Barbados' protesting their
communication to London. He signed himself 'A North
American' and printed the tract in Philadelphia in 1766.
On the title page of this tract, Shakespeare finds place with
the lines

> This word Rebellion hath froze them up
> Like fish in a pond.

It is out of Part I of *Henry IV*, where the half-hearted
opposition to Henry is compared to the immobility of fish
frozen in a pond, frighted by the word Rebellion. Dickinson not only knew the quotation but he knew its content
and hence its impudent pertinence to the Barbados situation. Furthermore he knew the passage too well to hunt
it up in a copy of Shakespeare and thus quotes it a little
awry.

The extent of one's knowledge of Shakespeare was a
matter of the particular person's environment. This is
illustrated in the life of George Washington. He was not
a bookish young man as his contemporary Thomas Jefferson was; neither was he a man of training in the learned
professions as Adams and Dickinson were. His talents
turned rather toward mathematics and toward practical

matters like surveying, farming on a large scale, and prospecting and fighting. He was early associated with Lord Fairfax, who came fresh from London with the aura of Addison's and Steele's friendship about him and a magnificent collection of books upon the shelves of his library. Washington probably did not spend many hours reading Shakespeare, or noting his language and style. Of course he knew him, and a one-volume edition of Shakespeare's works was inventoried in the Mount Vernon library at Washington's death.

In all his writings and letters there is only one reference to Shakespeare. This is in a letter written to a friend in the midst of the Revolution (October, 1778, from Fishkill) about the espionage and secret information which the British enemy had collected. No matter, thinks Washington, how much secret information they have about the American position, it will avail them no more than 'the baseless fabric of a vision'; for it will fall 'to nothing' before 'our arms' which 'they have to subdue', if they would win a victory. In this brief quotation from Prospero's famous speech in Shakespeare's *Tempest*, Washington shows no necessarily first-hand sense of the play. He might have known the passage as a general quotation. He does not even attribute it to Shakespeare.

Shakespeare on the stage, however, was Washington's delight. For Washington, as for any other fox-hunting, dancing, card-playing gentleman, 'the play', whoever the playwright, was a social function to be attended. He was certainly present at some of the performances of the famous Hallam Company who came out from London to Williamsburg in Virginia in the summer 1752. He was not at the performance of the *Merchant of Venice* on the opening night; for he was then on his way to Barbados with his half brother Laurence, who was seeking health in a change of climate. The first performance of Shakespeare which he certainly attended was in New York in the spring of 1773, whither he had gone to place his stepson, John Custer, in King's College. In his Journal under May 28th of that year, the entry reads: 'Dined with Mr. James Delancey and went to the play and Hull's Tavern in the evening.' According to the records, *Hamlet* was the play on that particular evening.

One deplores those laconic entries that great men record in their diaries. What one would give for some comment upon the performance or for reflections upon the ideas and moods of this play. But to Washington a play was a play; his diary is full of entries about procuring tickets and attending 'plays'. But when it was over, it was over. To criticize the technique either of the play itself or of the performance is after all a special business. Criticism is a disease, a delightful one but nevertheless a disease. The normal person knows that a 'play' is for his diversion, to be enjoyed when one is watching it and to be forgotten when it is over.

In the summer of 1787 when the famous Federal Convention that was to form the new Constitution was meeting in Philadelphia, Washington was present as a representative from Virginia. The four years between his farewell to his troops in 1783 and this summer had been devoted to his estates and to restoring his farming to something like its former prosperity. His reluctance to leave it and come to Philadelphia on political business was no doubt alleviated by the opportunity to see 'plays' by a good company in Southwark at the Opera House. There after a Saturday morning at the Convention, he went in the afternoon to listen to 'an opera called . . . The Tempest

. . . Altered from Shakespeare by Dryden'. The player's advertisement requested 'Ladies and gentlemen . . . to send their servants in time to keep their boxes'. No doubt Washington's servant claimed an important box. But what the great man thought of the show, he did not record.

After Washington was elected President and was living in the state and bounty that he thought became the head of this new nation, we hear of 'Shakespearean private theatricals', 'probably in the winter of 1790', 'in the garret of the presidential mansion before the magnates of the land and the élite of the city'. Washington Custis played Cassius. One wonders if the implications of this play, the split in power, the hints of demagogy and the instability of the populace, struck the first president of the new Republic with special emphasis. It would not be surprising if the wranglings of political Rome echoed with peculiar significance in the presidential ears on that winter afternoon in the 'garret of the presidential mansion' in 1790.

This survey of the representative thinkers of the Revolution and their attitude toward Shakespeare is far from inclusive or conclusive. Yet it should have some value as an indication of certain facts. The first is that Shakespeare was a commonplace in the eighteenth century colonial world. His name was familiar to all persons with any pretensions to culture. The degree to which his poetry and thought took hold of individuals rested entirely, then as now, on whether these people regularly drew sustenance from books or relied upon their contemporary world.

With Franklin who grew up into culture, it was natural that the new and outstanding movements of contemporary thought should arrest his attention. From Franklin's point of view Shakespeare offered nothing revolutionary, nothing startlingly new. His plays had achieved the sanction, dignity and, to a certain extent, the petrification of all accepted classics. No wonder Franklin had no time for them. Yet in the history of culture in America, the unquestioned prestige of the name and works of Shakespeare among all sorts of people argues much. Even though they misread him and misplayed him, his power over them was unbroken and undisputed.

CHAPTER VII

Shakespeare Fights the Revolutionary War: in Political and Social Parody; in the Performances of Officer-Actors, both British and American

THE literature of parody is always interesting psychologically. It takes the rhythm of some well-known passage, imbedded deeply in the public instinct, and creates for it new words and ideas, which by their sharp variance in meaning, combined with their strict agreement in pattern, are bound to set the reader thinking. Hamlet's famous soliloquy, 'To be or not to be', was deeply enough lodged in the American consciousness by the time of the American Revolution to make it the basis of political parody on both sides of the question, rebel and loyalist.

When that Boston newspaper, *The Massachusetts Spy*, edited by Zachariah Fowle and Isaiah Thomas, was only a month old, it presented in its pages, for the issue of August 11 to 14, 1770, a brilliant protest against British taxation in the form of a parody of Hamlet's famous speech. 'Be taxt or not be taxt—that is the question', it begins. It makes a clear statement of definite opposition to British mandates. This is interesting as early as the summer of 1770. It ponders

> Whether 'tis nobler in our minds to suffer
> The sleights and cunning of deceitful statesmen
> Or to petition 'gainst illegal taxes
> And by opposing, end them?

The dilemma with all its horrid consequences is clearly envisaged.

To live, to act, perchance to be all slaves,
Aye, there's the rub.

Who the author of this spirited parody was, is not certain. It might have been Isaiah Thomas himself, for he valued Shakespeare—at least in his songs. Thomas printed in a children's book, *Mother Goose's Melody*, after the war was over (first edition in 1786 and second in 1794), a whole group of Shakespeare's songs. It came out under the pleasing caption of 'Those [Songs] of that Sweet Songster and Nurse of Wit and Humour, Master William Shakespeare'. This 'songster' was taken seriously, too; for the section was 'embellished with cuts and illustrated with notes and maxims, Historical, Philosophical and Critical'. But whether Isaiah Thomas or another turned Hamlet's dilemma to such sharp account in the summer of 1770 is not important. The significant thing is that one could count on the public's familiarity with the Shakespearean passage to lend a fillip to the verses.

In the pages of the same *Spy*, some three years later, a whimsical contributor debates the value of presenting his creations in the public print. Though the passage is not definitely political, it uses the familiar *Hamlet* pattern. 'To *Print* or not to *Print?*' it begins, 'that is the question.' It goes on to ponder

Whether 'tis better in a trunk to bury
The quirks and crotchets of outrageous fancy,
Or send a well-wrote Essay to the press
(No matter which, whether on timed *Cowardice*
    or *Courage*)
And by imprinting end them.

This versifier was bitterly sure of the unimportance of the whole performance, for he concludes

> To print, no doubt,
> No more; and by our act to say we end.

Thus *Hamlet*, turned whimsically to light newspaper verse in 1773, moved forward amid the uses of a new adversity, the struggle for independence in a late eighteenth century British colony.

The Congress of 1774 passed a so-called 'association' or article of support of the Colonies against British aggression. It was 'carried into every community' and 'offered for the individual assent of every colonist'. Persons of importance who refused to sign it were likely to find their property and even their personal safety endangered. The British Loyalists in the Colonies felt that a great many persons signed this 'association' in order to save their skins, not because they were devoted to the colonial cause. Again Hamlet's searching soliloquy came to the fore. Some Tory set 'To be or not to be' to an analysis of the present situation. The composition, somewhere between 1774 and 1776, was first printed in the *Middlesex Journal* for January 30, 1776. It presents the awkward situation of the colonist who is asked to sign the 'association' and must choose either to refuse and suffer for his principles or to sign away his devotion to England in order to protect life and property in these daily more rebellious Colonies.

The parody is entitled 'The Pausing American Loyalist', and 'Loyalist' in this title clearly stands for allegiance to the British crown. 'To sign or not to sign', he debates with himself, 'that is the question.' He then lists the advantages and disadvantages of his act.

> Whether 'tis better for an honest man
> To sign—and so be safe; or to resolve,
> Betide what will, against 'associations',
> And, by retreating, shun them.

Then comes in the familiar humiliation of tarring and feathering.

> by that flight, t'escape
> Feathers and tar, and thousand other ills
> That Loyalty is heir to: 'tis a consummation
> Devoutly to be asked.

But flight, without money or property, even to England would not solve the problem.

> who would bend to fools,
> And truckle thus to mad, mob-chosen upstarts
> But that the dread of something after flight
> (In that blest country, where, yet, no moneyless
> Poor wight can live) puzzles the will.

He concludes bitterly

> ten thousands rather sign, and eat
> Than fly, to starve on Loyalty!
> Thus dread of want, makes cowards of us all;
> And thus the native hue of Loyalty
> Is sicklied o'er with the pale cast of trimming.

A broadside, printed and posted up in the streets of New York and Philadelphia in the autumn of 1778, makes reference to Shakespeare much less cleverly but yet with certain interesting implications. The French aid to the American cause was not proving very satisfactory, and the Loyalists were still hopeful of the triumph of Britain. In this broadside to the tune of 'Derry Down', they picture the colonials as having played out a farce called *Independence*. The broadside represents the Epilogue in which the Americans frankly admit defeat. 'Let Washington now from his mountains descend', one verse reads; and the next adds, 'who knows but in George he may still find a friend'. Shakespeare is invoked as a Briton. The Loyalists claim him to give prestige to their cause:

Old Shakespeare, a poet who should not be spit on,
Although he was born in an island called Britain.

Thus amidst the high feeling which marked the passage of the American Revolution, Shakespeare lights now upon the banner of Rebel, now of Loyalist, and lends his prestige to arguments on both sides.

THE PLAYING OF SHAKESPEARE DURING THE REVOLUTIONARY WAR

The opening of the American Revolution produced a wider activity in stage plays than had existed during the preceding quarter of a century. The performances, to be sure, were almost entirely amateur or, at best, semi-professional, but the frequency with which both British and Americans turned to dramatics to ease the boredom of a winter's encampment at Valley Forge, or the long years of British occupation of New York, shows very clearly the *class* attitude toward the theatre. People of the upper-middle class and upper class, the group from which the officers on both sides were likely to be drawn, regarded the theatre as diverting and fashionable and altogether one of the desirable things of civilized existence.

The opposition to the theatre in the Colonies, which had been coexistent with their history, came from the religious bigots and from the provincial groups of simple citizens whom they controlled. When the Congress of 1774 passed the regulation against all forms of diversion, as distractions from the life-and-death struggle in which America was about to engage, there was something of war hysteria in the prohibition. But there was also a good deal of the traditional suspicion of all 'fun'. It presented the essential point of view of the simple, hard-working citizen of Puritan or Quaker faith and of the man of plain, independent day-labouring stock. Work drove out sin; it was essential both to life and to goodness. When work was over, the place for a man was in the bosom of his own family or in bed getting ready for the next long day. Leisure and its diversions belonged to different sorts of people in a different sort of world.

The wording of the decree against diversions for the duration of the war, as passed by the Continental Congress, on October 20, 1774, shows what a large percentage of these simple, working people made up that body. 'We will in our several stations encourage frugality . . . and discountenance and discourage every species of extravagance and dissipation.' This has the ringing austerity of the seventeenth century Puritans. The 'dissipations' specifically named include 'horse-racing', 'cock fighting' and 'gaming' and, most pertinent to our discussion, 'ex-

hibitions of shews [sic], plays, and other expensive diversions and entertainments'. To be sure the motive seems
to have been as much the practice of 'frugality' and the
avoidance of 'expensive diversions' as fear of the moral
disintegration which attends such lightness. Yet the moral
disapproval is also distinctly there; often masking the 'inferiority complex', or the feeling that these pleasures of
'gentlemen' are something one does not understand, cannot share and therefore resents.

The diversity of opinion in various colonies on this
resolution was clearly foreseen by the Congress. The measure had to be approved separately by each of the colonies
in order to be effective. Some of them, notably Maryland, did not approve. These riotous devices of the upper
classes and the devil went on gaily in some sections
throughout the duration of the war. Besides, territorial
restrictions and prejudices were unavailing where military
control was in the ascendant. The officers, both British
and American, acted their way dashingly through the
Revolution, and in their revels the ghost of William
Shakespeare, often, it is true, 'strangely translated', had a
considerable part.

The most consistent and elaborate dramatic production
was in New York. The John Street Theatre was built
and waiting for the British when, under Howe, they captured New York in the end of the summer of 1776. By
1778 when Clinton had succeeded Howe as commander
of all the British troops in America, 'Clinton's Thespians'
were organized. The John Street Theatre now became
the Theatre Royal, and the troupe of young British officers, with its personnel frequently changing, played here
through the summer of 1783. The final treaty of peace in
the autumn of 1783 put a definite end to their revels.

Sometimes young men took the female parts, sometimes 'garrison mistresses' trod the boards. Though there were frequent assertions in advertisements and playbills that the proceeds went to charity, the profits seem really to have gone into the indigent and elegant pockets of the young officers themselves, whose kit and style must be maintained by some means or other. The 'quality' in the performers is clearly a drawing card. The advertisement in the *Mercury* for March 27, 1778, carries this tempting paragraph. 'The gentleman who is said to appear in *Othello* is eminent in tragedy and has figured, much to his reputation, in that distinguished part, some years ago in this city to a crowded audience.'

The next New York season in the spring of '79 at the Theatre Royal was even more gala. The *Royal Gazette* for February 24 announces that *Richard III* is in rehearsal. According to Dunlap, whose precise dates may be confused but whose general recollection is reliable, the old favourite, *Richard III*, was played three times during this spring; once, with 'a new comic dance' added 'by particular desire', and once 'with entertainments'. Its too familiar lines must have needed dressing up. The receipt book for the season, now in the library of the New York Historical Society, shows substantial box-office. *Richard III* took in the first performance £260/12/4, though the second performance fell to £146/15/0. The expenditure for costumes, scene shifters and 'lamps' (whatever that may mean) is listed. Wigs were very costly and the item 'for trimming a hat for Roderigo in Othello' is separately noted. But even when this was all paid, such fat receipts must have yielded a sizeable residue for the gaping pockets of the young 'military gentlemen' who favoured the audience with their histrionic art.

Governor Clinton seems to have had a box for the season. According to a notice in the *Mercury* for November 13, 1780, 'Several gentlemen having engaged Boxes for the season, their respective names are put on the doors of each box'. There is something distinctly 'settled' and 'elegant' about this procedure. New York already seems an urbane outpost of the 'town of London'. With the passage of another hundred years or less, another great New York entertainment, with boxes and names of occupants in brass plates upon their doors, will proclaim the rise of a quite different class, but yet a distinct class, in the New World which was then fighting so stubbornly for democracy and individual freedom.

The performances at the Theatre Royal continued throughout the summer. Urbanity was expected from the audience who graced these summer-night entertainments. There was a Moravian congregation in New York at this time, and a record of its members and how they were affected by the circumstances of the occupation was preserved in a diary in the handwriting of their pastor, Brother Shewkirk. Though he was a royalist, Brother Shewkirk belonged to a middle-class group who suspected the class above them and all their works, including their theatrical entertainments.

Under date of August 19, 1779, he made this entry: 'The military gentlemen [note the resentment in the phrase] amuse themselves with trifles and diversions.' He continues: 'Recently the walk by the ruins of Trinity Church has been railed in and painted green; benches placed there and many lamps placed in the trees, for gentlemen and ladies to walk and sit there in the evening'. It was distinctly a pleasure park set off for the enjoyment of 'military gentlemen'; for Brother Shewkirk adds, 'A band

plays . . . and a sentry is placed there that none of the
common people may intrude'. He sums the whole affair
up with this crushing phrase, 'a paltry affair'.

That this leafy promenade with seats, band and flirta-
tious ladies and their beaus by the side of Trinity Church-
yard had any direct connection with the John Street
Theatre cannot be proved, but the inferences are all in
that direction. That the band whose martial and senti-
mental strains whispered through this leafy retreat was
'the orchestra from the Play House' we know from another entry of Brother Shewkirk under June 5th of the
next summer (1780). He complains of the impiety of
the whole arrangement, maintaining that 'the walk at
Trinity Church had been increased in width so that the
posts had to be sunk into the graves'. He feels too that
the playhouse orchestra 'seated against the Church . . . gave
offense'. He concludes his pious stricture with this lamen-
tation: 'Profaneness and Wickedness prevaileth—Lord
have mercy'.

Shewkirk's aversion to this 'gentleman's' diversion,
though the gentlemen are those very British officers in whose
cause and on whose defense he relies, shows distinctly
the class differences of the period and the corresponding
divergences of opinion on entertainment and diversion.
Even if the walk by Trinity Church had no official connection with the Royal Theatre, it belonged to the same
general category of 'gentlemen's entertainments' and
evoked that same half-censure, half-envy from the class
below.

The season of 1779 at the Theatre Royal had several
Shakespeare evenings. They started off four nights after
Christmas with *Katherine and Petruchio*, which, to be
sure, is more Garrick than Shakespeare. Apparently the

play was not in rehearsal very long. Only three days before Christmas the company was advertising for a copy of the play. The *Royal Gazette* for December 22 carried a notice deliciously 'small-townish'. It seems that 'a gentleman purchased a set of Garrick's works' from the printer. This completely private and personal transaction could not go unnoted in a small town of the size of New York in the winter of 1779. The *Royal Gazette* begged the purchaser to 'resign the purchase over' to the theatre or failing that to 'lend . . . the particular volume that contains the comedy of *Katherine and Petruchio*'. Whether the 'gentleman' thus importuned through the pages of the local press obliged or not, we do not know. But the performance came off at the Theatre Royal, played on a double bill with *The Mock Doctor* on December 29th.

The season in the New Year of 1780 offered *Katherine and Petruchio* again in April and two performances of the inevitable *Richard III* with the characters dressed in the 'Habits of the Times'. Occasionally a member of the cast cannot appear because of a 'melancholy accident'. One sniffs a military engagement and remembers that this urbanity and gaiety are the lighter side of war. The next winter (1780–81) offered *Macbeth, Lear* and *Richard III*. Occasionally letters on the performances were printed in the *Gazette*. The comment is not in itself notable. The significant thing is that the standard is always the London performance. The London emphasis is still dominant in British New York. The next summer, in August of 1781, Cornwallis surrendered at Yorktown in Virginia and the Revolutionary War was practically won. Yet the British Theatre in New York continued. That winter *Macbeth* was produced and 'Between the second and third acts will be the favourite song of "Nancy in the Dale" '. The incongruity of this sort of interruption to high tragedy, one has learned to expect. Yet its occurrence here is the last stand of the old tradition. The western world was to create in the next few decades a new Shakespearean emphasis.

The following summer in New York saw 'Courtney Melmoth's monody, Shadows of Shakespeare' or as the condescending title ran, 'Shakespeare's Shadows Paying Homage to Garrick'. The performance was described as 'a most elegant compliment to the Memory of Garrick'. Thus the actor and the accent of his time overshadowed the great creator of the lines. But 'the old order changeth'.

The military echoes died hard. As late as the summer of 1783 (before Washington was to have his farewell dinner at Fraunces' Tavern and finally evacuate New York in November), a young Irishman, Dennis Ryan, and his wife, who had been playing regularly in Baltimore where the congressional prohibition of plays had never been adopted, were in New York. They produced *Richard III* with a company supplemented by 'gentlemen', and a *Macbeth* with 'characters by gentlemen of the Army'. The proceeds which accrued to the trim pockets of officers' uniforms were hard, indeed, to forego.

While the theatrical activity of British officers in New York from 1777 through the summer of 1783 is the most impressive example of a sustained dramatic interest during the American Revolution, there are plenty of evidences of play-acting behind both American and British lines in other places. As early as 1776, Burgoyne, that London actor, playwright and friend of Garrick, whose part in our Revolution has obscured these lighter interests, was in Boston. His farce, put on in that stronghold of Puritan activity, Faneuil Hall, in January of 1776, was broken up

by the announcement of an American attack on Charles-
town. What else he played that winter and whether
Shakespeare was included, we do not know. But he had a
regular company and printed handbills, copies of which
he ordered to be sent to the American commanders. His
association with Garrick must certainly have made him
conversant with the Shakespeare which Garrick had
played and adapted. The possibility of Shakespeare in
Boston in 1776 and acted in Faneuil Hall, tempts humorous speculation.

Howe's men, after his occupation of Philadelphia in
September, 1777, played at the Old Southwark. The
American Army, when they took over Philadelphia a year
later, also had performances there. In the spring of that
year, 1778, there was a theatre at Valley Forge. Washington was present and 'a very numerous and splendid audience', for a performance of *Cato*. Whether Shakespeare
was played is not certain. But the probability is strong.
The significance of all these dramatics, American as well
as British, during the war, is the evidence they bear for
dramatics and theatrical activity as a favourite diversion of
a certain social group. The opposition to the stage was
vociferous but it came from a very clearly defined and
circumscribed class.

A Shakespearean play, *Coriolanus*, buttressed the low
spirits of the American Army in New Hampshire at Portsmouth in 1778. One Jonathan Sewall wrote an epilogue
for this occasion, showing the figure of Coriolanus as a
man suffering from 'his country's base ingratitude'. This
epilogue, later printed, carried a footnote indicating that
Shakespeare's *Coriolanus* spoke for the American soldiers
and officers who felt that their efforts for their new country were not appreciated. 'General discontent', the foot-

note reads, 'prevailed in the American Army when this was written and spoken.' That the bitter and magnificent discontent of *Coriolanus* should thus echo with immediate application to the situation in Portsmouth, New Hampshire, in 1778, shows once more how universal Shakespeare's plays are. It must have been some officer, well versed in Shakespeare, who selected this austere and little-known play.

The American Army at Reading, Pennsylvania, in September 1781, enjoyed acting as a regular diversion. The letters of Lieut. Enos Reeves record their activities. 'We were as busy as possible', he writes, 'and as assiduous as if we expected to make a living by it.' He records performances of *The Revenge* and Garrick's *Lying Varlet*, and concludes 'so much for plays', as if they were a regular part of the life. There is no record of Shakespeare, but the probability is good. Wherever the regular theatrical taste prevailed, Shakespeare, such as he was, was a staple offering.

The playing of Shakespeare during the Revolutionary War shows that the theatre was still the exclusive property of the gentry. The cleavage of opinion on theatricals follows the cleavage between classes. Liberal and sophisticated taste was ranged against narrowness and prejudice. After the war, the new nineteenth century America was different. A new social set-up produced a new Shakespearean emphasis. Thus the Shakespearean barometer changes as the climate of opinion changes. Once more it establishes its validity as a measure of cultural development.

CHAPTER VIII

Shakespeare and the Magazines of America

IN THE magazine as we think of it today, there is always a tincture of contemporaneity. It belongs to and comments upon our own world as we live in it. If history is there, it will be the history of an idea or a situation or an object which persists into our contemporary world. If Shakespeare is there, the sense of Shakespeare in his own right will be used only as a take-off for the consideration of some modern production, or some present-day tendency. If this is true now when the world of periodical literature is wider and more inclusive than it has ever been, it was of course even more true in the earlier history of America.

Yet the chronological development of the magazine in America, if scrutinized for Shakespeare's place in it, reveals something interesting. The first American magazines began just before the middle of the eighteenth century. F. L. Mott in his valuable *History of the American Magazine* (1741–1850) shows what amateurish affairs these early magazines were. Difficulties of printing and mailing, lack of professional writers to contribute and the constant shadow of 'what is done at home in England' made the colonial magazines parasitic curiosities, in no way springing from or reflecting their immediate American environment. The lack of international copyright, combined with a paucity of colonial talent, led to the 'lifting' of generous portions from English periodicals. '*Aut scissors aut nullus*' was the literal truth about colonial magazines. Yet there were over forty magazine ventures in the Colonies between 1741 when the first one was published and 1789 when the nation had come into its own and was inaugurating its first President, Washington. The reason for this series of periodicals, persisting in spite of their financial and spiritual failures, furnishes an interesting psychological facet of the development of our country. The colonial editors felt that if England had periodicals, the Colonies must have them, too. Furthermore, if Englishmen happened to read these colonial efforts, they would see that the Colonies were keeping up their end.

Such a condition could not possibly conduce to a real periodical literature. That must spring from the contemporary scene, must be honestly representative of the most urgent trends of curiosity and thought in the public to which it caters. It is rather interesting, therefore, to find more Shakespeare material in the magazines of this period than in the later and essentially real national life of our country. It is the Shakespeare of the transplanted English gentleman, who exquisitely and self-consciously turns over his 'classics' (Roman or British) and evolves from them fashionable essays and poems. He wears his Shakespeare as he does his smallclothes and silk hose, knowingly and gracefully. Shakespeare enhances him; it does not dominate or possess him. In other words the Shakespeare in the magazines of the American colonies is a Shakespeare of prestige.

It tells the same story that we find in the Shakespeare on the colonial American stage. It was perhaps easier to swallow Shakespeare in a theatre, whither one bumped in one's coach, to see and be seen as much as to listen to the lines of the play. To read him and write about him in the chill privacy of one's library without benefit of an amusing after-piece and the savour of fashionable gossip with one's fellow auditors was much more taxing. Yet for the few correct literary gentlemen who imposed upon themselves this task, there was the reward of appearing in print as contributors to the colonial magazines. And if copies of these magazines went abroad, there would be the added pleasure of being read 'at home', of demonstrating to the 'town' that civilization had not been entirely submerged in the land of virgin forests and Indians.

What sort of Shakespearean comment did these colonial gentlemen produce? First of all there were parodies of famous passages, especially of the 'to be or not to be' Hamlet soliloquy. Such parody was a demonstration of ingenuity. Into the familiar mould, sanctioned by the prestige of Shakespeare's name, the colonial gentleman poured a new content. It might be a discussion of literary style: whether Pope was better than Quarles as a model; 'whether to live with Pope or sleep with Quarles', as it read in a parody appearing in *The New American Magazine* of 1759.

Incidentally this discussion among the critics and would-be critics on the style appropriate to English poetry never considered returning to the style of Shakespeare. It was not that they were too humble to dream of approaching his style. Not at all. They were rather embarrassed about his style. It was not sufficiently powdered and curled, not sufficiently self-conscious and elegant. Yet the prestige of Shakespeare's style dogged them, while they denied its lessons. To discuss style within the mould of a Shakespearean soliloquy and yet never to consider Shakespeare's own style as a model is a neat example of the paradox of Shakespeare's reputation. He was forever present in their mind and writing. Yet they could not entirely approve of him; nor completely enter into the largeness and romantic beauty of his world.

Ben Jonson in Shakespeare's own time had started this paradoxical attitude. He had combined idolatry of his great contemporary and censure in a single paragraph. Dryden had kept it up. Pope had done what he could. He had edited Shakespeare (for indubitably this rough Elizabethan was worthy of the honour of editing). But while editing, Pope had 'improved' him. So, too, our colonial gentleman of 1759 writes about English style within the mould of Hamlet's famous soliloquy, but never for a moment thinks of using Shakespeare's style itself as a general standard of perfection.

Another typically eighteenth century situation in which Shakespeare finds himself is recorded in the pages of the *New American Magazine or General Repository* for February, 1769. A gentleman writes in Horatian mood of the pleasures of country living. He pictures the colonial equivalent of Horace's Sabine Farm. He lists as essentials of rural contentment a well stocked farm, six slaves, a gracious wife, opportunity to revere God and country. An important source of happiness is his library, which contains his favourite authors. They are 'Swift, Shakespeare, Pope, Young, Addison and Gay'. All his favourites are eighteenth century authors with the exception of Shakespeare. But, whether read or misread, Shakespeare must be there in the library of this transplanted English country gentleman of the mid-eighteenth century.

Francis Hopkinson, writing an essay called 'The Extraordinary Dream' for *The Pennsylvania Magazine* in 1775, the very year of the outbreak of the American Revolution, discusses the garden of Poetry. In this garden ancient

126 SHAKESPEARE in America

poetry comes off with most blooms. It is infinitely greater
than modern poetry. Then, guiltily, Hopkinson remembers Shakespeare. It will not do to ignore him and so he is
allowed to set alongside the ancient blooms 'a few flowers
and evergreens'. In the same year and in the same magazine, 'T. W.', feeling moved to write an elegy upon 'Hope-
less Love', does so in the measures of Lear's famous speech
on the heath. It is a fantastic but impressive testimony to
the prestige of this little-understood but overshadowing
Elizabethan.

As the century comes toward its end, and the American
colonies have become the American nation, the magazines
still show Shakespeare. The Hamlet soliloquy is still being
parodied, with personal or political content within the
familiar frame. But there is a hint of the new 'idolatry'
which was changing the attitude toward Shakespeare in
England in the last third of the old century. The *Boston
Magazine* for March, 1785, reports the famous *Shakespeare
Jubilee* which had taken place first in Stratford and then
in London in 1769 under the skillful management of Garrick. Why Boston only got around to reporting this in
1785 is perhaps worth meditating. But it did report it.
Shakespeare was beginning now to be not only a figure of
prestige but a figure of inspiration to a world hovering on
the brink of new romantic taste.

To be sure there were still the die-hards. In the *Boston
Magazine* for this same year (1785–6), a conservative critic
maintains that Shakespeare 'in almost every instance . . .
has fallen short of nature'. What exactly the Boston gentleman means by 'nature' is not important here. It is enough
to note that Shakespeare is commented on adversely. But a
contributor to the *New Haven Gazette and Connecticut
Magazine* for the next year (February, 1787) balances the

Boston conservative's adverse judgement. In fact he more than makes amends in the direction of the new idolatry. If instead of Aeschylus, Sophocles and Euripides, Shakespeare and Milton had written before Aristotle, that great critic 'would have considered *their* works . . . and founded his maxims upon the evidence revealed'. This is indeed, the *amende honorable*. To dream of allowing Shakespeare to occupy the sacred throne of the classics and to suggest deducing from his practice the tenets of criticism was not to stay 'on this side idolatry' but to cross boldly over the line. This buried essay in the New Haven periodical of 1787 foretells both the rhapsody and the penetration of Coleridge and the other nineteenth century adorers of the Bard.

Thus Shakespeare in the pages of those unsuccessful, affected, highly derivative colonial magazines, reflects the history of the prestige and critical confusion which followed him 'at home' in England. His appearance in these pages is no guarantee of any reality that he had for this new Western world. As it existed in itself, America had not yet found how to hear what he was really saying. The magazines in which he was discussed were in no way representative of the new life that was going on over here. That life was still inarticulate, still submerged and unsung. But for the small group who aped British standards, the Shakespearean contributions in the colonial magazines are a provincial replica of the values 'at home'.

In the new American nation, Shakespeare had, as we have already seen in a survey of the American stage, a more widespread and more real influence. While the name of Shakespeare was still as useful as ever as an invocation of 'fashion' and 'prestige', there was a real response to his rhetoric and his vigour which was new. On the young

American national stage, Shakespeare gained as the new century got under way. Critics and philosophers paid more and more attention to him, and books on Shakespeare increased. But in the American magazine of the first half of the nineteenth century, articles on Shakespeare, outside of reviews of contemporary theatrical productions, tended to decline.

This simply means that the American magazine was now becoming a real magazine. It catered to that layer of the reader's life which was interested in contemporaneity. If actual performances of Shakespeare were going forward at the time, then Shakespeare in the form of dramatic reviews appeared in the periodicals. Dunlap, for example, did a good year and a half of reporting on the New York theatre for the *New York Magazine* between 1794 and 1796. He had a department in the periodical called 'The Theatrical Register'. Shakespeare's plays took their chances in this column with the others. But the appearance of Shakespeare in Dunlap's 'Register' is merely the news of the contemporary theatre. It does not in any sense represent the literary and philosophical interest in Shakespeare, which was reflected, however feebly, in the colonial magazines.

Joseph Dennie, to be sure, staunch Federalist and detester of the growing democracy, in his *Port Folio* (Philadelphia 1801) wrote on Shakespeare both in terms of contemporary theatrical productions and in more general terms of literary criticism. But the *Port Folio* was 'caviar to the general'. It was brilliant but reactionary, furiously turning its back on the way the new American nation was going. Several specialized periodicals, theatrical reviews with the magic name 'Thespian' in their titles, arose. The general magazines and newspapers tended more and more to carry a separate department of dramatic criticism. But in the main body of the magazine, articles on Shakespeare declined.

This is symptomatic of something very important in the history of Shakespeare in America. Though he was increasingly present as the new century unrolled, he was present not as a piece of contemporaneous American life. Rather he stood for theatrical entertainment, or culture— something to be studied, to be read with analysis, in clubs, under direction from the lecture platform, and finally in schools and colleges. He became pigeon-holed in two very important phases of American cultural development. But he lost footing as a natural feature of contemporary living. He was not taken for granted; not quoted or parodied easily by gentlemen for gentlemen. With the pressure of groups, widely unequal in background and cultivation, the Shakespeare of the elegant amateur disappears. In its place came the specific and self-conscious, almost grim, pursuit of him as an element of culture. He became very nearly compulsory. He was something that 'must be acquired'. The heavy hand of the pedagogue and of the Lyceum lecturer was laid upon his text. Editors carved him up. He was converted with charts, glossary, and notes into a medium for learning public speaking or for disciplining the young mind. He became a 'requirement'.

True this young American nation enjoyed its bondage. Shakespeare clubs spread all over the country. They met widely to read and debate points and then to end the evening with the decent neighbourly conviviality of iced cake and coffee served in the parlour. The members enjoyed being serious about the pursuit of culture. But the fact remains that they *were* 'serious'. The democratic American world laid strong and persistent hands upon cultivation. They fought for it. With that admission, one realizes that for something new, vigorous and commendable, something old that was urbane, civilized and unself-consciously sure of itself was lost. The grace, often ridiculously caricatured, yet essentially present in the old aristocratic world had gone. The new America *would* know its Shakespeare, willy nilly. And it did. Yet some fragrance, some balanced rhythm about the older amateur method fled and has never been recovered in the history of America's national pursuit of Shakespeare.

That is why, though interest in Shakespeare increased, it presented itself in the correct places, and yielded up the general pages of the nineteenth century periodicals to the vital matters of day-to-day general interest. The study of Shakespeare could not ride lightly here. It needed the label of its own special department. We even began to be self-righteous about our pursuit of him. The *American Review* of January, 1811, patriotically declared: 'The sterling poets of England, such as Milton, Shakespeare, Pope and Cowper, are read and admired here by that class of society, which, in Europe, scarcely aspires to the rudiments of letters'. That was probably partially true, though undoubtedly overstated in a spirit of spread-eagleism. But if Shakespeare was more generally read in America than in Europe, he was read, one admits regretfully, 'with tears'.

As the Civil War approached, there were fewer periodicals devoted exclusively to the drama. Complaints had appeared increasingly of the lack of American playwrights. The starring system, too, which often meant English acting, was deplored. Yet Shakespeare on the stage was more prominent than ever. But as regular magazine literature, he practically disappeared. Mott's survey of the American magazines from 1850 to 1865 has not a single reference to Shakespeare. This is not ultimately conclusive that material on Shakespeare did not appear, but the absence of references to him is roughly indicative. The public, on its magazine-reading side, was too preoccupied. Shakespeare in club, lecture hall or stage belonged after all to another and more serious side of one's nature.

But after the Civil War, as we move nearer to modern times, we are on more familiar ground. The business of writing on Shakespeare has become a profession. The magazine editor can again, as in the old eighteenth century, reckon on a sufficiently permanent interest in Shakespeare, especially if it is not too frequently asked for. Richard Grant White wrote on Shakespeare in the *Galaxy* about 1867–70. In the middle eighties Whitman was writing on Shakespeare in the *Critic*. Shakespeare, as a literary subject, even merited a magazine all to himself. Appleton Morgan's *Shakespeareana* (1883–93) was sponsored by the New York Shakespeare Society, and printed communications from Shakespeare clubs all over the country. Hamilton Mabie, editor of the *Outlook* and *fidus Achates* to all literary amateurs, ran a life of Shakespeare serially in the pages of his magazine. But *autres temps, autres mœurs*. The long arc of American magazine history, rising just before the middle of the eighteenth century and running up across the nineteenth, describes a curve of both commendation and regret: commendation for the explicit, success-seeking progress of a young and heterogeneous nation, heavy handed with its Shakespeare, yet possessing it almost universally; regret for that urbanity, that rather futile but graceful amateurishness with which the top layer of eighteenth century society wore its Shakespeare like a precious jewel, oblivious of the mob who could not even read.

CHAPTER IX

Shakespeare in the New Nation in Its First Fifty Years (1783–1840) on the Stage in Our Eastern Centres; Boston, New York, Philadelphia and Washington

WHEN the war was over and the last 'military' companies in New York and Philadelphia could no longer find any justification in the word 'military', the legitimate theatre in the new American nation began at once to gird itself up for a century of major importance. The old opposition on moral grounds which had yapped at its heels throughout the colonial period made a few last protests. These protests produced the usual 'dodges'. Shakespeare's plays appeared again in Philadelphia under the guise of 'moral lectures', on the evil consequences of sin; of jealousy in *Othello*, of ambition in *Macbeth*. It was the old colonial dodge practised again to meet the opposition of the City Fathers. But this lasted only for a few years. A leaven of newness, of fresh beginnings and magnificent aspirations was working in the new Republic which was to alter everything. By 1790 even Boston had given way, and public entertainment was free at last to make what it could of itself in this new world.

But of course no entertainment which must succeed financially, which must furnish what its public considers entertainment, can ever be free to express its own tastes. It is hedged around with a ring of taboos. It must really entertain. It must hit the public where it lives, have the emphases that fit in with the mood and taste of an audience, echo its ideals and its sense of incongruities, flatter it. At one and the same moment, it must both lead and be led by it.

The history of the American theatre in the eastern seaboard cities—Boston, New York, Philadelphia, Baltimore, Washington, and Charleston between 1790 and 1840—is one small but indicative facet of the larger history of American cultural values during these significant years. It reflects specifically the combination and recombination of social classes, the rise of prosperity, the tangible and intangible fashions in 'culture'. It shows the modelling and remodelling of standards which went on rapidly as one phase of our national youth gave place to the next, one dominant political group went down before another, one foreign influence obscured its predecessor.

Within this history of the American theatre as a whole, one single element, the playing of Shakespeare, is an even more sensitive barometer of the history of public taste than the theatrical production as a whole. Shakespeare's plays were constantly produced. Though accurate statistics are not particularly significant, it is interesting that at least one-fifth of all the plays offered in a season were likely to be by Shakespeare. The other oldsters, Middleton, Dryden, Farquhar, Otway, who had held their own valiantly across the eighteenth century, now disappeared. Shakespeare, alone, had survived, and had survived as a dominating choice in the new American theatre.

One would like to argue that this survival and prominence of Shakespeare are proof of the ultimate triumph of a classic: that great art never will be downed. One would like to hold up the hands of our young Republic by showing its unerring taste for 'the best' in its first national theatres. But this pretty deduction cannot be truthfully made. The reasons for the preponderance of Shakespeare over any other single playwright, in the first fifty years of our new era, are venial, material, snobbish; in short, closely tied to the accidental character of these groping, struggling years. Shakespeare in the theatre of the eastern cities was simply one manifestation of our rough struggle for self-realization as a nation.

He was there upon the boards of the Park in New York or 'Old Drury' in Philadelphia or the Federal in Boston, not because the theatre-going public of those cities were sensitive to his great art, but because he was vigorous (they *did* understand his primitive force) and for the equally important reason that he was the symbol of fashion, the link with England (though no one would have admitted this). He was the vehicle for declamation (and how young America liked declamation, political or theatrical), especially for declamation by famous actors who were doubly acceptable if they had come from England and had a background of successful performance at London's Drury Lane or Covent Garden. Surely there is something in these reasons for his popularity which would tempt a psychoanalyst, if there were a psychoanalyst of national personality. What were some of the underlying 'repressions', inferiorities, 'compensations' in the national psyche at that moment?

The fundamental contradiction with which one has to come to grips in our early national life is the intermingling of two sharp opposites, a 'democratic' and an 'aristocratic' view of life and society. It is a too simple and easy view of American development to picture the Colonies as full of independence, of belief in the individual man, and consequently of desire for a country and a system of government in which one could get forward by virtue of ability, supplemented by hard work. From such a simple premise it would follow that, according to the words of the Declaration of Independence in 1776, America fought against the domination of England, overthrew it and forever after enjoyed 'life, liberty and the pursuit of happiness' in what was to become 'God's own country'.

But it is not true that this late eighteenth century struggle, called the American Revolution, was a battle between democracy and aristocracy, in which democracy won and was forever after prosperous and triumphant. To be sure many soldiers who fought in that war believed this. It was the fire-eating challenge of many simple people in this new Republic. But of course issues are never as clear-cut as that. In the perspective of time, one sees that the origins of the American Revolution and its social and economic results were infinitely more complicated and infinitely more contradictory.

The essential thing to remember is that old traditions and ways of thinking did not abruptly terminate with the Peace of 1783. A new era with entirely new and consistent social ideology did not begin on the day when that Peace was signed. Nobody wanted social equality. What one wanted was freedom to get into the dominating class oneself. The new aristocracy, to be sure, was not inherited. Instead it was an aristocracy of brains and ability, measured in terms of the amount of personal property, or money, one could amass. It was nearer to a plutocracy than to aristocracy. But the new society aimed to have a dominant group, as much as the old English society had had. But that dominance was of a new kind, within the potential grasp of any individual if he had enough wits and drive to secure it.

First Hamilton and the Federalist group in the administrations of Washington and Adams (1789–1801) worked this idea for the domination of one group, the merchants and bankers of the eastern cities. Then with the administration of Jefferson, the domination was sought by another group. And so the warfare for control seesawed down the century. This fact was present throughout America, but it was 'suppressed'; it was not made articulate. What was said about 'democracy' was insincere, doubtless in most cases unconsciously so. Men chanted for 'democracy' but did not really want it or believe in it.

Thus the post-Revolutionary America presented by no means a clear-cut opposition to the world it had revolted from. It was full of the excitement of acquisition, interested in getting up in the world, keenly aware of the value of position, of belonging to the influential group which controlled things. It was ambitiously middle-class in its social philosophy. Though Jefferson is reputed to have amended a phrase in the Declaration from 'life, liberty and the pursuit of property' to read 'life, liberty and the pursuit of happiness', he need not have done so. The general course of American social development in the nineteenth century would have been more truly foretold if he had left the phrase unchanged. Americans were too vigorous, too primitive, too uncivilized to grasp the finer philosophic implications of 'happiness' as an ultimate goal. To their naturally limited and materialistic outlook, 'property' was the end to seek. And they are, perhaps, only now, after the passage of a hundred and fifty years of national life, beginning to doubt the rightness of their choice.

More superficial than this new idea of the socially dominant group was the lingering prestige of the actual aristocratic structure and fashion of England. These 'new'

Americans were after all only late eighteenth century Englishmen. Habits of thinking which had been rooted in
them from childhood had made the prestige of England
and of the English ruling classes a matter almost of instinct.
When the new America forgot itself, as it frequently did,
in these early years, it still 'dearly loved a lord'. No wonder
America presented a peculiarly contradictory idea of social organization. No wonder Fanny Kemble, writing
home to England from Baltimore in February, 1833, is
puzzled by 'the anomalous mixture of aristocratic feeling
and democratic institution'. She records the same confusion in her Journal (Philadelphia, October, 1832). 'The
anomaly', she says, 'is indeed striking. Democracy governs
the land; whilst, throughout society a contrary tendency
shows itself.'

Specifically, as one manifestation of this contradictory
American feeling about 'rank' *versus* 'the people' during
these years, stands the confused feeling about England.
American behaviour about things and persons English has
all the marks of an 'inferiority complex'. Americans knew
that their country was culturally inferior to England. Yet,
as is the way in such cases of inferior feeling, they were
too proud to admit it. They flew into rages at the smallest
'slight' which they fancied had been cast upon them by
the English. Undoubtedly a great many British travellers
in America, of whom Mrs. Trollope is the *locus classicus*,
did have bad manners in the books they wrote about their
experiences. Lowell's observation of 'a certain condescension in foreigners' was well-founded.

Yet there were, in the steady flow of visitors from England, a large majority who had been invited. They accepted their hospitality graciously and with a good deal
of admiration for the new American world. These inno-

cent guests must have felt that they were living on the edge of a volcano. For at one moment they were courted, deferred to, and perhaps in the next, for some fancied 'slight' or 'condescension', they were attacked and sometimes driven out of the country. America's attitude in all this is clearly the attitude of an adolescent with an inferiority complex. England still was, instinctively and in the marrow of their bones, the *beau idéal*. They coveted its praise, shrivelled at the mere thought of its disapproval, and were prepared to cover their chagrin with noisy protest and aggressive statements of their own superiority.

This attitude toward England is specifically illustrated in the record of the English actors who came over here to 'star', most frequently in Shakespearean rôles. It seems that the English actor was by very virtue of his 'Englishness' something to see in an American theatre. Some unconscious sense of the rawness of the new world, its lack of a culture of its own, made the culture of England, as embodied in English actors, who condescended to come to these shores to fill their pockets, something indisputably precious. The long succession of English 'stars', who travelled the circuit of the American cities all the way from Boston to Charleston and gradually took on the western towns, is a speaking testimony of America's adoration of English artists.

Yet linked to this tacit homage was a sensitiveness, an ease in taking offence, a violent anger at the mere suggestion of 'patronage'. It was easy to fan anti-British feeling into a riot at the Astor Place Theatre on a May evening in the spring of 1849 where an English actor, long welcome to these shores, was playing *Macbeth*. How he fled to Boston, barely escaping with his life, and took ship for England, is another story. But the wording of the posters inciting to riot is of significance here: 'Working-men', reads the invocation, 'shall America or England rule this city? . . . Washington forever. Stand by your rights. [Signed] American Committee.' And this was in 1849 when the Republic was already over fifty!

These national enthusiasms and contradictions were reflected in the theatres themselves. The new theatre buildings which sprang up in all the important eastern cities in the 1790's were built for a prosperous urban society. The arrangements were calculated to please the 'best' people, which meant the people with money to pay for entertainment. The pit or ground-floor seats were cheap and uncomfortable and represented in nearly all the contemporary prints without backs. The gallery, above the boxes, was noisy and crowded and had in some instances a section railed off for coloured auditors. But the chief glory of the building was the elegance of the boxes, usually in three tiers, in a manner suggesting the opera horseshoe, extending round the interior up to and onto the stage. Here one could see and be seen, could flaunt one's velvet and jewels as happily as the Elizabethan gallants had done in Shakespeare's day.

The first of the new theatres built in Philadelphia at Chestnut Street and 6th, in 1791, gave out with pride that its interior was after the Theatre Royal at Bath. Through twenty-five years of predominance among American theatres, it went by the affectionate nickname of 'Old Drury', because its standards were good enough to be compared with the best London theatres. The Federal Street Theatre built in Boston in 1794 by designs from the pencil of Charles Bulfinch was presumably of the same sort. New York's Park Street, opened in 1798, had a similar interior arrangement. The fact that theatrical entertainment was, in this new world, a source of money-making led the shrewd John Jacob Astor to buy The Park in 1805 and run it as a financial venture.

The $15,000 worth of improvements which he instituted before the theatre was reopened, shows clearly the way in which society was trending. He increased the seating capacity from the usual 2,000 to 2,700, 1,600 in boxes and 1,100 in pit and gallery. This distribution of numbers is interesting; there were more seats for the boxes than for pit and gallery combined. There were four tiers of boxes instead of the usual three. In the lower lobby there was 'a handsome colonnade with mirrors and fireplaces at each end, the whole lighted with gas lamps between the columns'. There were coffee rooms 'fitted in an elegant style', one exclusively for ladies. There were 'glass chandeliers' in the lower boxes. Most notable of all, in easy competition, apparently, with what was going on upon the stage, there was an 'oval mirror at the end of the stage boxes' which 'reflects the whole of the audience on the first row'. Remember that this was Astor's astute commercial project. It may safely be assumed that he knew what his American public liked.

Yet the seesaw between emphasizing 'class distinctions' and revolting from them can be seen throughout the history of these early national theatres. Wignell had no sooner finished his Chestnut Street in 1791 than a Philadelphia lady wished to purchase a box 'at any price to be fixed by the manager'. Wignell was tempted. He perhaps remembered the boxes, with names of British officers on the doors, in the Revolutionary days at the old John Street in New York. Yet he dared not accept the Philadelphia lady's offer. Such blatant flaunting of money and privilege might cause offence. In Boston, Bulfinch's new Fed-

HAYMARKET THEATRE, Boston, soon after the American Revolution.

eral Street Theatre was, rightly or wrongly, thought to be dominated by the wealthy and powerful Federalists. Bostonians outside the charmed circle charged that the stage on the Federal Street Theatre was used for Federalist propaganda in the form of gibes at the democrats and at the French theories of society which these democrats, such as Jefferson, espoused. This feeling led to the building of another theatre in Boston, the Haymarket, which, significantly, could not survive competition with the powerful Federal.

Thus episodes in management and accommodation, reflecting now 'differentiation' in society, now stout assertion of one common social level, checker the theatrical history of the period. When the new Chestnut Street in Philadelphia was built in 1822, it had three separate entrances for boxes, pit and gallery, respectively. The tender feelings of the pit were outraged, and handbills were issued. 'The national spirit of America', they read, 'has triumphed over the pride of European armies; shall that spirit slumber under the degradation of European distinctions?' Should it indeed? The answer was that it had slumbered quite complacently through years of these odious conditions and would continue to do so with only an occasional and fitful waking for protest. The three separate doors of the new Chestnut Street, however, were changed.

Presiding over this tremendous theatrical activity throughout the new America, with its turbulence, its display, its curious alternation of snobbish and democratic tendencies, was the spirit of William Shakespeare. Physically in the actual structure of the theatre building, he dominated. The critics' box at the first Park Street Theatre in New York, in which Coleman of the *Commercial*

Advertiser and Washington Irving, who wrote dramatic reviews under the pen-name of 'Jonathan Old Style', and other critics regularly sat during the season of 1800, was regularly called 'The Shakespeare'. The very name of Shakespeare was synonymous with theatrical activity. The frequency of his productions throughout these decades bore out the implication. When the New Park was built in 1821, the niche over the centre door was reserved for a bust of Shakespeare. The new Chestnut, opening in Philadelphia in December, 1822, advertised on the play-bill for the opening night that 'the tympanum immediately over the centre of the stage is chastely decorated with an appropriate design exhibiting the claims of Thalia and Melpomene to the genius of Shakespeare'.

But Shakespeare's domination of the American stage in these first decades of national life was more than a matter of homage in plaster busts. His plays were the *pièce de résistance* of every theatrical season, and performance in them was the ultimate test of an actor's ability. Yet on the same programme with Shakespeare, for the double-bill continued as it had in the colonial period, was the cheapest, fourth-rate sort of entertainment, in the form of farces, and variety actors of singing, dancing, and panto-mime. The continued presence of Shakespeare in the early nineteenth century American theatre does not have the flattering implications for our national culture that one would like to claim for it.

The more one ponders over the situation, the more one believes that the presentation of Shakespeare was a de-termined but external deference to prestige. Shakespeare was fashionable; it was always presented in England; go-ing to see it was 'the thing to do'. The psychology of its audiences was not unlike the psychology of modern audiences who attend the opera. Many love the music but many more go to see and be seen and to have the snobbish pleasure of feeling that their diversion has the seal of fashionable approval.

One cannot look at this indifferent and vulgar stuff which accompanied Shakespeare on every theatre programme from 1790 to 1840, without seeing that if the public could stand for this sort of entertainment, night in and night out, they could not have derived the fullest pleasure from the Shakespearean portion of the programme. Letters, journals and criticism of many gifted auditors and actors of the period show that a certain group were fully aware of Shakespeare's greatness. But they were not the majority, not the thousands who by their presence in these gas-lighted, mirrored and red velvet-hung auditoriums put money in the pockets of both producers and actors. To a certain extent one must have 'endured' the Shakespeare for the rest of the performance. One good thing about it was that the Shakespeare came first and was over with before the evening was half gone, so that one could settle down for the rest of the time to real pleasure!

It may seem to be putting the matter too strongly to argue that the playwright most frequently played, with the greatest prestige, was not enjoyed by the public who came out night after night to crowd the house and swell the box-office receipts. Possibly there is an ounce of overstatement in this contention but not more than an ounce. The reasons one is sure of its validity are very clear.

The passionate idolatry of Shakespeare which blossomed in England in the impressionistic criticism of such men as Coleridge, Hazlitt and Lamb and which entangled itself decoratively with the strands of German philosophy was reflected more crudely in the prestige of Shakespeare among the general public. On this larger group the nuances and refinements of the newer criticism, or better the newer appreciation, were quite lost. Instead there was regard for him as a great seer whose every word and every imagining was in itself a kind of revelation of the meaning of human life.

The attitude toward those rewritings and 'improvements' of Shakespeare's plays which had flourished from Dryden's day through the early career of David Garrick changed. About 1766, these light-hearted 'improvements' were seen to be not improvements at all, but the most damnable and patronizing acts of sacrilege upon the sacred body of the divine Shakespeare's plays as he had written them. Even Garrick began to be sorry for his acts of impiety and in 1776 declared that his alteration of *Hamlet* 'was the most impudent thing I ever did in all my life'. Shakespeare became almost a textbook of psychology. Maurice Morgann's famous study of Falstaff, in 1777, was almost a mental case history.

While the general public in England were not up to these refinements of analysis, yet they took the will for the deed, saw Shakespeare as a moral philosopher, went to public lectures on him. For, as R. W. Babcock has shown in his significant and revolutionary book, the idolatry of Shakespeare began in England at least a third of a century before Coleridge. Not only did people go to public lectures to hear the meaning of Shakespeare expounded, but the beauties of separate passages and scenes began to be emphasized, as if his pages were Sibylline leaves, each containing some potent prophecy.

These separate passages began to be collected in books of 'The Beauties of Shakespeare'. There were masques and jubilees, symbolically rendering homage. His bust was borne upon a triumphal, flower-bedecked car. The Muses of Tragedy and Comedy were in attendance. Garrick wrote the words for one such jubilee, which was held at Stratford in 1769. The streets and house fronts were decked with flowers, and a procession moved majestically to the church to read his epitaph publicly. The critics who had dared to offer adverse comments, notably Voltaire, were ostracized.

The reasons for this romantic reaction and whole-hearted acceptance of Shakespeare as a hero are a part of the social changes which are always operating to trans-mute one period in human history into the next. The social and historic counterparts of this change in the attitude towards a great literary figure are no concern of ours. But they lie there clearly discernible for the student of so-cial history.

The matter that does concern us here is the extent to which this new tendency in England, which was going forward in the crucial years just before and during the American Revolution, was reflected in the 'independent' American world. Though America had thrown off the political yoke of England, it yet followed at the distance of 3000 miles of ocean, item by item and phase by phase, the new idolatry of Shakespeare which had stolen upon its erstwhile English 'home'. In 1777, Maurice Morgann's prophecy of Shakespeare's future influence in the western hemisphere was no doubt more than half rhetorical. But in less than twenty-five years, it was to become literal fact. 'When the hand of time', Morgann wrote, 'shall have brushed off his present Editors and Commentators' and the French language in which Voltaire had dared to call him 'barbarian', 'shall be no more, the Apalachian [sic] Moun-tains, the banks of the Ohio . . . shall resound with the ac-

cents of this Barbarian'. How they did resound, before
Morgann's century was over and on down into the nineteenth, is the business of this present chapter.

What element of Shakespeare spoke to this new American era? In the popularity of certain plays, in the behaviour
of audiences, in the comment of the critics and the reminiscences of the actors themselves, lies the very interesting
answer.

The system of 'starring' English actors is itself one of
the most obvious clues to what the American public persistently wanted in Shakespeare from 1795 to 1835. A
'star' presupposes the high-lighting of the leading rôle to
the detriment of the play as a whole. The play becomes a
'vehicle' for a single famous actor. This is still true on
Broadway. One goes to see Katharine Cornell, or Leslie
Howard, or Gielgud, or Maurice Evans. Yet to a certain
extent, although these great artists are the chief drawing
card, 'the play's the thing'. Stars who are not 'supported'
by a skilful cast are not likely to survive long in our modern American theatre.

But in the theatre of our early Republic, affairs stood
somewhat differently. A relatively permanent stock company was maintained and was forced to adapt itself as
best it could to the meteoric presence for a few splendid
weeks of this or that star. The resulting productions must
have been anything but smooth. The circumstances of
theatre management at that time could not afford the
luxury of the right actor in the right part all through the
cast. It was a matter, at best, of makeshift.

The reminiscences of the stars themselves sometimes
make sorry protest at the stiffness and unsuitableness of the
local companies with whom, at a day's notice, they had to
act. Fanny Kemble, playing in Baltimore in January, 1833,

in a letter to a friend complains of having 'to drill a new set of actors'. Her days are spent on 'cold, dark stages, with blundering actors who have not had the conscience to study their parts'. Playing Juliet opposite a Romeo of the local company, she complains of 'my Romeo's inappropriate appearance in trunk breeches' with 'his unfortunate legs thrust into a pair of red slippers'. Doubtless his acting was as maladroit as his costume, yet the house was 'extremely full' and 'delightful'.

This discrepancy between the excellence of the star and the makeshift supporting company is not much emphasized in the contemporary criticism of productions. It did not trouble the theatre-going public as it would today. A world that took the heroics of Byron to its bosom, or that made Washington easily and quickly into a romantic legend, was a world interested in the individual. The exploitation of personal emotion was what the people wanted to see in life and on the stage. What they liked was a spotlight upon a hero, running the gamut of emotions with gesticulation and oratorical aid. The supporting cast was, to be sure, a necessity if one were to have a play, but the minor actors were definitely of minor interest. One could easily forgive makeshift and second rateness there, if the star were only 'strong' enough.

Sometimes, in fact, one did do away with the rest of the cast entirely and extract the meat from the sandwich for more concentratedly dramatic fare. Readings from Shakespeare were a real rival to the production of the plays as a whole. In New York, as early as the summer of 1791, a gentleman 'lately arrived from England' (seductive description), with a Covent Garden experience, gave readings from Shakespeare and others. Othello's speech in the Senate, the dialogue between Hamlet and the Ghost in

Act I of *Hamlet* were interspersed with favourite songs from Vauxhall. Two years later an actress 'of the Theatre Royal in London and Dublin' read selections from *Macbeth*, and Antony's soliloquy over the body of Caesar, along with readings from Milton.

This sort of entertainment continued to hold its popularity. Fanny Kemble deplores it. Hearing a gentleman argue that it was 'highly desirable to take detached passages and scenes from the finest dramatic writers and have them well declaimed in comparatively private assemblies', Miss Kemble explodes with well-bred fury. 'What!' she exclaims, 'take one of Shakespeare's plays bit by bit, break it piece-meal, in order to make a recital of it! Destroy the marvellous unity of one of his magnificent works, to make patches for declamation.'

Yet the 'patches for declamation' persisted. In the theatre itself the subordination and inferiority of the supporting cast must often have made the acting of the leading rôle seem like an evening of 'patches of declamation'. The public chiefly saw a Shakespeare play as a star's 'recital' and liked this distorted emphasis. The declaiming hero was peculiarly sympathetic at a time when public oratory flourished and the view of life was violent and none too subtle. The audience probably did not wish to forget that it was Cooper or Booth or Edmund Kean or Fanny Kemble whom they were seeing. The magic of Shakespeare's conception, freed from the accidental element of the actor's personality, meant nothing.

How did these 'stars' declaim their famous rôles? One of the earliest English importations was Thomas A. Cooper, a romantic looking young man who had made a success at Covent Garden in *Hamlet* in 1795. Wignell brought him to the famous 'Old Drury' in Philadelphia in 1796 where he captivated the audiences with *Hamlet* and *Macbeth*. The accounts of his interpretation show the typical romantic qualities. He 'relied', we learn, 'less on art than on impulse'. His memory was treacherous. Yet he possessed that fine heroic quality which enabled him to convey 'a sense of superb passion and power'. That was it; 'passion and power' combined with manly beauty, manners and a good voice. He was 'lent' by Philadelphia to New York in the early spring of 1798, where he played Hamlet and Romeo to delighted audiences.

His social status was very different from the one which all through the Middle Ages and Renaissance had classed actors with 'rogues and vagabonds', and had made them liable to arrest, *ipso facto*, for belonging to a vile trade. But now, the social prestige of acting in England which reached its height in Garrick and Mrs. Siddons was echoed in America, especially if the actor were English. Cooper had no difficulty whatever in stepping into New York society in 1812 by his marriage with Miss Mary Fairlie, the reigning New York belle.

He was still playing at The Park in New York in 1816– 18, when the American actor James H. Hackett was just beginning. Hackett's career extending up through the Civil War did much for the prestige of American acting and American dramatic criticism. He played in England almost as much as in America and printed aesthetic criticism of Shakespeare's characters. He was just enough younger than Cooper to come in for the literary and aesthetic analysis of Shakespeare which Lamb and Coleridge made so fashionable. He was familiar with Goethe and Schlegel, and his acting in London produced analytical reviews in the pages of the London *Times*.

Hackett exchanged long letters with John Quincy Adams on fine points of Shakespearean interpretation and had Adams' permission to print his opinions in a volume with Hackett's own Shakespearean criticism, entitled *Notes and Comments upon Certain Plays and Actors of Shakespeare with Criticisms and Correspondence.* This was published in 1863. It represents the fruits of a lifetime of thinking and acting Shakespeare. Though it appeared in the midst of the Civil War, Lincoln found time to write thanks for the copy which Hackett sent him. In short, Hackett's whole career, its international aspects, its combination of acting and critical writing, marks a new stage in Shakespearean prestige well beyond that which Wignell started with his importation of Cooper in 1795.

Hackett, looking back from 1863, estimated the acting of Cooper which he had seen as a young man in the New York of 1816–18 at The Park. He found that acting an interesting transition from the old conventions to the new romantic interpretation. He remembered certain parts of Cooper's acting as 'formal' and 'stiff'. His style of delivery was often 'cold' and 'declamatory'. By 'declamatory' Hackett meant clearly a conventional style of rhetoric. But along with this old-fashioned convention, he remembered something new and more congenial in Cooper's acting even at that early date. Cooper, says Hackett, sometimes broke away from the trammels of his original schooling with 'some very touching and effective *bits* [sic] of acting'. Thus propriety and conventions began to melt in the fires of subjective and romantic interpretation.

After the War of 1812 was concluded by the peace of 1815, this 'romantic' style of acting the leading rôles of Shakespeare became even more pronounced. Edmund Kean, who first appeared in America in 1820, had already succeeded in England with a style of acting in direct contrast to the traditions. His 'unstudied impulses of nature' had won him distinction as Shylock in a Drury Lane performance in 1814. His first New York season, opening with Richard III, and following with Othello, Shylock, Hamlet and Lear, brought one thousand dollars a night. When he moved on to Boston in the spring, his acting brought a frenzy of appreciation. The Boston managers 'approbated by the selectmen' (what a capitulation for the Boston City Fathers after more than a century of active opposition!) auctioned the boxes for a performance of *Lear*. Their promise of giving the 'proceeds to charitable institutions [in this case, the Boston Dispensary] meets the approbation of the public generally'. This same scheme of giving the theatre a 'worthy' object had been used in colonial America to quiet municipal opposition. One wonders to what extent the sterner side of Boston was still hostile to the stage and needed to be conciliated publicly.

There were other dangers of arousing American opposition, too. Kean, in spite of the advice of his managers, confidently undertook a summer engagement that year. The houses were thin, because people were away—as the managers had warned Kean that they would be. The audiences were so small that Kean refused to play. The public which had so recently adored him was furious and by their opposition virtually stopped his career in America for a time. Thus the lurking fear in the American breast that Britain condescended to us and would, for a caprice, break a mere American contract, rose in a strong wave of anti-British feeling and cruelly punished Kean's pocket for this act of British hauteur.

James Hackett, looking back to the season of 1826 in New York, has an interesting comment on Edmund Kean's acting. It was definitely in the new romantic tradition and had been approved, as Hackett remembers, by those arch-romantics in England—Byron and Hazlitt. 'His face', says Hackett, 'beamed with intelligence and its muscles were plastic and suggestive of the passions.' To Hackett, the romantic and complicated part of Hamlet seemed Kean's best. But the general public, he recalls, preferred something more external and melodramatic. Kean's Hamlet was less well received, he says, than the 'most popular and invariably attractive part of Richard III'. The old colonial favourite—violent, villainous and blood curdling—still held sway. The new subtleties of acting pleased the critics, but they lagged in the rear of popular appreciation.

Hackett's memory of Kean's facial expression, 'plastic muscles', shows the significance for this type of acting of the projecting or 'apron' stage. In Shakespeare's own day, the platform projecting well out into the audience had made facial expressions an effective instrument. Now the new Chestnut Street, or Old Drury, of Philadelphia in the 1790's had an apron projecting twelve or fifteen feet from the proscenium arch and 'ran past the first section of boxes'. Thus the actor was in close physical contact with his audience and could stir them as a political orator stirs a crowd. This was how Burbage and Edward Alleyn in Shakespeare's day won and held their audience. It is a romantic thought that the early national stage in America offered the same physical equipment for the same sort of declamatory acting.

This fashion of stage construction persisted. In 1822 when a new theatre was built in Philadelphia on the site of the 1794 Wignell building, the playbill advertised boxes 'in the style of the Covent Garden Theatre, London' and commented that the 'mass of the audience [is] within 35 feet of the Stage . . . an advantage which the best theatres in Europe do not possess'. The Park in New York (opened in 1798) has, according to the sketches of the interior, the same apron stage. The unconscious effect of this nearness to the audience upon the actor was considerable. An English star, imported by America in the 1930's for the acting of Shakespearean rôles, Maurice Evans, played on a slightly projecting stage and came to the very outer edge of that projection, moving his audience by an almost physical contact. It is more than a coincidence that this spell-binding in the theatre ran parallel to the political eloquence by which Webster and Calhoun were swaying the destinies of our new nation.

Another British actor who played Shakespeare to American audiences in this high romantic style was Junius Brutus Booth. He had played Iago to Edmund Kean's Othello in 1817 in London. Thence via Madeira and Virginia he opened in New York in the early 1820's with the inevitable *Richard III* and followed it with the rôles of Othello, Brutus, Hamlet and Lear. Booth's new method of acting contrasted with the old-fashioned convention of 'studied attitudes and enunciation'. All the critical comment on the acting of Shakespeare in the 1820's and 1830's reveals enthusiasm for the newer type of acting. Mary Ann Duff, who was probably the most successful actress in New York in the twenties before the arrival of Fanny Kemble in 1832, was praised for 'the unity of her conception' and her 'separate existence during the continuance of the play'.

Of course the older, more studied and traditional interpretation of Shakespearean parts existed alongside of this newer, more subjective conception. For no new style entirely eclipses its predecessor. Furthermore, as Shakespeare became the stalking-ground for literary and aesthetic criticism, the 'studied' actors came in for appreciation of their 'scholarship'.

The English William Charles Macready who appeared in America in the twenties and again in the forties, and whose playing of *Macbeth* in 1849 was terminated by the Astor Place Riot, was an exponent of this 'scholarly' rendition of Shakespearean parts. He had had a classical education in England and had expected to be a barrister. Naturally when he turned actor instead, his performance was characterized by 'scholarly reading of the text'. Hazlitt called him 'the best tragic actor with the exception of Mr. Kean'. But even Hazlitt prefers the new romantic acting of Kean.

The Kembles, Charles and Fanny, father and daughter, exemplify in their acting the survival of these two styles, side by side. Charles Kemble, brother of the famous Mrs. Siddons, when he opened in New York in *Hamlet* in 1832 was commended for his 'elegance'. Hackett looking back upon that winter calls Kemble's acting of Hamlet 'prosy and measured' and complains that 'he never seemed impulsive'. Of Kemble's Falstaff (of *Henry IV*, Part I) Hackett's criticism attempts to be favourable. Kemble's Falstaff was 'chaste and sensible'. These circumspect adjectives applied to that 'mountain of flesh' are not without their humour. Hackett adds that there was 'no mellowness, nor unctuosity' about the performance. He concludes with desperate frankness 'it was very dry and hard'. Charles Kemble, one readily sees, with his style of 'elegant' acting, was definitely outmoded.

His lovely daughter, Fanny Kemble, on the other hand, whose subsequent career in America was so full of tragedy and romance, was all 'fire and impetuosity' in her acting. Her *Journal of a Residence in America* (1835) and her correspondence during her two years of acting here in company with her father (1832–34) reveal indirectly a great deal about the American public's taste in acting. The American audiences were the object of her careful scrutiny.

At the opening in New York of her father's *Hamlet* (September, 1832), she sat in a private box. 'The house was crowded', she says. 'The audience, we were assured, was enthusiastic beyond all precedent.' Yet she needed to be assured. The 'elegant' acting of her father was undoubtedly disappointing. She comforts herself for this slightly cold reception of her father by saying in a letter to Mrs. Jameson (the famous author of *Shakespeare's Women*), 'ranting and raving in tragedy, and shrieks of unmeaning laughter in comedy are not, you know, precisely our style and I am afraid our audiences here may think us flat'. This reflection on the crude taste of the American audience is only a rationalization to cover the defects of her father's old-fashioned style. For when they acted together, as in *Katherine and Petruchio*, 'the pit rose to us like Christians and shouted and hallooed us as I have been used to hear'. 'Going up the stairs', she adds, 'we heard three distinct and tremendous cheers.' And at the conclusion of their Boston engagement in the spring of 1834, 'the phlegmatic Bostonians' 'shouted', 'cheered' and 'crowned me with roses'. Surely it was her 'fire and impetuosity' in the rendering of Shakespearean rôles and not her father's 'elegance' that drew the halloos and the crowns of roses.

Yet for our early nineteenth century American public, the charm of 'Britishness' would largely offset defects in acting. In Miss Kemble's letters and journals the lure and the peril of their British background are constantly reflected. She and her father arrived in this country with letters to the President, to Henry Clay, and Daniel Webster. The prestige of great British acting of Shakespeare was charmingly attested for the Kembles in one of their walks about Baltimore while they were playing there in the winter of 1833. 'We came to a print-shop', she says, 'whose window exhibited an engraving of Reynolds' Mrs. Siddons [Fanny Kemble's aunt] as the Tragic Muse and Lawrence's picture of my uncle John in *Hamlet*. We stopped before them and my father looked with a great deal of emotion at these beautiful representations of his beautiful kindred.' Then she offers the emotional context of the episode. 'It was a sort of sad surprise', she writes, 'to meet them in this other world where we were wandering, aliens and strangers.'

No doubt the Kembles did feel 'aliens and strangers' amid the unfamiliar and somewhat crude phases even of a city like Baltimore in 1832. The surfaces of life were indeed different. Yet the spiritual affinities with 'Our Old Home' were strong. The print seller displayed British actors of Shakespeare in his window and the Baltimore theatres produced British stars in Shakespearean rôles for their American public.

Even in the hinterland beyond the Alleghenies Miss Kemble's British self was honoured. She relishes the story that a print of Lawrence's portrait of her, 'carried by a peddlar beyond the Allegheny Mountains' was auctioned off 'at an egregious price' to 'a young engineer who . . . went out there upon some railroad construction business'. Sir Thomas Lawrence's portrait of a great British actress of Shakespeare, finding its way across the Alleghenies in a pedlar's pack, was put up at auction to the engineers of a railroad project which should bring the 'wilderness' into touch with the Atlantic seaboard and Europe. Thus old and new, British civilization and American pioneering, tacitly admit their commonality.

Yet at the drop of a hat (one uses the phrase advisedly) this tribute to Britain was likely to change to anger if even a touch of British condescension was surmised. The younger Kean (Charles) was comparing notes on this strange young America while visiting the Kembles in New York. He was giving them reminiscences of his experiences in 'various southern and western theatres'. In a performance of *Richard III*, 'some of the underlings', said Kean, 'kept their hats on while he was on the stage'. They were remonstrated with and replied, 'Fiddlesticks! I guess we know nothing about kings in this country'.

The ghost of the old moral opposition to the theatre was still evident to these British visitors. Dr. Wainwright, 'rector of the most "fashionable" church in New York . . . expressed great delight' to Miss Kemble 'at having an opportunity to meet us in private'. He explained to her that 'his congregation (and this was the most 'fashionable' in New York, remember, of the year 1832) are so strait-laced that he can neither call upon us nor invite us to his house, much less set his foot in the theatre'.

In Boston the great William Ellery Channing, exponent of Unitarianism, author and traveller (his anti-slavery activity came later), allowed Miss Sedgwick to bring Miss Kemble to call. The conversation naturally turned upon Shakespeare and his Juliet. The focus of Channing's question to Miss Kemble was 'if at the present day and in our present state of civilization, such a character as Juliet could be imagined possible?' This must, for Miss Kemble, have been a moment calling for all her power of acting. She had been brought there by 'Miss Sedgwick' and she was in the presence of a cultivated and prominent American figure. What her answer was she does not record. But she confides to her paper that 'I was a little disappointed, in spite of his greatness, his goodness and a reverence and admiration for him'. Nine years earlier Channing had visited Coleridge in England. If the conversation turned upon Shakespeare, one shudders for Coleridge's estimate of American culture, if he considered this famous Bostonian representative!

The most pronounced feature of the acting of Shakespeare in the first third of the nineteenth century in America was the enormous preoccupation with the leading rôle, its rhetoric, its rendering, and the personality of the actor who through it reached out for public laurels for himself. The American public regarded the play as a vehicle for a romantic hero, impersonated by a famous actor in high rhetorical style. This taste was both satisfied and probably partly created by the willingness of English actors to make money in American theatres and by the acumen of American managers in securing them. The 'fashionableness' of Britain in this belligerently independent America was a strong contributing factor to the system.

There was a flood of 'imitations' of British Shakespearean actors in their most famous rôles. Apparently if one could not have Kean or Kemble in person, the next best thing was to have an imitation of his rendition. The implication is significant. It was not, one sees, primarily Shakespeare as such that one cared for but the famous actor. In these imitations, the play as a whole was quite thrown away, and the high spots of poetry and rhetoric were offered with the gestures and inflections of the great original skilfully mimicked. Shakespeare was astutely butchered to make a fashionable American holiday.

On the Washington stage in August 1817, it was announced that 'Mr. Thompson, in imitation of Mr. Kean, the English actor, will perform three of the principal scenes in *Richard III*'. One might imagine that Washington, being small and new, had to put up with imitations because it could not tempt the great originals themselves to visit the town. But 'imitations' were fashionable everywhere. Philadelphia, a theatrical centre, not only displayed the British acting lions themselves, but also enjoyed imitations. The Philadelphia *Aurora* for March 9, 1819, records: 'By particular desire Mr. Duff will give imitations of celebrated performers: Mr. Kemble as Hamlet; Mr. Cooke in Richard III, etc.' In the spring of 1823, we read in the pages of the *Democratic Press* of Philadelphia: 'at the request of many friends H. Wallach has consented, for the first time in public, to attempt imitations of the following celebrated actors, Mr. Kemble as Coriolanus, Mr. Kean as Richard III, etc.'

Probably never since Shakespeare's own day were the lines of his plays and the creations of his imagination so completely subordinated to a place below the actor. Shakespeare, to be sure, had seen himself as a theatre manager and had regarded playwriting as the construction of the necessary vehicle in which to present his actors in his theatre. It was only the two centuries after his death that elevated these scenarios to a position of importance as literature. They were still of unimpaired prestige in early nineteenth century America but their success was a success of reputation. The thing that made them palatable to the theatre-going public was the fire and rhetoric of their chief rôles. Thus the ghost of Shakespeare, the producer, sees eye to eye with his nineteenth century successors.

The new American nation, once under way, began to

produce some great actors of Shakespeare within its own
shores. The name of James H. Hackett is one of the earliest in the field of distinguished acting of Shakespeare by
Americans. It has for the twentieth century a familiar
ring, for through his son, James K. Hackett, the tradition
of distinguished acting has been kept alive into our own
day. Hackett's ancestry was typical; he was the son of a
Dutch father and an American mother. He got into the
theatrical world after a failure in the business world. But
the theatre itself was becoming a part of the business
world, what with John Jacob Astor taking over a New
York theatre purely as a financial investment. Certainly the
opportunities for distinguished acting both in America and
in England (for Hackett often played Shakespeare in
London) continued throughout his life and up to his
death, after the Civil War, in 1871.

There are several things about both the actual circumstances and the quality of Hackett's Shakespearean acting
which make his career indicative of what the Shakespeare
stage in America was like. In the first place, he left a
printed record of his impressions of Shakespearean acting
and interpretation. This record came out in 1863 under
the title of *Notes and Comments upon Certain Plays and
Actors of Shakespeare with Criticisms and Correspondence.* It is fair to say at once that Hackett's quality in the
field of literary criticism is less notable than in the field
of acting. But within the pages of his book he printed (by
permission) Shakespearean criticism by no less a person
than John Quincy Adams, lately President of these United
States. Hackett sent a copy of his new volume to the
wartime President, Lincoln, and received a note of acknowledgment.

These facts illustrate the prestige of the Shakespearean

actor in this period. He assumed his place along with other artists and was courted and flattered by persons of prominence. Furthermore, Hackett, born in the first year of the nineteenth century and living into the 'reconstruction' after the Civil War, was in a position to witness most of the great acting both in England and in America during a period of theatrical expansion. He not only was a large part of all these things but his book is a sensitive record of the impressions they made upon him. 'These papers', he says in his Preface, 'have been written at intervals in the course of many and now by-gone years.'

The impression in these pages of his own acting of Shakespearean rôles is very clear. The thing that characterizes them all, not only in Hackett's own view but in that of the newspaper critics who reviewed his performances, is that they are highly conscious renditions. Hackett studied the part critically. He laid one speech against another to see whether the two parts hung together or what light a speech, expressed later in the play, might throw on something which the hero had said earlier. He had his own annotated versions; he even practised the editorial art and made textual emendations according to his own idea of what Shakespeare really wrote.

In Hackett, the actor tries to get inside the skin of the 'character himself', to live him and act him as he was magnificently conceived in the brain of Shakespeare. His acting differs from that conventional rendition of the parts with a gesture here, a drop of the voice there, a step forward in another place, according to set tradition. It is probably the ultimate stage in the subjective study of a 'hero' which began in England just before the American Revolution. The Goethes and the Coleridges and Hazlitts have made their impression. Interpretation has, in the case of a truly ambitious actor like Hackett, become a philosophical and psychological matter.

This deepening is concretely illustrated in Hackett's own account of his acting. In 1828, he appeared in the rôle of Iago at The Park. The *New York Evening Post* carried a signed review of the performance. In this account, the whole emphasis is on the critical interpretation and imaginative conception of Hackett. The reviewer quotes from Hazlitt and praises the originality of portions of Hackett's conception. In his own note on this press comment, Hackett admits his 'innovations of conception' in playing Iago and confesses to 'nice subtleties in collating the text' of the play.

And his performance, what of it? Its subtleties are recognized by the dramatic critics of the press. But what of the audience? The poor public is always in the rearward of the intellectual pioneers, and this scholarly performance of Iago is no exception. Hackett bemoans the fact that audiences have 'scarcely one educated critic among them'. They are not capable of 'applauding or condemning' his new interpretations. They prefer Iago 'in a black wig and with heavy black eyebrows'. To the subtle villain of Hackett's studied performance, they prefer 'the characteristics of a bare-faced ruffian'. An actor's popularity, Hackett moans, lies in the hands of 'the uninstructed and impracticable majority of play-goers'. Their 'notions' may be 'false' but they are 'settled'. And in this 'settledness' lies fortune for the actor.

Hackett's career, indeed, seems to have been a delicate balance between what the critics applauded and what the public wanted. He had first made his reputation on the American stage by his wonderful powers of mimicry, taking off brilliantly in his Dromio the twin servant in

Shakespeare's *Comedy of Errors*. Such 'staples' of popular entertainment established him. In his most famous Shake-spearean rôle (that of Falstaff, with which he conquered England in 1832), he put theatrical appeal above aesthetic criticism. Playing the part again in London in 1839, he comments to his Journal that the character of Falstaff was 'designed for stage effect'. Any high-flown criticism that declares that Falstaff is 'beyond the reach of histrionic art' can, he asserts, 'only originate in a hypercritical and fantastic imagination'. Bravo, Hackett. In a period when Lamb was claiming that Shakespeare read was likely to be better than Shakespeare acted, this note of sanity from an actor is welcome.

Yet the niceties of aesthetic criticism always tempted him. And he dabbled in them sufficiently to satisfy his literary self and to bring him into contact with other fashionable critics. In his later life it would seem as though sometimes the critical knowledge of a part spoiled its essential theatricality. Of a performance of Falstaff in London in 1845, Hackett comments that he has 'made the character a practical study' for 'the greater portion of my professional life'. That is all very well. But when he adds that he feels 'ready to maintain my conception with the poet's text and its most obvious interpretation', he belongs more to the study and the after-dinner conversation than to the public stage. Such emphasis imperilled his laurels as an actor. One is therefore not surprised to find that when he played Falstaff in London in 1851, the comment in the London *Times* for June 27 gives his performance the damning adjective 'conscientious' and adds 'you always see the pains he takes'.

This struggle in Hackett's acting between the standards of the theatre and of the study is symptomatic of what was good and bad in the Shakespeare of the first half of the nineteenth century. If the rendering of parts was too superficially theatrical, the performance became mere claptrap and sensationalism. The critical and psychological interest in the nature of Shakespeare's characters, which found voice and commanded wide attention in the pages of Goethe, Lamb, Coleridge, Hazlitt and their American fellows, was no doubt a good influence upon Shakespearean acting. It turned the superficial rant into something artistic and real. Hackett's career is a concrete instance of this. Yet it also illustrates the peril of removing Shakespeare completely to the study and there dissecting his creations as if they were 'case histories'. Hackett hits a mean between theatricality on the one side and philosophical analysis on the other, when he reminds the London critics in 1839 that Falstaff was designed 'for stage effect', not for analysis by any 'hypercritical and fantastic imagination'. But the prestige of his critics and their distinguished society sometimes overcame him and earned for his London Falstaff of 1851 the dubious adjective 'conscientious'.

The prestige of Shakespeare and of the actors who interpreted him in this period is illustrated in the account of Hackett's correspondence with John Quincy Adams. Adams had been all his life a devoted reader of Shakespeare's plays and a witness of their performances all over the face of the earth. 'I have been', he says in 'Extracts from the Mss of a Celebrated Person', which Hackett by his permission printed in the 1863 volume, 'man and boy, a reader of Shakespeare three score years'. A 'pocket edition of him' had been in 'my Mother's nursery library'.

Remembering Abigail Adams' reference to Shakespeare in those love letters she wrote to her husband (the first John Adams) during the early days of the Revolution, one is not surprised that a pocket edition of the bard was in the nursery library she used for her children. Her famous son, 'at ten years of age', was as familiar with Shakespeare's 'lovers and his clowns as with Robinson Crusoe, the Pilgrim's Progress and the Bible'. The conservative company which Shakespeare keeps on the nursery library shelves of this late eighteenth century lady is as it should be.

Adams was started early and had been an avid reader of Shakespeare and the Bible all his life, though 'always recognizing', he adds, 'the precedence of veneration due to the Holy Scriptures'. But luckily he had not been merely a reader of the plays. He had 'seen almost all the plays of Shakespeare that are ever exhibited upon the stage'. Specifically in England he says 'there was scarcely an eminent performer at Drury Lane or Covent Garden, for the space of thirty-five years, from 1783 [when Adams was sixteen] to 1817 [when he became secretary of state for Monroe] but I have seen grapple with some of the persons of Shakespeare's drama'.

It would not have been difficult, then, for James Hackett to meet Adams in Washington in 1837, during those years when Adams, having had the highest office in the gift of the nation, returned to the floor of the House and was doing valiant service as a Representative. Shakespearean actors were a matter of importance to Adams. As a result of this personal meeting in Washington, Hackett had sent Adams his 'manuscript notes' on *Hamlet*. Undoubtedly these were the basis of Hackett's essay on *Hamlet's Soliloquy on Suicide*, which was printed in the 1863 volume. The scholarship in this essay, the pertinent quotations from Schlegel and Goethe, and the philosophical speculation on the character of Hamlet must have interested Adams.

He replied to Hackett from Washington, February 19, 1839. The circumstances of the letter are interesting. Adams is writing at 4 A.M. (a very dark hour in February), 'snatching as I do', he says, 'from the *morning lamp* [original italics] to commune with a lover and worthy representative of Shakespeare upon the glories of this immortal bard'. Hackett, when he prints the letter, footnotes this passage. 'It was Mr. Adams' custom', he says, 'to rise at 4 A.M. and dispatch all his *private* affairs, that they might not interfere with his *duties* in the House of Representatives.'

The atmosphere of duty in high places combined with a philosophical interest in Shakespeare, all expressed in a long letter written by the 'morning lamp', from an ex-President of the United States (and from Massachusetts, too) to an American Shakespearean actor, shows what changes had come over Shakespeare in America. Can it be, at long last, that America has 'come of age', lost its provincial prejudices, and come not only to a true estimation but possibly to an overestimation of the importance of Shakespeare?

The criticism of Hamlet which Adams records in that February letter is remarkable. It is better than any of the later comment on Shakespeare which Adams wrote and turned over to Hackett in 1845. It is detached from an overemphasis upon morality, which is not true in the later comments. It goes to the psychological basis of Hamlet's tragedy with startling similarity to the latest twentieth century criticism of English scholars, like G. B. Harrison and Dover Wilson. It seems not to have the slightest whiff of Victorianism about it. 'Under the unsupportable pressure of despised love, combined with a throne lost by usurpation [in 1936 this was one of Dover Wilson's newest emphases] and a father murdered by a mother and an uncle', writes Adams. The analysis is original. The habitual turn of Hamlet's mind, he says, 'to profound meditation' coupled with a conduct 'always governed by the impulse of the moment' explains him. Under his lamp in a private letter, Adams seems to have thrown aside the conventional attitude of his time.

Hackett was just leaving for England when Adams' letter came. He answered it from 22 Charlotte Street, Bedford Square, London, in July, 1839. His own comment on Hamlet is quite different from Adams'. It has the characteristic 'moral' emphasis of the period. While he knows his play, his grasp of the underlying human situation is highly conventional. As criticism it has no importance. But as an indication of the extent to which the criticism of Shakespeare and the acting of Shakespeare were bound to each other at this moment, it has significance. Hackett forthwith transcribed the Hamlet correspondence which had passed between him and Adams. 'Published throughout the land', he says, it 'was attracting great attention from critical admirers of Shakespeare'. The theories about Hamlet's character, in fact, became so generally interesting that Hackett, himself, was persuaded to play *Hamlet* at The Park in New York, to illustrate his own conception of the part. Thus the complete reversal of the original position of the plays is achieved. Hamlet has become primarily a critical problem; the playing of it is merely a concrete illustration, a demonstration if you will, of the critical theories involved.

Hackett's comment on his great contemporary American actor, Edwin Forrest, is not unprejudiced. Yet from its very exaggeration, one sees that Edwin Forrest represents the high romantic tradition of Shakespearean acting.

But Forrest's performance was untempered by critical study. His career, beginning in the West, and moving eastward via the playing of minor Shakespearean rôles under Edmund Kean in Albany, covers the same period as Hackett's. Like Hackett he played London and the English provinces in 1836 and again in 1845. It was on one of these English provincial tours that he was, or fancied he was, hissed at the instigation of the British Macready. For this real or imagined slight, Forrest paid Macready off with the Astor Place Riot of 1849.

Forrest's acting had the violence and romantic frenzy which the time and the typical audience adored. He played Mark Antony at the Bowery in New York to crowded houses before 1829. He played with 'untutored, savage spontaneity'. He was skilful at 'depicting the emotional experience of turbulent characters'. His acting was sometimes characterized as full of 'swaggering Americanism'.

But this last phrase is only partly true. Hackett's acting was equally American, surely, yet at its best it seems to have been anything but 'swaggering', and at its worst it was too painstaking and studied. Forrest suffered from lack of subtlety, too strong and unshaded an interpretation, too merely villainous with a capital V. Hackett deplores his playing Lear with a 'countenance inflexible, stern and forbidding'. His make-up is too conventional. The eyebrow, says Hackett, is 'too shaggy and willowy', and the beard 'covers some useful and important muscles of the face'. This caricature of the irascible old king, according to Hackett, makes Forrest 'incapable of depicting effectively the alternate lights and shades of benevolence and irascibility'. Yet the American public liked Forrest and for five decades, up to 1871, he enjoyed national favour as an actor.

Charlotte Cushman, contemporary with both Forrest and Hackett, shows the same romantic style of acting. Descended from one of the original Massachusetts Puritans, she at last paid the score against the old opposition to acting by being one of the most popular actresses of her day. After failure in a singing career, she succeeded as Lady Macbeth at the Bowery in 1836. She was very tall and 'somewhat ungraceful and awkward in her movements', so that she easily stole into the romantic male parts of Shakespeare. She played Romeo in 1837 and Cardinal Wolsey from *Henry VIII* in 1849. She was in England at intervals, including most of the period of the Civil War. Her English critics attest to her romantic style of performance. She has 'an amount of emotion', says one, 'that we believe . . . never exceeded in any one performance'. 'Melodrama in excelsis', says another. And writers recall that 'when she came upon the stage, she filled it with the . . . brilliant vitality of her presence'.

In these star performances the rest of the cast was subordinated. It was not from them that the added pleasure came. The accompanying diversions lay rather in the interpolation of spectacle, such as the funeral procession in *Romeo and Juliet*, the coronation of Anne in *Henry VIII*, the foresters' dance in *As You Like It*, the entry of Coriolanus in a triumphal car to the tune of 'Hail, the Conquering Hero Comes', or the acrobatic display of the witches in *Macbeth* with their 'grand aerial car'. Yet there was beginning to be adverse criticism to this sort of thing. As early as January, 1798, the *New York Magazine* carried a protest on the witches in *Macbeth*. It said that the recent production had 'converted [the witches] into a shocking deformity'. It protested 'grimaces and gestures so ridiculous and disgustful [sic] that the audience would have acted with proper dignity had they driven them with hisses from the stage'.

Yet diversions were a very welcome sauce to the rather strong meat of Shakespeare itself. In a city like Charleston where 'society' was prominent, the plays had many charming local touches to whet the interest of the audience. *Hamlet* in Charleston in 1795–96 was played 'with a new Parlour Scene executed in most masterly manner'. 'Portia and Nerissa in breeches under the figured character of a lawyer and his clerk, was a happy thought' for a performance of *Romeo and Juliet* in Charleston in 1793. 'It must ever be pleasing as it tends to show female virtue triumphing over false delicacy.' A performance of *Henry IV* in the winter of 1794–95 was followed by 'a grand ballet' and a farce, written 'by a gentleman of Charleston'. The song from Handel's Judas Maccabeus, 'Return, O God of Hosts', enlivened the funeral procession in a midwinter performance of *Romeo and Juliet* in Charleston in the season of 1795–96. On February 22nd of that year, the performance of *Richard III* was appropriately accompanied by a 'song in celebration of Washington and Liberty'. This, falling in the midst of Washington's Administration, must have enlivened the evening with a fervour of patriotic feeling. Whether the tyrannous career of Richard III was meant to suggest any thoughts on the recent British tyranny so magnificently overcome by the Father of his Country, one wonders.

The scenery and costuming grew steadily more elaborate and more realistic. It was clearly another source of entertainment. The account of losses from a fire at the Chestnut Street in Philadelphia, in 1820, includes a lament for 'splendid English scenery' and itemizes such contrivances as 'chapel scenes' among the losses. 'The whole of the dresses from Lord Barrymore's wardrobe' were burned as were those 'from a French establishment recently purchased'.

After-pieces of sheer 'trash' continued. In Philadelphia in the winter of 1831–32, there was a spirited protest when *Richard III* terminated at the end of the third act because of the actor's asthma. Something called 'The Evil Eye' was substituted. The audience sat through this. But when the curtain went up on the after-piece, a farce called 'Raising the Wind', we read that 'some gentleman blackguard threw a large piece of plaster extracted from the roof of the pit passage, with some force upon the stage'.

Such tangible criticism from American audiences, even in Philadelphia, New York or Boston, was not uncommon. The actor 'seized the offending missile and hurled it back'. Thereupon a 'general row ensued, in which stoves were overturned . . . lights being rapidly extinguished'. No wonder decorous Boston had established with the opening of the Federal Street Theatre (1794) a 'master of ceremonies' to prevent indecorum, such as hurling of apples and stones at the orchestra. No wonder the Astor Place Riot of 1849 was so easily instigated. The vigorous, turbulent new America was still in the stage of 'direct action'. Its critical protest to the theatre was in physical terms; its standard of entertainment and diversion was correspondingly primitive.

Yet Shakespeare for a thousand complex reasons dominated this vigorous young American stage. The index of plays in Philadelphia, Baltimore, Washington and Alexandria from 1800 to 1835 is made singularly complete by the survival of the diaries of both the managers, Wood and Warren. These are made available in the invaluable vol-

ume of R. D. James, *Old Drury of Philadelphia*. In checking through it, one sees the steady presence of Shakespeare.
There is a wealth of unknown and indifferent plays. There
is much trash. But always Shakespeare interlards it. In
Baltimore out of about 375 plays, there are 13 Shakespearean titles. Each of these titles is played more than once.
Great favourites like *Richard III, Macbeth, Hamlet*, were
each offered 14 to 18 times. Philadelphia saw 21 of Shakespeare's 36 plays offered during those 35 years. *Richard III*
was seen there 60 times; *Hamlet*, 43; *Macbeth*, 42; *Romeo
and Juliet*, 33; *Othello*, 29; *Lear*, 25; *Merchant of Venice*,
24.

To maintain this wide popularity and frequency of performance, Shakespeare must be 'adapted' to the wide
range of popular taste. The pageant, *Shakespeare's Jubilee*,
illustrates this popular taste. It was a symbolic spectacle,
designed with words by David Garrick in 1769 for presentation at Stratford in September of that year. It caught
the exact feeling for Shakespeare, 'idolatry' if you like,
which was to mark both the popular and the scholarly
attitude toward him for the next seventy-five years. It was
one of those ephemeral things which by accident became
the very essence of contemporary and future feeling.

In England this was immediately realized. Boswell wrote
about it; the pageant itself was transferred to Drury Lane.
From there it spread to the young American Republic. It
was performed in New York in the spring of 1788, advertised as having run at the Theatre Royal, Covent Garden,
London, for ninety-nine nights. 'The whole', reads the
announcement, 'will conclude with a triumphal car, containing the Bust of Shakespeare, crowned by Time and
Fame, and attended by the different characters, Banners,
Trophies, and Transparences [sic], a Roundelay and

Chorus'. Another performance in Charleston in the spring of 1793 advertises that the Shakespeare Jubilee will conclude with 'a striking representation of the Monument of Shakespeare as in Westminster Abbey'. The 'device' was still being given as late as March, 1814, in Philadelphia.

Perhaps it is not too fantastic to see in the 'bust of Shakespeare' upon a 'triumphal car', 'crowned by Time and Fame', a tangible presentation of what Shakespeare was in the minds of the people of that day. A bust, a truncated Shakespeare if you will, a thing of beautiful and rhetorical passages and high moments of acting, but not a whole man or a whole play. The prestige of this bust is a prestige established by Time and Fame. He *is* great and admittedly great. Not the public's business to question why but simply to go and pay adoration to dramatic poetry sealed with the approval of Time and Reputation. His high moments, like his bust mounted on a triumphal car, would bring thrills to the audience. Around those moments, intervening or following, would be other sources of arresting entertainment, choruses, roundelays. The theatrical equivalents of the Transparences, Banners and Trophies would be the spectacles and farces and dances which shared his programme. In attending one would be paying deference to this 'bust', this monument, at the same time that one was getting one's money's worth in a rattling good evening of thrilling entertainment.

So for the moment we leave Shakespeare among the rhetoric, claptrap and diversified entertainment of the American stage in the East during the first forty years of our Republic. That he was served reverently and intelligently by many actors, critics and auditors we cannot doubt. That he was 'the big noise' and thrillingly so for thousands of less discriminating theatre-goers is equally certain. That the sensitive appraisers of his wit shrank from this fact is true. But it is both an amusing and a comforting thought that Shakespeare himself would have been mellowly at ease with trapeze performances and vulgar farces and dancing and singing, and even with a ruffian audience. He did not shrink from 'mixing his head with other men's heels', though his great contemporary, Ben Jonson, took him to task for it. Shakespeare would have applauded his early nineteenth century American managers. He would have loved his conglomerate public.

CHAPTER X

Shakespeare on the Ohio and Mississippi Frontier
(1810–1850)

THE name of William Shakespeare dominated the western frontier theatre. At first glance it may seem surprising that this virile and adventurous world, which perforce bent all its energies to subduing the wilderness and surviving, should have any time or any appreciation to bestow upon Shakespeare's plays. In spite of the critics, who have never relinquished their game of emphasizing the subtleties of his art, Shakespeare is as much a playwright of melodrama, oratory and blood-stirring violence as a poet of subtleties. The pit in his own day knew this; it was these qualities that brought them to fill his Globe Theatre and make him well-to-do. The subtler members of his audience, sitting in their quilted taffeta and pearls, somewhat withdrawn from *hoi polloi*, in stage boxes, found exquisite poetry and delicate analysis of the meaning of life. For these elements are in his plays as much as the blood and rhetoric. But there were not enough of such men—as there are perhaps never enough of them—to make a profitable audience. Something simpler, more obvious, more crude formed the basis of his plays. It was this that the Elizabethan ground-lings and the backwoodsmen and river boatmen along the Ohio and Mississippi recognized and went to enjoy.

There were other reasons for his presence in the world of frontier entertainment. Practically, he was in the repertory of the actors who struggled out there by wagon and flatboat from the eastern coast and from Britain itself. They put on Shakespeare plays because they knew them. He also had a 'snobbish' value. Some western dwellers, who honoured culture and craved it, were glad to see Shakespeare and imbibe a little of the sophistication and fashion of the East. To see him was an 'opportunity'. The presentation of his plays, too, proclaimed that the frontier was not abysmally ignorant. It was keeping within range of things back East.

The chief reason for entertainment of any kind is that it shall entertain. And certain of Shakespeare's plays (one must admit that the western circuit inclined to play a few, like *Richard III, Hamlet, Othello, Julius Caesar*, over and over again) *did* entertain. The plays drew picturesquely various kinds of audiences, from twenty to two thousand: in rooms over billiard rooms or adjoining saloons; in flashy interiors decorated with red velvet, chandeliers and tiers of boxes; in the 'cities'—if one can call a town of 20,000 a city—and in the villages under the Cumberland Gap. Ladies, harlots, negroes (carefully railed off from the quadroons), famous politicians like Houston and Henry Clay, fur-traders, rivermen, English travellers—they were all there.

One does not want to push the parallel between Elizabethan London's theatrical circumstances and these of the American frontier too far. Obviously Elizabethan London and the banks of the Mississippi were very different. Yet it must be remembered that England as a modern nation was just coming of age in Shakespeare's lifetime. The first formal theatre building in England was only sixteen years old when he came to London. There was still plenty of playing on improvised stages in the courtyards of public inns, in town squares on temporary scaffoldings, in country houses in one end of the great banqueting hall. Players still 'travelled' and took the rough and tumble of the 'road', as Prince Hamlet so conveniently discovered.

The same sort of circumstances attended performances in the young western world. The Irish actor Tyrone Power (whose grandson entertains twentieth century America) toured the western circuit and describes a scene at Natchez on the Mississippi in 1835. He was hurrying back in time for his performance at the miserable little theatre by the graveyard in Natchez not far from the famous river pirates' cave. On the road he passed the people who were coming to see him. He noted their 'broadleafed Spanish hats', 'high leggings' or 'cavalry boots and heavy spurs'. Their saddle cloths were 'of scarlet or light blue', with 'gold or silver lace'. To his European mind the parallel to the audience of Elizabethan days was immediately present. 'So many fine horses', he says in his reminiscences, 'with their antique caparisons, piquetted about the theatre recalled the palmy days of the Globe and the Bear-garden.'

In the summer of 1833 Sol Smith, 'strolling' with two wagons and teams from Kentucky into Georgia by way of the Cumberland Gap, stopped with his troupe at a little town called Tuzewell. The only available place for playing was the dining room of the hotel. It had 'a sort of landing-place or gallery, about 6 feet long and 2½ feet wide'. There 'our heavy tragedian' (who afterward became a celebrated Mormon preacher) rendered the 'Seven Ages' speech from *As You Like It* to an audience of twenty. The improvised stage, the picturesque career of the actor, the interruption of Shakespeare's lines by transactions at the neighbouring bar—'set down that julep'—all this 'local colour' is different in hue but not different in kind from a good deal of trouping in Shakespeare's own day. Probably his own plays, when the plague closed the London theatres and the actors 'travelled', had been put on in equally 'informal' circumstances. Yet the patina of centuries of reverence is on those lines from *As You Like It*. Their mingling with the landlord's transactions over a julep in a remote Kentucky inn of 1833 is the essence of romanticism. It is a crude illustration of the famous definition of the romantic quality, that it is 'beauty added to strangeness'. Certainly the lines are traditionally beautiful and the setting is picturesquely strange!

The range in kinds of buildings where Shakespeare was played and in the make-up of the audiences is significant in itself. It reflects in general a pioneer world, full of makeshifts. Occasionally in a centre like New Orleans where the wealth of the planters made life expensive and showy, there was a magnificent theatre building. But the fact that theatrical entertainment, with its almost invariable seasoning of Shakespeare, was constantly wanted all over the western frontier shows that it had a real value. It was not merely a fashion; it was a staple of existence.

When young Noah Ludlow, who had come out from Albany to Kentucky by wagon and flatboat with Drake's travelling players, arrived at Lexington in 1816, he found a theatre improvised from the second floor of an old brewery. It was seventy-five to eighty feet by twenty-five to thirty feet and adjoined what he discreetly calls, 'a room for the sale of beer'. The seats, he says, were arranged in an amphitheatre and were covered with canvas and painted. The audience must have been real theatre-goers for there were no cushions and no seat-backs to ease them over boring moments.

Here Ludlow and his fellow troupers opened with

Shakespeare's *Taming of the Shrew* in the popular adaptation called *Katherine and Petruchio*. Shakespeare for the opening gave the company what prestige it would. Here, later, they played *Othello* and the *Merchant of Venice*. A young 'super' named Plummer played Portia's servant. He was the son of the local Methodist preacher. But there was apparently nothing in the upbringing of this religious sect which forbade tobacco, for young Plummer was 'a great tobacco chewer'. He spoke his lines, Ludlow remembers, 'revolving his enormous quid of tobacco in one cheek'. His mispronunciation of a word and the rebuke of the manager offstage were easily heard by the audience in this smallish room. They burst into a roar of laughter which broke up the progress of the *Merchant of Venice* for ten minutes. It is not the crudity of this performance that is important. It is the fact that under such circumstances Shakespeare was played and that enough people came to see it to make it a practical part of the offerings by which these valiant troupers kept themselves alive.

The first theatre that Ludlow owned was in Mobile, in 1825. He makes as much of it as he can, saying that it had sixty feet on the street and ran back one hundred and ten feet. It had a pit and two tiers of boxes which accommodated between five and seven hundred people. The centre of the upper tier was for the 'coloured population'. It being Alabama, there was a subdivision of this section for 'quadroons' who 'would not condescend to mix with those that had purely negro blood'. Thus the colour line was already being drawn in 1825. The stage was equipped with six 'scenes', as well as 'wings' and 'borders'. It sounds impressive. But Sol Smith, who quarrelled and lied his way in and out of partnership with Ludlow, says that it was merely 'fitted up over a billiard room'. What 'stock' productions of Shakespeare Ludlow may have put on here, we do not know. But the next year Thomas A. Cooper, the English artist who came to New York, made himself famous in Shakespearean rôles and married New York's reigning belle, was playing in this funny little Mobile theatre such rôles as Macbeth, Richard III and Hamlet. If Cooper played Othello, one wonders what the 'quadroons' in the centre of the upper tier made of the play.

Miscaloosa was four hundred and eighty miles by water down the Black Water River from Mobile. Thither Ludlow and his company repaired for the summer of 1825. They played in the 'ballroom' of the hotel. The hotel manager offered this room free, thinking he could make a tidy sum from the increased sales in his barroom on the nights of performances. Miscaloosa boasted twenty-five hundred souls. Drawing only on this public Ludlow played three performances a week all summer. *Macbeth* was among his offerings.

Perhaps the most picturesque circumstances in which Shakespeare found himself under Ludlow's management were in Louisville, in the summer of 1829. Ludlow planned to join forces with a circus manager and to offer a 'combination of dramatic and equestrian performances'. They planned to put up a ring and a stage 'in every town that we could stop at'. For the first stand, Ludlow took his troupe to Cincinnati where he rented an old bathhouse which had an adjoining ring and makeshift stable for the horses. He opened with Shakespeare's *Katherine and Petruchio;* whether before or after the bareback riding, we do not know. After two weeks of this equestro-dramatic arrangement, the circus man left Ludlow with the theatre on his hands. It is interesting that he turned for support to Shakespeare. He played *Julius Caesar* for his benefit.

Apparently it was not sufficiently lucrative. Ludlow, surveying a summer which had begun with horses, remembered his trick-dog Nero. 'Finding', he says with unquenchable courage, 'that my *bipeds* could not fill the
treasury, I had recourse once more to the *quadruped*, my
never-failing dog *Nero*.' Thus what Shakespeare's *Julius
Caesar* could not secure, Ludlow's *Nero* won.

Not only was Shakespeare played against these frontier
settings. The advertising of a new company, bidding for
the favour of a town, decorated itself with Shakespearean
quotations. Francis Courtney Wemyss, an English actor,
who had played frequently in Philadelphia, came to Pittsburgh in 1833 to open a theatre. Pittsburgh was, of course,
a seething point of junction on the journey to the frontier.
It was where one left the wagons and took to the flatboats. Wemyss was appalled by the prospective audiences
of miners and boatmen. They were likely, he said, to hiss
a man 'because he dressed like a gentleman'. But he went
ahead. He renovated the local theatre, converted the pit
into a 'parquette'. According to William Knight Northall,
a brilliant and intelligent theatre-goer and critic in New
York of the thirties and forties, a 'parquette' was merely
a name used 'in the more fashionable theatres in the city'
for 'the good old pit'. The fact that Wemyss applied this
'fashionable' nomenclature in Pittsburgh is an index to
the kind of appeal he tried to make.

The gallery at the Pittsburgh theatre jeered everyone
who took a seat in this new-fangled 'parquette'. Yet one
notes that the seats *were* taken. Wemyss's advertisement
of his new venture in the *Daily Pittsburg* [sic] *Gazette*
promises to make the theatre a place of 'rational' amusement. In confirmation of this highly moral intent, he
quotes from Hamlet's advice to the players (III, ii, 24

seq.): 'To shew Virtue her own feature, Scorn her own image.' But Wemyss boggles his quotation to strengthen its moral emphasis:

> Shew Virtue her own features;
> *Vice* her own image
> And the age and body of the Time, his form and
> pressure.

For Shakespeare's *Scorn* he substitutes *Vice*. Thus Wemyss can quote Shakespeare to his purpose in the frontier town of Pittsburgh in 1833.

When Joseph Jefferson, aged eight, set his face westward with his father and mother on an acting venture in 1838, they arrived ultimately at 'the new town of Chicago'. It 'had just turned from an Indian village into a thriving little place'. It had two thousand inhabitants. As the young Jefferson got off the packet boat, 'saw and hammer . . . bright and muddy streets . . . calicos . . . blue and red flannels . . . bar rooms' greeted his eye. The theatre was new with 'stuffed seats in the dress-circle' and a curtain. Over the centre, symbol of something traditionally precious though surely little understood, was 'a medallion of Shakespeare'. The crude drawing of this medallion tickled Jefferson's fancy. He remarks that the bard is 'suffering from a severe pain in his stomach'. Under the medallion is the obvious Shakespearean quotation, 'One touch of nature makes the whole world kin'. Crude and obvious, if you like. Yet in this new town, ringing with hammer strokes and waving with calico and red flannel, it was Shakespeare who was chosen for the presiding genius of the theatre.

But Shakespeare was not always associated with so

Courtesy of Louisiana Historical Society.

FIRST St. Charles Theatre, New Orleans 1835.

crude a background. The first St. Charles built in 1835 by
Caldwell, the English actor and promoter who had been
making financial and dramatic history in New Orleans
for the past fifteen years, was the equal of any theatre in
the East. Tyrone Power writes in his *Impressions in
America,* that he had expected 'noisy planters from the
up-country and boisterous Mississippi boatmen'. Instead
he found 'the belles of the city', 'coiffée with the taste
which distinguishes French women in every country'.
They occupied the pit, too, which was unusual in America.

The presence of ladies in the pit perhaps explains the
urbanity of the audience during Power's visit. Northall
regrets, in his *Before and Behind the Curtain,* that it is not
the American custom for ladies to sit in the pit. 'We have',
he says, 'been accustomed to see ladies occupying a seat
in the pit in England.' He regrets that they 'are excluded
from the pit of our [American] theatres for . . . it leaves
the pit without the softening and refining influence of
woman's presence'. Apparently the first St. Charles in
New Orleans felt the benefits of this refining presence.
With its parquette and 'dress-boxes' it seemed to Power
'decidedly the most elegant looking auditory of this country'. While Power himself did not play Shakespeare at the
St. Charles, New Orleans during these years was a great
Shakespeare town, and the St. Charles audiences saw many
Shakespearean productions.

One suspects that the St. Charles was on its good behaviour for Tyrone Power. An imposing theatre did not
always have manners to match. One knows this from Ludlow's account of the new St. Louis theatre, opened in
1837. Next to the St. Charles it was the most imposing
theatre building in the West. It was lighted by 'spirit-gas'.
There were 'branch lamps suspended around the front of

the boxes' and there were footlights of 'square tin boxes'.
It had three tiers—dress circle, family circle and gallery
—just as a modern London theatre has, as well as a 'par-
quet'. There were balustrades of 'handsome cherrywood'.
There was a saloon for gentlemen with refreshments and
a retiring room for ladies. This all sounds very grand. But
Ludlow reckoned somewhat without his audience. He
records that the ladies' retiring room was closed because
the ladies did not use it, and so much loud talking issued
from the 'gentleman's saloon' that it had to be closed. He
also had to refuse admission 'to any female who did not
come accompanied with a gentleman'. So in spite of the
cherry balustrade and the chandeliers and rows of boxes,
it was an audience that was likely to turn rough.

An address in rhymed couplet, written for the occasion,
graced the opening night. It was full of references to
Shakespeare, the master who did

> all our feelings scan,
> Each nook, each recess in the heart of man.

The characters of his plays are evoked. 'Banquo's Kings',
Lear, 'Sweet Ophelia', Romeo and Juliet. There was the
sense, too, that a remote outpost was commemorating a
European past and preserving it for a world only rich in
a future. The new St. Louis theatre is called 'thy first
temple in the far far West'. There was a hope that 'stars'
may 'arise hereafter in the West'. Many Shakespearean
'stars', English and 'Western', played in this theatre immediately after it was opened.

What kind of Shakespeare was played in these theatres?
In general, the adjective for it is 'amateur'. And this, too,
in the best sense of that word. The actor, acting and
audience were in close interrelation to one another. There

was a moment-to-moment adjustment of the conditions, crude though they were, to the spirit and desires of the audience who came to watch the show. There was, in other words, a reality about Shakespearean entertainment. It had to respond to the listener or be yelled off the stage. The audience were a creative element in the performance. Their naïveté and whole-hearted response shaped it.

When the great English Shakespearean actor, Cooper, was playing Othello in the little town of Cincinnati in the season of 1821–22, at the line, 'Here comes the lady', which is the cue for the entrance of Desdemona, from the audience 'a country lass of sixteen, named Peggy . . . stepped from the box plump on the stage and advanced toward the expecting Moor'. Whether Sol Smith embroidered this tale or no, it is symptomatic. The complete and self-forgetful absorption in the play, by those who sat out in front, is the point. It represents a simple and whole-hearted capacity to be 'taken in'. It is a quality of people not sophisticated or sated with too much diversion. As the famous British actor, Cooper, saw the buxom young Peggy stepping toward him across the footlights, he would have been both amused at her simplicity and stimulated to play even more skilfully, if his rendition of *Othello* had deceived her into thinking it was life.

Peggy was an impromptu amateur performer in Shakespeare. But there were many 'gentlemen' spread all over the West and South, who 'knew their Shakespeare'. When a band of strollers came to town, they delighted, at a moment's notice, to attach themselves to the show for the duration of the local engagement. This underlying familiarity with the lines of Shakespeare by persons whose business was not acting, shows to what extent his great imaginings had filtered into the basic structure of the western world. At Greenville in the autumn of 1832, Sol Smith found 'two local gentlemen' who were anxious to act 'the celebrated quarrel scene of Brutus and Cassius in Shakespeare's *Julius Caesar*'. They were, it seems, 'familiar with the text, having at various times taken part in it at school'. Cassius' costume for this occasion is symbolic; it is half the conventional melodramatic hero and, where suitable costume failed, half plain, everyday North Carolina clothes of the 1830's. It is a noble makeshift, reflecting the enthusiasm which surmounts difficulties and blends contradictions into a spiritual whole.

Cassius claimed 'a large spangled shoulder cloak' and a 'slouched hat and feathers'. So far his costume belonged purely to the stage villain. But beneath these magic garments he wore 'a stock, gray wig with a very long tail . . . nankin pantaloons, boots, spurs, gauntlets', etc. Thus early nineteenth century Carolina and dateless stage villainy combine in one telling costume. His companion, Brutus, had less flavour. His only 'fancy dress' appurtenance was a 'Turkish scimitar'. For the rest he had his own 'two pistols in his belt, gauntlets . . . and a ruffled shirt front'. Yet these two gentlemen were above incongruities. With the use of burnt cork, they gave themselves heroic 'black whiskers' and won an enormous success. They were so good that an encore was demanded. But they had no more Shakespearean passages by heart. The resourceful Smith 'put a volume of Shakespeare into his [Cassius'] hands' and the death scene on the plains of Philippi was read through on the spot with additions from prompter and manager.

The 'professionals' themselves often were forced *en tour* to resort to amateurish devices. Sol Smith and two fellow actors found themselves in want of a lodging for

the night when they arrived, in the course of their wan-
derings, at the village of Greensburg (near Pittsburgh) in
1823. They 'sang for their supper' to the tune of scenes
from Shakespeare's *Richard*. Their wardrobe was entirely
extempore; Richard in a 'common soldier's coat' (perhaps
a moth-eaten survival of the buff and blue of the late Continental Army). The royal Henry appeared 'in a scarlet
kilt', and Catesby 'in a Roman shirt'. Yet the Greensburg
inn found this Shakespeare worth a free bed and breakfast.
'The three strolling gentlemen made enough', says Smith,
'to pay for their lights, lodging and supper and returned
(presumably to Pittsburgh) next day poor as they went.'

The creative audience again entered in when Smith and
Ludlow deliberately took their troupe to play Shakespeare
in Milledgeville, Georgia, in 1833–34, because the legislature was in session there. They played through the whole
session, offering generous draughts of Shakespeare—*Macbeth*, *Lear*, *Romeo and Juliet*, *Merchant of Venice*,
Richard III and *Much Ado*. The actors were constantly
aware of their specialized audience and played to them.
When the pressure of state affairs necessitated night ses-
sions toward the end of the legislative period, the audience
suffered. Sol Smith has the appropriate comment for the
situation. 'A plague', he cries, 'on both your houses.' In
the widest and most constructive meaning of the word,
there is something 'amateur' about this season. It is not
Shakespeare played in routine fashion to a usual public; it
is Shakespeare personally adapted to the ears of the
Georgia legislators in their moments of relaxation.

The knowledge of parts and speeches which reposed
in the heads of auditors everywhere, whether among the
Georgia State Fathers or the gentlemen of Greenville,
North Carolina, or in a thriving centre like St. Louis,

made a close interrelationship between actor and listener. They both made parts of a thrilling evening. Once in the St. Louis theatre of 1839, the entertainment was composed of 'acts from various [Shakespearean] plays'. 'I found no difficulty', says Smith, 'in finding Hamlets, Shylocks and Richards in abundance, very glad of the opportunity to exhibit their hidden powers.'

Sol Smith's records of his theatrical life in the West are undoubtedly inaccurate. The picturesque episodes surely lose nothing in the telling. Yet with allowances for his 'theatrical' imagination, one finds confirmation in his pages of the immediacy and vitality of the Shakespearean tradition on the frontier stage.

Picturesque elements lend a kind of glamour to the history of Shakespearean playing. The Indians ride in and out of the theatrical picture. For a performance of *Pizarro* in Columbus, Georgia, Smith had bargained with a chief for twenty-four Creek Indians (to furnish their own bows, arrows and tomahawks), as supers. The payment, 'fifty cents each and a glass of whiskey' was apparently satisfactory. For they turned up the next day, offering themselves—tomahawks and all—for that evening's performance, which happened to be *Macbeth*. What disappointment must have reigned in the proud savage breasts when Smith 'most positively declined their valuable aid'. Considering the various transformations that the witches of that play had undergone in the preceding century, it is a wonder that the Indians were not adopted for this scene. The dance around the cauldron could surely, with slight change, have been transformed into an Indian war-dance.

The 'redskins' turn up again in the theatrical records of the early forties. This time in Florida, during the second Seminole War. A certain William A. Forbes, travel-

INDIANS in Shakespearean costume at time of Second Seminole War in Florida. 'The theatrical wardrobe ... fell into the hands of the Indians who, dressing themselves up as Romans, Highlanders or Shakespearean heroes, gallopped about in front of the very fort.'

ling with his troupe from one military station to another
without an armed escort, was attacked by Indians. Two
of his company were captured and butchered. But what
is more to the purpose: 'The theatrical wardrobe . . . fell
into the hands of the Indians, who, dressing themselves
up as Romans, Highlanders or Shakespearean heroes, gal-
loped about in front of the very fort, tho' well out of
gunshot'. Later when they were taken, they were 'decked
in the habiliments of Othello, Hamlet and a host of other
Shakespearean characters, for', says Joseph Jefferson who
vouches for the story, 'Forbes was eminently legitimate'.
There is the point. A travelling troupe playing American
garrisons in Florida during the Seminole War, must carry
equipment for the production of Shakespeare.

The mishaps and accidents in specific performances
keep this record of Shakespeare in the West warm and
alive long after the passing away of the frontier, when a
century of national life has already rolled between. The
story of old Stanley, ex-manager and keeper of a barroom,
keno table and faro bank at San Antonio, Texas, in the
early forties, is full of flavour. Hearing that Jefferson was
playing at Houston, the old man rode three hundred miles
through dangerous country to urge him to bring his
troupe to San Antonio.

Jefferson, remembering Forbes and the Seminoles,
thought the venture too risky. But he kept Stanley for a
performance at Houston in the title rôle of Richard in
Shakespeare's *Richard III*. Stanley rehearsed, 'gesticulating
wildly and roaring out the soliloquies'; he 'accumulated
raw cotton' for the necessary hump on Richard's villainous back. The Houston audience is an integral part of the
show. They never forget Stanley, never believe that he is
Richard. When he woos the Lady Anne, a voice out in

front shouts that the old villain already has two Mexican
wives back in San Antonio. This is 'amateur' with a vengeance; yet under it all is the prestige of Shakespeare no
matter how picturesquely travestied.

During this Houston performance of Richard, the hero's
'ostrich plumes' caught fire from 'the spermaceti chande-
lier'. This sort of lighting lent an element of suspense to
many a Shakespearean production. 'The footlights of the
best theatres in the western country were composed of
lamps [fed by odorous sperm oil] set in a "float".' Smith
describes the rôle of the sperm lamps in a performance of
Romeo and Juliet at St. Louis as late as 1845. An imported
star, Ellen Tree, was playing Juliet in the balcony scene.
She saw flame flare up in the wings. Between the impas-
sioned lines of the play, she gestured wildly to someone
off-stage to use the swab and the tub of water which were
always provided for such occasions. 'It was not unusual',
says Smith, 'to see Richard III or Hamlet just before en-
tering upon the stage, catch up a swab and dash it upon
the rising flames, which if not attended to were likely
to burn up the Tower of London, or the royal palace of
Elsinore.'

But even when the eastern stars came West, as did
Ellen Tree, the crudities of even the best theatres affected
their performance. One could not play Juliet with quite
the same accent, if sperm lamps were flaring in the wings.
The performance, too, was bound to suffer a kind of distortion which high-lighted the leading part, made an evening of splendid oratory, interrupted by more or less
painful intervals of 'local support'.

There is a fascinating parallel between the taste for
oratory in Shakespeare's day and in this early American
frontier. Burbage and Alleyn who shouted out the great

rhythmical and rhetorical speeches of Elizabethan plays knew precisely what they were doing. They were suiting their manner to a public more easily moved by the periods of oral declamation than by quiet reading of the printed page. Many of Shakespeare's audiences both in his own Elizabethan London and in the St. Louis, Cincinnati, Mobile, and New Orleans of the western world could not read.

But they were all the keener listeners. Their ears responded to the piling up of rhetorical phrases, their nerves reacted to a wide range of emotional pitch in the voices of the actors. By the combination of rhetoric and declamation, Elizabeth moved her army on the eve of battle, and Clay and Jackson exhorted their political constituents. Sometimes the rhetoric was offensive to the playwright. Shakespeare, through the Hamlet of the scene with the players, deplores that style of declamation in which the actor 'mouths it', 'saw(s) the air', 'tear(s) a passion to tatters'. It only pleases the groundlings whose appreciation is won by 'noise'. Yet Shakespeare, in his own person, knew that the groundlings must have their 'noise'. He gave it to them in plenty. His followers, playing up and down the banks of the Ohio and the Mississippi, were faced with audiences who, for the same reason, preferred 'noise' to finesse.

As one looks at the social setting out of which the frontier audiences came, and the supposedly more 'cultured' audiences back East, too, one sees everywhere the dominance of oratory. Stout hearts and rough circumstances call for highly seasoned style. It was not by accident that Henry Ward Beecher, who had left New England for the West in 1832 and returned in triumph to the pulpit of the Plymouth Church in Brooklyn in 1847, was called 'the Shakespeare of the pulpit'. Over his audiences, as Constance Rourke shows, 'he poured the flood of an accumulated and primitive excitement'. His oratory was own brother to the oratory with which Shakespeare was played in the contemporary theatres of the eastern seaboard and the western frontier. When his Brooklyn congregation built him a new church it had 'broad galleries and rows of seats . . . placed in a close curve'. The platform from which his rhetorical cadences descended projected into the audience somewhat as the stage of Shakespeare's Globe had done and as many of the American stages were doing.

The reason for this arrangement was psychological. Beecher understood it perfectly. His new platform was, he said, 'built on . . . the principle of social and personal magnetism, which emanates reciprocally from a speaker and from a close throng of hearers'. The element of 'catching fire' is well understood in all ages that live by oratory. So John Donne had preached from the high pulpit of St. Paul's in London. He spoke to his congregation 'like an angel from a cloud'. So Shakespeare's lines had hurtled round the 'wooden O' of the Globe Theatre. The 'Sweet Swan of Avon' made 'flights' in his theatre 'upon the banks of the Thames'. So the Shakespearean actors of this period in America and the preachers in the Brooklyn pulpits or in the revivalist meetings in the western wilderness spoke in flights of oratory.

All the great figures, East and West, who dominated this period, were orators. Often they were theatrical in bearing. There was Daniel Webster, whose farmer neighbors described him as having 'an eye as black as death and a look like a lion's'. He was, as Van Wyck Brooks points out, a man 'with an all-subduing personal force'. Posterity is inclined to laugh at Beecher's exaggerated theatricality, but he was geared in sensitive adjustment to his time. When toward the end of the war, Lincoln was asked 'whom he considered the greatest of his countrymen, [he] answered, after a moment's hesitation "Beecher" '. And this was the man whose pulpit was a veritable stage and who understood that the voice of the orator was 'a magician's wand'.

If one were not gifted as orator, one could at least lecture on oratory. John Quincy Adams delivered at Harvard in 1806 a series of *Lectures on Rhetoric and Oratory*. 'Harvard', writes Brooks, 'was prepared to hear the doctrine, sanctioned by Cicero and Demosthenes, that while liberty was the parent of eloquence, eloquence was the stay of liberty.' The small theatre of the Mississippi and Noah Ludlow, the western theatre manager, are many removes from J. Q. Adams and the Harvard of 1806. Yet Ludlow appraised the Shakespearean acting of his visiting stars, Macready and Booth, by oratorical standards. He quotes Quintilian on the charm of 'natural' oratory, and 'putting the actor in place of the orator', awards the palm to Booth. Even Ludlow knew that oratory and acting are but two forms of the same art. When Bancroft set his hand to the *History of the United States* (beginning to appear in 1843), he wrote 'like a Fourth of July oration'. He apostrophized the West in oratorical periods which eminently suited their tastes:

Crowd fearlessly to the forests [he exhorts]; plant your home in confidence, for the country watches over you; your children grow around you as hostages, and the wilderness at your bidding surrenders its grandeur of useless luxuriance to the beauty and loveliness of Culture.

To 'the beauty and loveliness' of Shakespearean culture, especially in its kinship with oratory, the West was peculiarly attuned. What was already an essential emphasis in eastern theatres and churches and on political platforms, was intensified on the frontier. The extreme perils and exuberance of frontier life made everything in the West more highly coloured. The language in which towns were settled, wildernesses subdued, was larded with picturesque metaphor and image which made the frontiersman famous. Judge James Hall who travelled down the Ohio by keelboat in the 1820's writes that when the frontiersman becomes excited his language is 'redundant with exaggerated form and figures of comparison'. When one of these frontiersmen strayed into an improvised theatre, over a billiard room, or adjoining a bar, and heard declaimed from the rickety stage Antony's oration over the dead Caesar, or Macbeth's 'Out, out, brief candle', he recognized, though afar off, some kinship with his own flamboyant speech.

When, in 1834, Dr. Daniel Drake, who had moved from New York to the Kentucky frontier as a baby, came to summarize the characteristics of the West in which he had lived for forty-nine years, he describes its taste as 'strong rather than elegant'. 'The literature of a young and free people will, of course, be declamatory . . . our natural scenery and our liberal political and social institutions must long continue its [the literature's] character of floridness.' To the western ear, attuned to its own extravagance, with strong nerves demanding violent responses, the great and near-great speeches of Shakespeare roared out magniloquently from improvised stages, spoke with congenial accents. There was a happy synchronizing of young Elizabethan and young western-world tendencies.

A young would-be actor had an interview with Sol
Smith, the manager, in 1841. His qualifications were in his
own words, that 'I can speak *orations* and I think I could
learn to act out plays in a short time'. The gift of oratory
was a great milestone on the road to acting. When Smith
asked this young man what 'orations' he could speak, the
answer was significant. Mark Antony's oratory, as Shakespeare had conceived it, ranked with John Quincy Adams'
and Patrick Henry's. Flesh and blood Americans and the
creations of Shakespeare's brain, like the Mark Antony of
his *Julius Caesar*, are lumped together as 'orators'. A nice
rendition of their rhetorical utterances is the stepping stone
to a career as an actor.

For a thousand good reasons, inherent in the times and
the social setting, Shakespeare dominated the frontier
theatre. There is a set of reliable statistics, based on the
most careful and intricate survey of the stage, made by
R. L. Rusk in his *Literature of the Middle Western Frontier*. Professor Rusk makes a study of over seven thousand
performances which took place in five significant western
centres in the forty years between 1794 and 1840. He
chooses one newspaper in each town and from it collects
all the notices of theatrical performances through these
years.

Upwards of a thousand different plays were put on, but
'a comparatively small number of plays were the favourites
which made up the programmes of the bulk of the performances'. Among these favourites Shakespeare ranked
first. 'Of all dramatists', writes Professor Rusk, 'Shakespeare was not only credited with first rank in every opinion directly or indirectly expressed by western writers,
but was actually given first rank in the matter of the total
number of performances of the work of any one author.'

Specifically Rusk's statistics are equally impressive. 'Of the 7594 performances recorded [in the five dominant centres in the years 1800–1840] 433, or more than one in eighteen, were of Shakespearean plays.' These carefully compiled statistics of an ingenious and acute scholar support the impressions deduced from contemporary social emphasis.

In the lives of the men who were concerned with the frontier theatre, one sees evidence of the prestige of Shakespeare. To have an apposite Shakespearean quotation either on the tip of one's tongue or on the title-page of one's book was to put the seal of culture upon one's personality or one's literary work. The two outstanding managers of the frontier circuit grace the openings of their books of theatrical reminiscences with Shakespearean decorations. Noah Ludlow's *Theatrical Life As I Found It*, published at St. Louis in 1880, bears upon its title-page lines from Othello's touching speech at the end of the play (V, II)

> Speak of me as I am:
> Nothing extenuate, nor set down in malice.

The play, act and scene where the quotation is found are not given. It is enough that it comes from 'Shakespeare'. Shakespeare with his handfuls of tragical speeches was ready for quotation wherever the sentiment was appropriate.

Ludlow leaves out a significant word in his title-page quotation. Apparently the lines 'lived in his memory' inaccurately and he set them down without checking up in a copy of Shakespeare. The book is dedicated to Edwin Forrest, with the obvious Shakespearean passage: 'After life's fitful fever, he sleeps well'. The first chapter, too, is headed by the line 'All the world's a stage'. Decked with these evergreen laurels, Ludlow's book gets under way.

Sol Smith, Ludlow's rival and partner, opens his *Theatrical Management in the West and South* (New York, 1868), with the same impressive decorations. His title-page bears a lovely passage from *All's Well:*

The work of life is of a mingled yarn—good and ill together.

In the Appendix, Smith works out some 'models' for his epitaph. On the stone he wants two Shakespearean quotations, one from *Macbeth* on 'Life's but a walking shadow, a poor player', and one from *As You Like It* on 'All the world's a stage'. Thus living or dying, this opportunist strolling player, Sol Smith, would give the fillip of distinction to his mean shifts and ups and downs in the theatrical world by lines from Shakespeare. That these lines were spoken 'in character' in particular plays, Smith cared not a whit. They were pure Shakespeare, speaking across the gulf of centuries directly and personally from one theatre man to another and lending the aura of their prestige to his miserable little life.

Lines from Shakespeare's poetry were always cropping up in appropriate situations of daily life among the actors. As Ludlow went westward from Albany to Kentucky in 1815, with Drake's company, they left wagons and horses at Orlean, near Pittsburgh. They transferred to a flat-bottomed boat, called an 'Ark' or 'Broadhorn', and went drifting down the Allegheny on their way. Ludlow recalls how 'Old Drake' waked them in the morning, after night anchorage, with what he calls 'a touch of Shakespeare'. It was a highly appropriate 'touch', being that lovely de-

scription of morning in *Romeo and Juliet* where Friar
Lawrence is setting out with his 'osier cage' to collect
herbs. 'The grey-eyed morn smiles on the frowning night.'
To sleeping boys, who dreamed of theatrical success so
persistently that they were willing to endure this rough,
dangerous and utterly unfamiliar journey in their 'floating house of small dimensions', Drake's use of Shakespeare
to rouse them to the struggles of the day must have been
both ludicrous and inspiring. As the wild banks of the
Allegheny re-echoed to his 'double-basso voice', they all
must have felt that crudely as the great tradition was distorted by the wildness and strangeness of this frontier
world, yet it still was the great tradition and they were a
very part of it. Perhaps the rosy light of memory coloured
this incident in Ludlow's old mind as he wrote his reminiscences. But occasions of this sort must frequently have
occurred.

Once Drake's party had planned a night on shore and
reserved a bedroom in a near-by house. When they went
to the house to go to bed, they found two Dutch mule-
attendants already established in their rooms. These 'merchants' had a huge flatboat and 'mules on board intended
for the Southern market'. As a result of their cargo, the
Dutchmen smelled to heaven and must be removed if
Drake and his men were to enjoy a night's rest. How they
'put on' the ghost scene from *Hamlet* to scare the muleteers is gleefully recorded in Ludlow's reminiscences.

As the cock crew, the ghost (in iridescent garments
from the property chest) glided 'stealthily along through
the woods to the back of the house' and entered at the
back door. While 'Sam Drake was delivering the following words in the true Hamlet style', there was such raising
of hair on the Dutch pates and such issuing of Teutonic

oaths from the Dutch mouths as surely never accompanied
these famous lines of Shakespeare before. The muleteers
were thus routed, and after this 'fitful fever', Drake's
company slept peacefully in their hired room. Surely any
owl or prowling wolf along the wooded shores of the
Allegheny that night must have furnished strange and unfamiliar 'glimpses of the moon', to this Anglo-Danish
ghost who slipped glistening past him.

Not only was Shakespeare on the tip of the tongue
among theatrical people but it was fashionable among amateurs of the theatre and gentlemen of culture. Smith records with pride that Mirabeau B. Lamar, Esq., candidate
for Congress and afterwards President of Texas, 'had
Shakespeare at his tongue's end and could quote him
directly and at pleasure'. Smith adds that Mirabeau 'fenced
well and was otherwise highly accomplished'. A knowledge of fencing and an ability to quote Shakespeare per-
tinently are badges of the accomplished gentleman and
lend stature to a future 'President of Texas'.

Not only is Shakespeare coupled with fencing, but he
finds himself bracketed along with darky minstrelsy. Scott,
a traveller on the steamboat up the river between New
Orleans and St. Louis in 1844, included among his accom-
plishments 'snatches of the fashionable negro songs—called,
for fashion's sake, *Ethiopian melodies* [Smith's italics]—
quaint sayings and quotations from Shakespeare' which
were 'at his tongue's end'.

This 'fashion' of Shakespeare was used for all it was
worth to combat the moral opposition to the stage on the
western frontier. If there was opposition to the stage in
New York City, there was even more vociferous opposition in the new West, where religion in its most emotional form—in revival meetings and frenzied new cults—

ran the theatre a close second as a source of entertainment. Perhaps there was some subconscious realization that 'Hallelujah' religion and oratorical Shakespeare were off the same piece. A too thriving theatre might draw from the congregation of the camp ground. At any rate, the war cry of immorality was raised all over the frontier. Records of theatre life are full of answers to the charges.

When Sol Smith, a stage-struck boy from a log cabin, began to hang about the Green Street Theatre in Albany and sneak in for a peep at a performance, he hid one day in a coffin used in the melodramatic scene between Richard and Anne in Shakespeare's *Richard III*, and thus got onto the stage. He makes a good story of the fright which he gave the four 'supers'. While stowing away the coffin after the show, they discovered strange sounds inside it, dropped the coffin and ran. He records that they 'immediately joined the Church', that one 'became a notorious preacher' in whose sermons the theatre always came off badly.

This tall story of Smith's is an allegory of the whole situation. The theatre fascinated the people who abused it. They were afraid to be interested in it and so they inveighed against it. Henry Ward Beecher, whose methods in preaching were so theatrical that he was called the Shakespeare of the pulpit, would doubtless have liked to go to the theatre. Yet he avoided it all his life 'saying that attendance would involve him in endless explanations'. He faced the fact that the religious element in America were against it and as the spokesman of this group he dared not go against their opinion.

Beecher, in fact, made an attack upon the stage from a Boston pulpit in 1843 and the intrepid Sol Smith answered him in a *Defense of the Stage*. Smith's *Defense* reads like all the Defenses of art against the charges of

FELIX DARLEY shows the players' consternation at the Green
St. Theatre in Albany in the early eighteen-hundreds, when
young Sol Smith was nearly stowed away in a coffin used in
Shakespeare's *Richard III*.

immorality, from Horace down. The same time-honoured arguments occur. If the Church would not stand aloof but would lend its support to the purifying of the stage 'the drama might flourish as the adjunct of Christianity'. 'Practical lessons acted before the auditor at the theatre . . . are more lasting and consequently more useful.' One remembers that the colonial theatre had adduced the same arguments in its defense.

The prestige of Shakespeare's name was undoubtedly useful in allaying the suspicion of evil. A troupe playing Cincinnati in 1815, opening with *Hamlet*, printed on their playbill a couplet which strove to emphasize the cultural and moral value of the performance.

> Source of refined and rational delight,
> Thro' *joy* to *virtue* see the stage invite.

The playbill further enjoined 'an audience of the *good people*'. Caldwell, bidding for the attention of Cincinnati in 1832, reminds in his newspaper advertisement that 'the theatre is among the first and highest schools of Literature and the Arts'. By an easy transition, one got from Shakespeare as cultural to Shakespeare as 'fashionable'. In 1831, Louisville was treated to what Caldwell advertised as 'Shakespeare's fashionable comedy', *Much Ado*.

The weighty name of Shakespeare was always a protection. Ludlow playing *Richard, Othello, Macbeth* in Frankfort, Kentucky, in the spring of 1817 complains that 'my personal respect [was] brought into question because I was an *actor*'. Sometimes, as in colonial days, a religious sect could express its opposition to a theatrical company by bringing an injunction against the opening. This happened in Springfield, Illinois, in 1839 when Jo Jefferson, as a boy, was making a western tour with his parents. He recalls how a young lawyer of Springfield called upon the manager of the company and offered his services free to secure for them the right to play. The young lawyer made an harangue before the council, full of tact, skill and humour. He traced the history of the drama and showed its advantages. When one learns from Jefferson that the young lawyer's name was Abraham Lincoln, one is not surprised that the injunction was removed and the company opened their performances.

As one looks over the history of theatrical production along the Ohio and Mississippi, between 1800 and 1850, one sees the predominance of English influence. Where English theatrical management dominated, of course Shakespeare dominated. Both Drake and Caldwell, great managers of the West and South, came originally from England. The whole throng of great Shakespearean stars who came West to play, especially in the thirties and forties, were those same English actors who had been in eastern centres like Boston, New York and Philadelphia. Aside from the stars, there are glimpses of obscure young English actors sprinkled here and there among the western wilds, playing Shakespeare violently. Ludlow, when he first entered Kentucky, found a young English actor at Frankfort whose father had played at the Royal Theatre in London and who, himself, rendered Dr. Caius of Shakespeare's *Merry Wives* with peculiar brilliance. This infiltration of English-trained actors into the frontier meant, of course, the preservation and emphasis of the Shakespearean tradition on the western stage.

The conjunction of British actors and the frontier is romantically illustrated in the showboat of the Chapman family. William Chapman, Senior, had played in Covent

ENTERTAINMENT on the flat-boat or broad-horn on the Mississippi. Forerunner of the Show Boat.

Garden with Mrs. Siddons. With his family of three sons
and two daughters, he had come to New York about 1827
and had played Iago at the Bowery in 1828. Thence they
had apparently drifted westward. They turn up most picturesquely in Ludlow's reminiscences in the year 1831 or
'32. Ludlow recalls the day when he saw head up the
Cincinnati river front 'a large flatboat, with a rude kind of
house built upon it'. It had a 'ridge roof' and a flagpole on
which was bravely flying a pennant with the word 'Theatre' upon it. This was the famous floating theatre of the
Chapmans. It plied between Cincinnati and New Orleans,
stopping 'at every town or village on the banks' where
there was a prospect of 'sufficent audience'.

The showboat was beautifully adapted to the chances
and changes of a frontier world. It utilized the great river;
it reached the tiniest settlements; it was movable; and
when any trouble or opposition scented the air, the Chapmans had only to loose the hawsers and drift away into
safety. No wonder they were able soon to substitute for
the flat-boat a steamboat 'filled up very comfortably after
the fashion of a theatre'. Although the Chapman family
were all born on British soil and trained in the British acting tradition, they floated on the North American rivers,
and among the most uniquely American social setting.
Shakespeare was the staple of these British actors. The
father had played it in New York before he came West.
And the talented children, Caroline and William, Jr.,
made Shakespearean history in the theatre of San Francisco in 1852. Though there is no specific reference to
Shakespeare on the Chapman Showboat between 1830
and '40, they must have played it there, too.

The late Ashley Thorndike, gifted American Shakespearean scholar, in an address on 'Shakespeare in America'

before the British Academy in London, in 1927, was impressed with the romantic juxtaposition of Shakespeare and the raw setting of the new American world. 'An extraordinary chronicle', he said, 'might be gathered of the various and peculiar conditions under which Othello was wooed and Hamlet soliloquized upon the American scene.' The British Chapmans on their Mississippi flatboat, probably playing Shakespeare along with dancing, singing, and acting in blackface are surely a picturesque part of this 'extraordinary chronicle'.

Judge James Hall, who drifted down the Ohio by keelboat in 1820, records the need for entertainment on these tediously long days when the current of the river held the wheel. He remembers boat songs, compounded of 'poetry dressed in rags and going on crutches'. There was dancing. The whiskey jug helped to put 'life and metal' into the dancer's heels. 'Old Pap' with 'Katy', his beloved violin, made music to pay for his potations. Slipping into the mould of this local amusement, the British Chapmans, with the tradition of Covent Garden in their keeping, adapted the lines of the greatest English poet to the rhythm and drift of 'the lazy stream'. It was symbolic in adaptation to locale, in method of presentation, and in its welcome reception, of the way in which Shakespeare captured the American frontier in the first half of the nineteenth century.

CHAPTER XI

Shakespeare in the California Gold Rush

THE story of Shakespeare in California from 1848 to the eve of the Civil War is a combination of crudity and sophistication. It is easier to see the pressure of social background here than in the older and more complex sections of the country. For while California prior to the Mexican War of 1846 had a long history, it was not an American history but one in which Spain, France, England and Mexico had played the major part. When in 1848, by military and political machinations California became American territory, the social trends and influences had yet to be made and felt.

The first dozen years of California as a part of America are years of acquisitiveness. First, the territory itself was stolen. Then, although the legend of gold had hung over the Sierras for centuries, the discovery of the actual metal 'was delayed until American operation arrived'. In the tailrace of John Sutter's sawmill on the American River, 'something that glittered and was gold' set a force in motion which was to 'trouble the surface of American life' in picturesque and violent ways for the next decades. This was in January, 1848. In less than six months 'more than half a million dollars' worth of precious metal' had been secured. Within fifteen months, seventeen thousand persons had sailed away from the eastern shores, not to mention the hordes pouring overland. The California which had had seven hundred American residents in 1845, had, according to the census, ninety-two thousand in 1850 and three hundred eighty thousand by 1860.

There was not only a miraculous growth in wealth and population; there was, too, a miraculous development in the theatre. From a non-existent stage, five years brought dramatic activity to a point where the theatre was more sumptuously housed than the drama on the east coast. The names of the most gifted actors, British and American, appeared in the leading rôles. The sizes of audiences and prices paid for admission were, too, phenomenal. The fact of the matter was that California's gold was fabulously powerful; it was used lavishly to buy the best things that life offered. Significantly for the history of Shakespeare in America, Shakespeare on the stage was considered one of those 'best things'.

The plays were garnished with the pleasures of the gambling table and the saloon, the pleasures of gilded interiors and audiences raining tiaras and gold brooches upon the stage. Certainly, too, that 'makeshift' quality of production, which marked the touring performances of the stars in the East, the uneven 'support' in minor parts, the final presentation before the play could achieve smoothness in rehearsal, all these things were true of Shakespeare in California in these feverish 'gold rush' years. But that he was there in such abundance, displayed on such flamboyant red plush, is the notable thing. It proves once more the unquestioned power and prestige of his name, though real appreciation and the true estimate of his power may have lagged far behind.

In California, the strictly moral element in society which had forbidden and checked dramatic productions in the East simply did not exist. The civic and religious opposition to the theatre which the Puritans and Quakers brought

with them from England, as a large part of the spiritual
cargo with which their small ships were crammed, had
been embattled against the stage for over two hundred
years. In places like Boston, it had successfully prevented
the existence of any theatre until after the Revolution. In
New York and Philadelphia, the managers and actors had
toed a very sharp line. They were always conciliating the
opposition, giving benefit performances for public chari-
ties, asserting the gentility and cultivation of their actors,
invoking the prestige of 'society' for their productions.
Even in Virginia and Carolina, there was always present
the rumbling of moral opposition.

But here in California, ravished from Mexico and turned
into a great potential source of wealth to any man with a
pick and shovel and a stout heart, there was no conservative social element, no hostile moral tradition to fight. In
fact, the theatre itself, especially the Shakespearean theatre, became a mark of tradition and culture. At last the
wheel had come full circle, and the production of Shakespeare in the San Francisco of the early fifties was a tangible proof that this new West had spliced its newness into
the long cable of the English cultural past. Instead of being
on the side of the bohemian and the radical, he was now
the very symbol that California was an established cultural
unit. Thus 'the whirligig of time brings in its revenges'.

A breath of adverse criticism of the theatre on moral
grounds comes from 'Mrs. Robinson'. She was the wife of
one of the earliest professional entertainment men, 'Dr.' or
'Yankee' Robinson. This 'Dr. Robinson' was born in
Maine. Association with Barnum had exorcised any stiff-
necked morality with which his native Maine may have
endowed him. Whether Mrs. Robinson came from Maine,
is not certain. But at any rate, she disapproved of all her

husband's theatre world and sometimes made him trouble. It is amusing that this breath of opposition seems likely to have blown from the rock-ribbed conscience of far-away Maine. But it blew to little purpose in the warm, golden haze of San Francisco.

The theatre buildings themselves are a piece of material evidence on the nature and quality of Shakespearean production in California in the fifties. The 'palatial' California theatre began at Sacramento at the very mouth of the mines, in 1849. The New Eagle, opened there in the autumn of 1849, shows beautifully the Janus-like quality of these new buildings. It was partly a mining-camp entertainment hall and partly an echo of the established and sophisticated theatre of the East. It had canvas walls and a roof of sheet iron. At its door was the familiar round tent which housed an elaborate gambling arrangement. But it also had, in imitation twice-removed of the eighteenth century London world, a 'dress circle', 'parquette' and drop curtain. It cost seventy-five thousand dollars to build and was operated at a cost of six hundred dollars per night. It soon closed, probably because of the high cost of operation. But its dual nature, half frontier amusement-hall and half sophisticated theatre, is significant.

In San Francisco, the history of the theatre buildings is equally revealing. Gambling and the theatre there were 'inextricably interwoven' and 'every theatre had a bar at its entrance'. In other words, the frequenters of the California theatre could have the amusement they were used to. But over and above that, they could have something more. They could have theatrical performances, just as they had had them at home, back East. They had the 'best', which meant Shakespeare played by the 'best' actors, eastern and foreign stars.

Tom Maguire, who was an early and successful producer in San Francisco, was originally a famous gambler. He had been an illiterate cab-driver who rose into the career of gambling. And he never left the gambling field: it simply occurred to him that theatre production was the best gambling of all. One remembers that Jacob Astor in the New York of a generation earlier had had the same notion: that investment in the theatre was the finest sort of money-making game. The fact that both of these men, who had no sense of the theatre as art, yet poured their fortune into the material equipment for the stage, argues volumes for the important function of the theatre then in the lives of the American public.

Tom Maguire's first Jenny Lind Theatre in 1850 was, true to expectation, over a gambling saloon. But it had also the traditional features of an eastern theatre and in luxurious fashion. It could seat two thousand, had a wide stage and spangled drop curtain. It is described by Constance Rourke whose collection from both printed material and oral tradition in California has made her *Troupers of the Gold Coast* a uniquely valuable book. Tom Maguire's first Jenny Lind had 'richly gilded proscenium boxes, gilded ceiling and panels of deep rose'. Here in the year 1850 were produced *Macbeth, Hamlet, Much Ado*. The 'miners . . . swarmed from the gambling saloons and cheap fandango houses to see *Hamlet* and *Lear*'. No doubt many of them, who had lived in small towns back home, had longed for a chance to visit the city theatres of New York, Boston or Philadelphia. Here at last in this outlandish faraway world, they had found both gold and some of the precious things they had longed for, to spend it on. Fires were frequent and when Tom Maguire's third Jenny Lind rose from its ashes in October of the next year

(1851) it had an even more gorgeous red and gold interior against which young Junius Brutus Booth and his company played *Henry IV*.

Yet there was nothing 'esoteric' about all this. Shakespeare took his place, without embarrassment, among the robust pleasures of gaming and drinking. It was as it had been in his lifetime on the south bank of the Thames in Elizabethan London. Rowe's Amphitheatre of 1849 was primarily a circus tent. Yet *Othello* drew audiences there apparently as easily as bareback riders. The American Theatre, opening also in 1851, flaunted a pit, parquette, gallery and gilded dome. The draperies and lamps were notable. The first tier of boxes was supported by Corinthian columns. And Shakespeare was invoked in the 'poetical salutation' of the opening night. All this seems to be in the grand tradition and far removed from the gambling tents and the bars. Yet Dr. Robinson, who had wandered from Maine by way of the American amusement world, made some trenchant criticism of the bogus quality of California's Shakespearean production. It was in the 'poetical salutation' which he composed for the occasion. The lines run:

> Could we tonight the eternal slumbers break
> Of Avon's bard and bid the dreamer wake
> The astonish'd muse would bid the Poet turn
> And sleep again beneath the honoured urn.

No doubt the tone of reverential declamation in which these lines were read on this opening night concealed the sly implication that Shakespeare's ghost would be affronted by the poor quality of the production. But the nasty criticism is there, slipped in by the wise little Doctor. As Constance Rourke observes: 'There were plenty of theatre-goers who realized that some of these new ventures failed to fulfil the highest theatrical traditions'. It was *not* the best Shakespeare, though red velvet and Corinthian columns and eastern or British actors featured in its production. Yet it was there and it was popular. For artistic oversight there was the compensation of 'warmth in the audience as well as humour; something palpable and genial . . . all but floated in the air'. His essence would out, at least in scattered speeches, whether the production as a whole was smooth or rough. And the magic of his name bound this crude new world as with a spell.

The great tradition in Shakespearean acting was represented by persons who could adapt it to frontier conditions. Caroline and William Chapman, who played Shakespeare at the Jenny Lind in San Francisco in 1851, had been brought up by an English father who in his youth had played with Siddons at Covent Garden. From Covent Garden to Mississippi showboating was an arc which the elder Chapman could span with ease. These, his two most gifted children, had the same artistic elasticity. After playing the eastern centres in the forties with distinction and fame, they came to Tom Maguire's palatial Jenny Lind Theatre in San Francisco, in a variety of Shakespearean and other rôles. Junius Brutus Booth, then thirty, was already in the West and was joined at just this time by his brilliant father, now fifty-five, and his younger brother Edwin, a boy of eighteen.

Combining with the Chapmans, the Booths opened in the summer of 1852. They played *Hamlet, Macbeth, Othello, Richard III*, and packed the Jenny Lind for two consecutive weeks. The performances must have been a combination of contradictory traditions. Caroline Chap-

man had in her ten years of showboating on the Mississippi
learned 'to cast away nearly everything of fixed tradition'.
The elder Booth, on the contrary, who had been born in
England and lived the first twenty-five years of his life
there, 'played within a ritual . . . by which every touch of
action or of business had long since been prearranged'.

This combination of traditional acting and new flexibility crowded the Jenny Lind to the doors. Another five-
day engagement at the Adelphi in the same summer was
an equal success, concluding with the *Merchant of Venice*. In this combination of Booths and Chapmans in 1852,
the naturalness of acting in the younger members of the
troupe offset the elder Booth's stiffness: and their lack of
form was balanced by his finish. San Francisco audiences
were sufficiently cosmopolitan to receive both strains of
interpretation and to like the combination.

But when the elder Booth tried Sacramento in this same
summer, he failed. Sacramento was too near the mines; it
produced a too exclusively 'new-world' audience. Yet the
younger Booths and the Chapmans were able to tour the
mines and give them what they wanted. The Chapmans
went there in the autumn of '52. And Edwin Booth, a
temperamental youth of eighteen with a great career before him, was a strolling entertainer in the mines throughout the winter of '52. With the agility of the younger generation, he could entertain the camps with the part of Iago,
as he had learned it from his father, or, when that failed,
sing for his supper to the strumming of his banjo.

After the elder Booth's sudden death on a Mississippi
River boat in 1852, the young Booth and the Chapmans
opened again in Tom Maguire's new theatre, San Francisco Hall. They presented an enormous number of plays,
including Shakespeare. But the old charm, perhaps lent by

the flavour and decorum of the elder Booth, was gone. They were too facile and too expeditious even for this bold new San Francisco world. There were complaints of 'too many plays' and of performances 'not sufficiently finished' and of lines not 'well learned'.

By 1856 Laura Keene's Shakespearean offerings, venturing a half dozen performances of *Hamlet*, *Macbeth* and *Richard III*, and producing such lesser favourites as *Coriolanus*, argue a fairly sophisticated Shakespearean taste in her San Francisco audiences. To be sure, she played with 'extravagances', but this was the extravagance of all Shakespearean production in that period, whether in London or in San Francisco. If the magnificence of her 'mountings' choked the spiritual grandeur of Shakespeare's lines it was not the fault of frontier taste. It was a manifestation of that Victorian world to which, seen from the angular and chromium austerities of our twentieth century, belong the comfortable contours of a pincushion. San Francisco was not behind London in its display of red plush.

The swing from excessive admiration of any form of art to reaction, often in the form of burlesque, is common enough. With Shakespeare in California it happened in a briefer space of time than in more slow-moving portions of the world. Any classic lives in the shadow of imminent parody. Parody or caricature or burlesque is a by-product of admiration as well as an indication of scorn. The shadow of parody has always pursued Shakespeare. In his own lifetime, a cool head like Ben Jonson's could easily detect those portions of his plays where the riotous exuberance of his fancy had betrayed him. As he receded from the common touch down the long vistas of the centuries and became a 'classic', his mere eminence and sanctity invited parody. Hamlet's famous soliloquies lent their pattern to controversial verses just before the American Revolution.

It is not surprising, therefore, to find that the new, high-tension world of California in the days of the Gold Rush soon got through its awe of Shakespeare, soon found the frequent production of him boring. The miners 'could finish lines from Shakespeare before they were spoken'. There was something about this familiarity which bred a delicious and high-spirited contempt. They were at ease in Zion. When McKean Buchanan, an accomplished gambler as well as a Shakespearean actor, played to the miners in the late fifties, Constance Rourke describes the kind of Macbeth he put on. He 'strode onto the stage', she says, 'amid blue fire, in a slouch hat'. It is not fantastic to see in this presentation of *Macbeth*, a semi-western costume. He wore 'a long black cape'. He stood with 'arms folded high, ominously patting one arm with a huge yellow gauntlet'. Here is the swaggering, western braggart, daring his enemies to come on and take their medicine.

While Miss Rourke does not suggest a specific burlesque here, there is the hint that Buchanan's *Macbeth* adapts the Elizabethan hero of 'Lay on, MacDuff' to the parallel conditions in western mining camps. Contemporary realism overlays the strangeness of Shakespeare's language and reveals the universal 'bad man'. The miners enjoyed, too, 'a black-faced Mr. Othello', though excellent productions of Shakespeare were held 'in recent memory'. This does not mean that the day of serious Shakespeare in California was over. His popularity was very great in the decades after the Civil War. The things burlesqued are permanent. One simply chooses, for the nonce, to shake oneself free of their sobering import and to gambol lightly and affectionately around their time-tested sobriety.

Shakespearean travesty in California in the late fifties is

ILLUSTRATION from a skilful parody of *Hamlet* in George
Edward Rice's *An Old Play in New Garb*, Boston 1853. The
sketch shows 'Laertes Polonius' sailing for France.

a reflection of a tendency felt all over the country. In the
Folger Shakespeare Library in Washington, D.C., there is
a whole sheaf of paper-covered pamphlets and other travesties, ranging in date from 1820 to 1925. Sometimes they
are done by persons of taste. George Edward Rice's *An
Old Play in New Garb*, printed by Ticknor & Fields, Boston, 1853, is a skilful and tasteful parody of *Hamlet* in
rhymed couplet with charmingly incongruous illustrations. *The Hamlet Travestie*, New York, 1820, parodies
the misplaced learning and ingenuity of pedantic commentators. *Hamlet, A Dramatic Prelude in Five Acts*, by
James Rush, M.D., printed at Philadelphia in 1834, is a
take-off on medical quackery. These adaptations of Shakespeare to the parody of contemporary social issues are the
jeux d'esprit of cultivated professional men. They use the
familiar idiom of Shakespeare to grind their particular axes.

But the more typical sort of travesty in the Folger is of
the same sort that rejoiced the miners of California in the
late fifties. There was a whole series of these paper-
covered plays devised for amateur production. One such
series, published by 'The Happy Hours Company', No. 1
Chambers Street, New York, about 1870, is inspired by
the prominence of the negro in the Civil War. It is called
'The Ethiopian Drama' Series. The paper cover bears a
stage with footlights. Beneath the curtain appears a large,
grinning darky face, above polka-dotted collar points. The
title-page reads: HAMLET THE DAINTY [a dubious
pun on Dane] / AN ETHIOPIAN BURLESQUE / or
/ SHAKESPEARE'S HAMLET / Performed by /
GRIFFIN AND CHRISTY'S MINSTRELS / By
G. W. H. Griffin, Esq. / Author of 'Rooms to Let'.

There are three scenes and eight pages of dialogue.
Hamlet and Horatio are darkies, frightened by a ghost

who obviously is 'from the South'. The ghost tells how
he was murdered by a 'gallon of brandy' while taking his
afternoon snooze at the gin-mill. It is not very funny. The
provocation to titter arises from the temerity which adapts
a classic to a homely evening's entertainment in terms of
a contemporary social problem. The 'Happy Hours Company' which prints these travesties advertises the sale of
'Wigs, Beards, Moustaches, etc., for Amateur Theatricals'.
We wish them all a happy evening in their Victorian parlor or church vestry.

The significance lies in the extent to which a knowledge
of Shakespeare has penetrated the American consciousness.
In this same series appear *The Comedy of Errors, Shylock*
and *Othello,* of which last the Folger Library has a copy.
In this *Othello* we read that Brabantio had thought to produce his daughter, Desdemona, through Barnum when off
she goes with a 'nager called Othello'. Songs about Dixie
intermingle with the dialogue. The text, as a whole, is a
dismal failure from the point of view of wit. Yet this sort
of thing continued. The Hamlet Travestie was adapted in
San Francisco in 1876 by 'the Shakespeare Club'. In it
Tilden, Roscoe Conkling, and Grant appear. Hamlet in
the closet scene looks 'here upon this picture and on this'
and discovers

Roscoe Conkling's curls: the front of Grant himself.

There were less ambitious parodies. *Gus Shaw's Original Comic Songs,* a yellow paper-covered volume, published in New York, 1857, and now in the Folger Library,
parodies Shakespeare's Seven Ages with no point save that
the Elizabethan social setting is supplanted by American

social background. The lines on the old-age of man describe a time when

> like sheep what's got the rot
> All our senses go to pot.

It's the temerity of taking the classic Shakespeare and translating his theories into the parlance of sheep-herders and farmers. Whatever fun there is, lies there. *Beadle's Dime American Speaker*, N. Y., 1863, offers, besides selections from Beecher, Edward Everett, Poe and Tennyson, a 'piece' entitled 'The Case of Mr. Macbeth'. In it Macbeth is presented as 'hen-pecked' by Mrs. Macbeth, a 'Scotchwoman' and a 'Tartar'.

On the cover of *Beadle's Dime American Speaker* is a picture of a boy declaiming against the background of a draped American flag. The whole thing is significantly American. Boys must grow up to be orators, to move their country and to get their own way in this wide land of the American flag. They must get 'culture' with the minimum of time and effort. Tennyson, Poe, Beecher, are offered. So freely and completely was Shakespeare appropriated that a comical interpretation of the family dilemma could be applied to his Macbeth and declaimed amid guffaws, to a delighted American audience. But no matter how casual and brazen its touch, America could not and did not wish to escape the tacit dominance of its British models.

When the California mining camps of the late fifties laughed at the antics of 'a black-faced Mr. Othello', they were not necessarily retrogressing from a higher standard of Shakespearean entertainment. Shakespeare mounted in

gilt and plush, or set off with burnt cork, played over
saloons and behind gaming tents or amid Corinthian columns and gas lights; Shakespeare rendered in the Covent
Garden tradition, or in the new naturalness of an original
American technique, came with the Gold Rush to California. It was one of the most precious treasures which the
new gold could buy. Nuggets straight from the shaft fell
at the feet of the actors of his magic lines. In more civilized San Francisco, they fell onto the stage in the form of
'diadems and watches, golden flowers and jewelled
brooches'. The presentation of his plays reflected the ins
and outs, the ups and downs of the California spiritual
climate in those tense and feverish years. But however distorted, Shakespeare was there as one of the most precious
things they could buy for themselves with their new
fortunes.

CHAPTER XII

Shakespeare Enters the American Consciousness by Way of the Schools and Colleges *

THERE is a certain generation of living Americans to whom the line 'Friends, Romans, Countrymen, lend me your ears' is a kind of secret-society joke. The repetition of this line, in stentorian tones, acts as a password: it admits one to a familiar company who share a common memory. It is a memory partly boring, partly ludicrous and partly stirring: a memory of a high school class which laboured from day to day through something long and cumbrous, called *Julius Caesar* by one William Shakespeare. The thing was too long and the class staid on it too many weeks to enable one to grasp it in its entirety; what the whole show was about, one never knew. But day by day there were sections of text to read, words to be elucidated by notes 'in the back of the book'. In the class itself there was the minute-to-minute peril of being asked the meaning of a word or phrase. There was, too, the rare chance that some particular speech, rolling itself out in loud, metrical oratory, might send a chill down one's spine. Sometimes these heroics might be turned into fun. The Roman mob could be pictured, detaching its ears and handing them over generously to the speaker. One could reproduce the situation deftly in pantomime. Boring, thrilling or humor-

* For suggestions throughout this chapter I am indebted to Henry W. Simon for his scholarly study, *The Reading of Shakespeare in American Schools and Colleges, An Historical Survey*, New York, 1932.

ous as the memory may be, it *is* a memory. It has left an indelible impression.

The history of Shakespeare in American education, secondary and collegiate, reflects the veers and flaws of American opinion. Its curves fluctuate with the geographical sections of the country and with the dominant moods of successive decades. The story as a whole is full of contradictions. It has the same paradoxical qualifications that one remembers from the high school class in *Julius Caesar;* it is by turns boring, ludicrous and thrilling.

Prior to the American Revolution, Shakespeare as a formal part of education in the colonies is non-existent. The erotic lines from Shakespeare which found their way into the private notebooks of some Harvard boys in the mid-seventeenth century existed there to be secretly enjoyed when the day's assignments in Harvard courses were forgotten. It is not unpleasant to think backward from the 'bad eminence' of Shakespeare in most twentieth century college and university curricula, to these happier American collegiate days. Then undergraduates slammed to their books on the requirements of the mere professors, and turned for private joy to lines out of Shakespeare. This historical perspective might well cause the modern pedagogue to ponder on the obliqueness of the young human animal in whatever century. What he is told to read in direct assignment, loses its charm by the very act of telling. What he finds for himself, as he waywardly adventures among books on his own initiative, becomes his treasure trove.

At the time these young Harvard men were enjoying Shakespeare privately, President Dunster in his administration of Harvard College was busily engaged in reproducing 'on the banks of the Charles, the ideals he had found established on the banks of the Cam'. There was no course in Shakespeare at Cambridge (England) nor any likelihood of one for over two hundred years. In this new Massachusetts, the crying need was for learned ministers of the Gospel. Dunster's whole curriculum was constructed 'to raise up a class of learned men for the Christian ministry'. Surely this Shakespeare, this common stage-player so recently dead, who had crept into the folds of noble and royal protection in his own day and had won favour among the Cavaliers who followed, was the arch-enemy of all that Dunster wanted Harvard to stand for. As for Shakespeare in the common schools, this, too, was unthinkable. If he was not fit for the university, he was not fit for the dame school which wrote and read and figured and never forgot that 'in Adam's fall, we sinned all'.

After the passage of nearly a hundred years, after the eighteenth century was half gone, Shakespeare, educationally at least, still stood in the same position. According to the resolutions passed in October of 1753 by the General Assembly of Connecticut 'the one principal end proposed in erecting a College [Yale] was a learned, pious and orthodox ministry'. To courses in Shakespeare the doors of such colleges were still closed. The professors were examined by the overseers of Harvard for their 'soundness' and 'orthodoxy'. If these professors took pleasure in profane literature, especially the literature of the stage, it was no part of their professional equipment.

As for the common school in the mid-eighteenth century, it was distinctly conditioned by class consciousness. Governor Berkeley in Virginia thought the simplest and happiest policy was to preserve the common people even from the danger of literacy. The indentured men and other stout 'workers' who were migrating to America and forming something like a 'frontier' on the western boundary of the seaboard colonies were too busy keeping alive by their own hands to resent the lack of popular education. The common schools of New England continued their practical tyranny in the useful art of literacy. Their pupils learned how to keep accounts on weekdays and fear God on Sundays. And this was sufficient.

But just then, about 1750, something new and different began to be in the air. In the history of Shakespeare on the colonial stage, a new prosperity and a closer linking of American colonial enterprise with British business brought a new opportunity for entertainment to the colonial world.

Yet this presence of Shakespeare on the stage had no effect upon the possibility of getting him introduced into American education. But just about 1750 there spoke out certain forward-looking idealists and untrammelled thinkers who conceived of education as something broader than mere professional training. English literature seemed to them an advisable addition to the traditional studies. If their theories had been put into practice then, Shakespeare would perhaps have appeared much earlier in our educational system. Luckily for us these men put their ideas and schemes down on paper. Their pamphlets and brochures make interesting reading. In this liberalizing programme there was a possibility for the reading of Shakespeare.

Franklin's proposals, for instance, for 'an English School' at the Philadelphia Academy in 1749, had two places in it where Shakespeare might have been used. In his 'second class', among passages suitable for oratorical training, he lists 'a speech in a tragedy, some part of a comedy'. For his 'sixth class' he prescribes 'the best English authors'. Under both these general heads, Shakespeare might have been used. In fact, Shakespeare was actually suggested to Franklin as a specific requirement for this 'English School' by his friend Samuel Johnson (the American of that name).

But innovation, such as this would have been, is hard to establish. Besides, the American Revolution was looming over the horizon. There was no leisure time for experimenting with new educational ideas.

Even after the Revolution, as late as 1785, Franklin on revisiting the Philadelphia Academy found no hint of broadening educational theory. Fresh from Europe as he was and full of the new winds of social doctrine that were blowing, it is small wonder that he was discouraged. He found too much reading of the traditional Greek and Latin in their originals and too little of the education suited to the new conditions of the new American citizen. He took his pen in hand again and wrote in 1789, *Observations Relating to the Intention of the Original Founder of the Academy of Philadelphia*. In it he deplores 'in mankind an unaccountable prejudice in favour of ancient customs and habitudes'. Especially, he might have added, in those men whose business it is to shape the educational policy for the young. He draws an amusing European parallel. When wigs, curled and pomaded, became the fashion, men no longer needed hats to protect their heads. These hats, furthermore, were a nuisance; if worn they would disarrange the puffs and curls of the wigs. Yet men were so accustomed to hats that by sheer force of tradition they provided themselves with them and carried them under their arms. Hence the phrase *'chapeau bras'*. Franklin then draws the parallel with the outmoded curriculum of the Philadelphia Academy. 'The still prevailing custom', he writes, 'of having schools for teaching . . . the Latin and Greek languages, I consider therefore in no other light than as the *chapeau bras* of modern literature.'

The forsaking of the *chapeau bras* of traditional curricula and the substitution for them of English literature in general, and of Shakespeare in particular, came slowly. From 1785 onward, however, a book which lauded Shakespeare and quoted from him was used in many of the American universities, such as King's College [now Columbia] and Yale. This book was Hugh Blair's *Lectures on Rhetoric and Belles Lettres.*

Now the entrance of Shakespeare into the conservative American stronghold of traditional education, under the respectable aegis of Hugh Blair, is one of the pleasant little jokes of our history. Hugh Blair was a famous Edinburgh preacher and professor; these facts spelled safety for anything he might write and publish. He had occupied successively the famous pulpit of the Presbyterian High Church in Edinburgh and the newly created Chair of Rhetoric and Belles Lettres in Edinburgh University. He had retired in 1783 from his lectureship and put his lectures into book form. This Scotch preacher and teacher, friend of Hume and Adam Smith, made frequent use of Shakespeare both in his lectures and in the book for which they furnished the basis.

To be sure Shakespeare is handled with the usual eighteenth century prejudices. He is scolded for not knowing the rules of poetry. But he is lauded, too, and generously quoted. 'Touching the heart', Blair declares, 'is Shakespeare's great excellency.' Shakespeare is a bulwark of virtue and morality instead of a seduction of the devil. His characters make speeches which 'are at once *instructive* and affecting'. He is 'great' and 'altogether unrivalled' in tragedy and comedy. Thus by way of the Scotch Presbyterian, Blair, Shakespeare as 'great', as 'instructive' and 'touching the heart' enters, unchallenged, into the educational scheme of America.

He does not seem to have made much stir for several years to come. Probably American professors did not stress the pages of Blair in which Shakespeare was discussed. Perhaps the young gentlemen who sat in their classes were inattentive to his attractions. For whatever reason, the real story of Shakespeare in American schools and colleges begins well after the Revolution. Yet the seeds for ideas of education as a source of individual growth and social peace had been sown. On the eve of the nineteenth century, they began to bear fruit, though it was at first and for many decades scraggly and misshapen. A new social world was demanding a new kind of education. First the schools and, at long last, the colleges acceded to this demand.

Declamation and oratory were at once the bane and the blessing of the new secondary school education. They entered by way of the school reader. The history of the school reader is also the history of Shakespeare in American school education for many years to come. The new democracy had brought with it, as democracies always have since the days of Socrates and the Sophists, a perilous chance for the person gifted with oratory to get on in the world. If one learned how to move people, one had only to stand in pulpit or on campground and lift up one's voice. Then personal prominence would follow. Or if one's tastes leaned in a political direction, one could use the same technique on the campaign platform and climb to power and influence in the state. The history of the United States is full of individuals who actually succeeded by these methods. It is no wonder, then, that the secondary school began at once to work on a system which should give every girl and boy the necessary training for these ends.

As happened in the history of the American stage, we went for ideas to England, though nothing made us more angry than to be reminded of this fact. In England in the late eighteenth century, there was a good deal of activity in the field of teaching elocution. Among the best passages for practice in declamation were, of course, speeches from Shakespeare. No doubt this rhetorical interest in Shakespeare had been stimulated by the Shakespeare of the stage.

The study of rhetoric by amateurs became popular. Books of passages suitable for declamation, with instructions on how to read them, began to appear in England. One such collection of pieces for rhetorical rendition, called *The Speaker*, was compiled by William Enfield, and went through six editions in England in the last quarter of the century. Forty-six out of the two hundred and sixty-nine passages he collected were, as one would guess, from Shakespeare. There was an American edition of *The Speaker*, published in 1799. It had no great American vogue; it was too expensive a book and perhaps a trifle too early. But its numerous passages from Shakespeare were a treasure for American pillagers, and by its publication in Philadelphia a trend and a tendency were clearly defined.

Another English importation of a book of passages for declamation had a wider American influence, and into the bargain, a humorous and ironic history. It was *Lectures on the Art of Reading* (1775) in two volumes. It contained many Shakespearean passages and was widely studied and adapted by American editors of schoolbooks.

The compiler of these lectures was Thomas Sheridan, British actor and educator.

On the adaptation of Sheridan's reader to American schools, it would seem that the long colonial quarrel between acting (especially Shakespearean acting, for Thomas Sheridan was a famous interpreter of Shakespearean rôles) and the decent and sober forces of society was likely to be settled. This Thomas Sheridan, son of Swift's famous Dublin schoolmaster and father of Richard Brinsley Sheridan, had really been led to an interest in education and the place of rhetoric in it, by way of his experience as an actor. He had played Hamlet at Covent Garden, in 1744, with distinction. He took over the management of the Theatre Royal in Dublin, in 1747, and did many constructive things for the Irish stage. Being the son of a schoolmaster and the father of a gifted son whose education was important, Thomas Sheridan became interested in the problems of education. Because of his theatrical training, he believed that oratory was indispensable to a gentleman's education. Thus the immoral stage and the chaste training of youth at last met.

Thomas Sheridan lectured on his educational plan at both Oxford and Cambridge. These universities rewarded him after their fashion. They bestowed upon him the M.A., listened politely to his programme and did precisely nothing about it. He returned again to the stage but he never lost his interest in the function of oratory in education. We hear of him in France studying its system of education, and in 1769 he embodied his ideas in a brochure called *Plan of Education for the Young Nobility and Gentry*. Certainly in the career of his own son, Richard Brinsley Sheridan, training in oratory yielded a rich return. He not only became a great actor and playwright but had a career in Parliament where his gift of oratory in the impeachment of Warren Hastings made British history.

Thus Shakespeare and the training of youth are identified in the theory and practice of Thomas Sheridan. The combination bears spectacular fruit in the theatrical and parliamentary career of his son Richard Brinsley Sheridan. That Thomas Sheridan's *Lectures on the Art of Reading*, embodying these principles and using Shakespeare as the 'indispensable' aid in 'the teaching of elocution', should become the source of ideas and passages for 'American editors of schoolbooks' is both amusing and touching. At last it makes some amend for the long outlawing of Shakespeare and the stage by the sober forces of American social betterment.

Yet there lingered in the compilers of these American Readers, some fear of the immorality in Shakespeare. Though they used his speeches they usually did not give the act, scene and line lest some inquiring adolescent should look up the play and thus open the way to the contaminating power of the theatre. Sometimes they withheld the title of the play and even Shakespeare's name. The middle-class fear of the stage died hard and the forces of religion and morality were still to be reckoned with. The McGuffey Readers were typical in their handling of Shakespeare. They had, outside of New England, the widest distribution and the greatest influence.

McGuffey's career was calculated to give a keen sense of what was needed for American children. He knew the social and private circumstances of the American family as it existed all over the central states in the 1830's. He was of Scotch origin. This vouched for his strict moral bent combined with a shrewd sense of how to make a living. Like many boys with a leaning toward book-learning in those days, he could always earn money by teaching for the next lap of his self-made career.

In the University of Miami at Oxford, Ohio, his stripling person might well have bent beneath the imposing title of 'Professor of Ancient Languages'. This was in 1826. Six years later he had added another whole province of learning to his equipment and sat, apparently with ease, in the Chair of 'Mental Philosophy'. Meanwhile, he had become a licensed preacher in the Presbyterian Church. He had now the prime requisites for dealing with the young. He was a man of religion and learning. The order is significant. Thus eminently equipped he became President of Cincinnati College in 1836 and appropriately combined with his presidential duties the professorship of 'Moral and Intellectual Philosophy'. It is a title to inspire confidence. McGuffey apparently carried the portfolio with assured ease; for nine years later (1845) he was still lecturing, now as the 'Professor of Natural and Moral Philosophy' at the University of Virginia.

It is easy to be satirical about McGuffey and about the struggling, superficial and often misguided educational efforts of his time. People were determined to have 'universities' and lectureships with imposing titles. It was the ambition and not its pathetically inadequate fulfilment that mattered. McGuffey's feet were on the ground. If this had not been so, he could not have produced a series of school readers so delicately attuned to the exact stage of provincialism, intellectual and moral, through which America was then struggling. No matter how shrewd the business methods of his publishing house were in 'putting across' these readers, the editorship of the books themselves was the ultimate reason for their astounding success.

230

McGuffey hit the educational and social ideas of his time exactly. It is perfectly natural, too, that these educational and social ideas should seem to us ludicrous, though in their own time they made excellent sense. America was aware of itself as a new nation. Individual Americans saw, stretching ahead, vistas of personal and family achievement. Their children must learn to speak correctly, to stand on their own feet and move an audience. For in this direction lay the possibility of power both in Church and in State. Also, if it could be conveniently achieved at the same time, they must acquire 'intellectual background'. Poetry, geography, history, famous speeches of the past, all these things were good to know for themselves; though their chief purpose was to give 'practice' to the boy or girl in the art of oratory.

Intellectual background, however, if it were not carefully selected, might bring to the child all sorts of strange and wicked ideas of life and society. These ideas might be too 'foreign', too pagan, too radical. For the American youth must not be educated at the expense of the fine moral inheritance which the origins of the Colonies had transmitted to them. The intellectual world, which might mean the European past, was full of ways of thinking that America had violently turned its back upon. It would not do to let that world come flooding in again upon the young, without careful editing. Thus American education for the whole first half of the nineteenth century moved in the leading strings of religion and morality. And McGuffey's Readers simply met the situation.

As late as 1911, H. H. Vail, writing his *History of the McGuffey Readers*, still preserved the emphasis as it had been in McGuffey's day. 'Their [the Readers] greatest virtue', says Vail, 'consisted in the choice of masterpieces

in literature which [and here the order is significant] by their contents taught morality and patriotism, and by their beauty served as a gateway to "pure literature".'

For the opening of this last mentioned and less important gateway, Shakespeare bore the chief responsibility. For in the McGuffey Readers very little of what the world calls 'great' literature, except Shakespeare, appeared. And even Shakespeare was there not because he had, in the mind of McGuffey, a great literary claim, but because he had been handed down as the best possible material on which to practice 'reading'. The fact that the most influential British Reader, with its large number of Shakespearean passages, came from the pen of a Shakespearean actor, probably never entered the mind or troubled the dreams of McGuffey.

The McGuffey Readers began to flourish in the thirties and burgeoned through several decades. The *Rhetorical Reader* of 1844 had six Shakespearean passages. The *Eclectic* or *Sixth Reader* of 1853 had even more. The name of the play was not mentioned. Sometimes a selection was given a title by which the class could see at a glance what moral lesson was implied. A passage from *Othello* was not identified except by the caption 'The Folly of Intoxication'. There are delicate and tragic moral problems in *Othello*, but surely intoxication is not one of them! The drunken scene (Act II, Sc. III) is a piece of Iago's villainy. If he can persuade Cassio to drink too much, he can use him for his plans. And poor Cassio, who knows he has a weak head, resists Iago's offer of wine:

> *Cas.* Not tonight, good Iago: I have very poor and unhappy brains for drinking: I could well wish cour-

tesy would invent some other custom of entertainment.

His final yielding is only a matter of courtesy.

It is amusing to see this piece of Elizabethan manners
excerpted and distorted out of all recognition, to show
American boys of the 1850's the folly of drinking too
much whiskey in frontier barrooms. Often the Shakespearean passages are not given any personality of their
own. They appear in the introductory section of the
Reader as illustrations of 'Principles of Elocution'. Shakespeare frequently exists solely to illustrate 'Inflection' or
'Gesture'.

In the *Fifth Reader* there is printed a scene from the
Merchant of Venice with the caption 'Shylock or the
Pound of Flesh'. The scene (IV, 1) opens in the usual text
at 'Venice. A Court of Justice'. The Duke of Venice enters to hear the trial. The dialogue begins:

> *Duke.* What, is Antonio here?
> *Ant.* Ready, so please your grace.

In McGuffey's Reader the dialogue reads:

> *Judge.* What, is Antonio here?

The substitution of '*Judge*' for '*Duke*' in a courtroom
scene argues volumes. Old-world society and the business
of titles has at last come across the Atlantic and has suffered a 'sea change'. Thus *Duke* turns up strangely 'translated' into *Judge* in the new democratic western world.

In this same Reader a passage from *Hamlet* is preceded
by a paragraph on Shakespeare's life. It is a masterly
adaptation of means to the end desired. In it Shakespeare
emerges as the ideal of a good provincial middle-class
American. There is everything substantial, thrifty and

law-abiding about him. 'He was married when very young to a woman eight years his senior.' In London he was 'joint-proprietor' of the theatre. He 'accumulated some property' (the phrasing here is a triumph). He was 'buried in Stratford Church'. As is the hope of the 'big' man of the corresponding American town, 'a monument has been erected to his memory'. Nothing more circumspect, more admirable, more neatly embodying the American middle-class theory could be devised. The facts are historically true; but the emphasis reveals the hand of the master, Mc-Guffey!

When Hamlet interviews the travelling players and asks for their repertory of pieces, he thinks not in terms of whole plays but in terms of particular speeches illustrating a particular emotion or mood. Remembering a play they had produced, Hamlet graciously explains

> One speech in it, I chiefly loved.

Hamlet then starts off reading the speech. Warmed by the Prince's graciousness, the player, there and then, begins to declaim it. When the scene is over and the troupe has left the stage, the passionate 'reading' of the speech by the actor lingers in Hamlet's memory. It moves him to a great soliloquy. If an actor merely by reciting a speech

> in a fiction, in a dream of passion
> Could force his soul so to his own conceit
> That from her working all his visage warm'd,

if, in the name of mere play-acting, a man could do this, then

> What would he do
> Had he the motive and the cue for passion
> That I [Hamlet] have?

It is an extraordinary scene. It is pertinent to think of this scene in connection with the American School Reader and its use of passages, separate speeches, for declamation. One sees that the fashion for selecting separate speeches out of plays and declaiming them to move people is as old as *Hamlet* and has, by implication, the sanction of Shakespeare himself. In the most recent and revealing twentieth century studies of Shakespeare, this fact is realized. Shakespeare's plays, of course, are aesthetic wholes. Each part does in a way hang on every other part. But there is another way of regarding them. In Shakespeare's own day, or in Garrick's or in Gielgud's or Maurice Evans', the play is not a whole but a series of beautiful shreds and purple passages, a set of moving rhetorical speeches.

It was not rank heresy, then, for William Enfield when he compiled his rhetorical Reader, called significantly *The Speaker*, to arrange his Shakespearean speeches under such headings as 'Pathetic Pieces'. Enfield's method was followed in America. A book entitled *Elements of Elocution*, by John Walker, Boston, 1810, advertised a 'Complete System of the Passions . . . exemplified by a Copious Selection of the Most Striking Passages of Shakespeare'. *The American Common School Reader*, compiled by J. Goldsbury and William Russell, the latter a teacher of elocution at Phillips and Abbot Academies in Andover, was a competitor of McGuffey. It had sold one hundred thousand copies by 1845. In it the types of emotion were catalogued in such categories as Astonishment, Amazement, Extreme Amazement, Horror, Grief, Moderate Grief. Each type of emotion was illustrated from Shakespeare. This arrangement must have had the sanction of John Quincy Adams, for the book was dedicated to him 'by permission'. It is pleasant to think that it also would have had the sanction of Hamlet's player and Hamlet and of Shakespeare, himself.

How definitely this American training in rhetoric was a preparation for a later career in pulpit or legislature or courtroom (for theatre, too, though this fact would not have been admitted) is shown by the absence of elocution in a volume constructed exclusively for 'young ladies'. Ebenezer Bailey, Principal of the Young Ladies' High School in Boston, in the 1820's compiled *The Young Ladies' Class Book*. It is full of passages from Shakespeare. But there are no instructions for elocution, nor use of these passages for declamation. Instead, the Shakespearean bits, safely anonymous, illustrate those poignant moral situations which are supposed to be the peculiar province of the tender young female. A spicy passage from *Measure for Measure* turns up under the caption 'A Sister Pleading for the Life of her Condemned Brother', and the scene in *Lear* between Lear and Cordelia is headed 'Scene of Filial Affection'. Thus Shakespeare, all unguessed, melts the gentle heart of the home-keeping young lady. Not only has he no breath of the stage about him but not even a whisper of the public platform. *Autres temps, autres mœurs.* This venture of Bailey's was apparently in exactly the right vein, for the book had gone through twenty-six editions by 1844.

From some Readers of the period all foreign literature was excluded in a burst of misguided patriotism. The Abbott Brothers, one of them of 'Rollo Book' fame, would naturally have some delicacy about including Shakespeare. This would be especially true in a volume bearing the title, *Mount Vernon Readers: A Course of Reading Lessons Selected with Reference to their Moral Influence on the Hearts and Lives of the Young*. No

Shakespeare, in any form, could enter through these for-
bidding gates. In certain Readers, notably those of Charles
W. Saunders, which had a circulation in the academies of
New England, Shakespeare, carefully emasculated, was
allowed to appear. In the Saunders' *High School Reader*
(N. Y., 1856) Henry V's famous speech 'Once more into
the breach' suffered excision of a large number of lines.
The line

   Cry 'God for Harry, England and Saint George!'

was carefully edited to read

   Cry 'Heaven for Harry, England and Saint George!'

Thus was vulgarity turned into refinement in the high-
school readers of the fifties.

   Yet all this while America was crowding to the theatres
and seeing there a good deal of Shakespeare. One cannot
explain the presence of contradictory attitudes toward
Shakespeare in the American schools and on the American
stage merely by saying that the theatres represented urban
taste and the schools the more provincial country districts.
For this is not true. The theatre, with Shakespeare frequently in its repertory, penetrated the hinterland. The
same schoolbooks were used in city and country. What is
more likely true is that within the same person lodge two
distinct attitudes toward Shakespeare. One of these attitudes held Shakespeare highly desirable to see on the stage;
the other attitude believed in tempering all educational
schemes, whether they included Shakespeare or not, to
the business of 'high moral influence'. The young must be
taught what is ennobling. That, when school was over, life

itself would be waiting at the schoolroom door with its kaleidoscope of moral and immoral elements, irrevocably interlaced, did not trouble the educators of the young. Besides, the stage still was anathema to one large section of the American public. This group, with admirable consistency, would, of course, object to the use of plays or portions of plays as such, in the Readers which their children used.

But there was already a promise of much broader and sounder use of Shakespeare in American education. George S. Hillard, not primarily a teacher at all, but partner in the law firm of Charles Sumner, owner and editor of the Boston *Courier* and Elizabethan scholar (he edited Spenser's poems), was writing schoolbooks as early as the 1830's. In these he omitted Shakespeare, not for moral reasons but, as he explicitly states, because 'sublimities and beauties lose most of their value when separated from the connection in which they stand'. Better no Shakespeare than Shakespeare truncated.

Thirty years later, in the sixties, when vast changes were coming over the whole American educational scheme, Hillard put out some notable Readers. These surrounded the Shakespearean passages with biographical, critical and explanatory notices, so that the student was at least aware of the whole from which the part was taken. The same thing happened in Readers compiled in the South and West. At last the reading of Shakespeare was to be taught not by an arbitrary set of symbols and directions for gestures, but by understanding the meaning of the lines.

Richard Edwards' *Analytic Sixth Reader*, N. Y. and Chicago, 1866, bravely maintained that 'the thoughtful reading of Shakespeare affords mental discipline of the highest order, for it fully taxes the thinking powers and brings the reader into contact with some of the most exquisite poetry to be found in literature'. The long struggle of America to put Shakespeare into his proper perspective as one of the great gifts to civilization was, after nearly two hundred and fifty years, at last achieved.

Thus much for the history of Shakespeare in school Readers up through the 1860's. The remarkable school editions of the plays in their entirety by the gifted Henry Norman Hudson and William J. Rolfe belong to the history of American editors of Shakespeare. The highlighting of particular speeches, the rhetorical rendition of them, the inability of the pupils to see the play as a whole, all these ills descend from the peculiar treatment of Shakespeare in the school Readers up to the Civil War. They *are* ills; but on the other side they are also blessings. By this method, deformed as it was, Shakespeare has become a national classic. Misunderstood, often boring, often laughed at, his work has yet furnished a kind of common cultural experience. As Dr. Adams, Director of the Folger Shakespeare Library, said on the day (April 23, 1932) this great and beautiful Collection was opened to the public:

If out of America, unwieldy in size, and commonly called the melting-pot of races, there has been evolved a homogeneous nation, with a culture that is still essentially English, we must acknowledge that in the process Shakespeare has played a major part.

The history of Shakespeare in the American colleges in the nineteenth century is, until after the Civil War, less creditable than the corresponding history in the schools. There were too great obstacles to the recognition of

Shakespeare as a suitable subject for college study. The first was what one might call the 'gentleman's tradition'. It was assumed in England, and therefore in America, that an English boy of gentle tradition grew up knowing the classics of his own tongue. He took them in with the breath of his native land. It would be completely super-fluous to submit himself to the boredom of courses in these subjects as a part of his regular college training. This as-sumption was in the majority of cases quite false. But it was strong enough to keep Shakespeare out of English and American colleges.

In America some college boys did read him, even though he was not a requisite. In Harvard about 1806, 'the young men were passionately given up to the reading of Shake-speare'. Then Munroe and Francis' *Complete Shakespeare* (Boston, 1807) was subscribed for by ninety-nine out of one hundred and seventy-five undergraduates at Harvard; Brown had twenty-eight subscribers; Union, seventeen; Dartmouth, seven. This does not necessarily guarantee de-lighted private hours spent in poring over the pages. Yet young men of the period, such as Longfellow, *did* read Shakespeare for pleasure. In some instances, then, this sweeping assumption that young gentlemen who were born speaking English (whether in England or America) would know the classics of their own language without benefit of specific college instruction in these matters was justified. But, whether justified or not, it was a potent factor in keeping the very idea of a college course in Shakespeare out of educational programmes.

The other great enemy of the idea was the fact that American colleges from early colonial times were pro-fessional schools, not liberal arts colleges. The conception of the American college as a place to which a young person goes for four years of 'growing up' amid liberal and cultural surroundings is only as old as the eighteen sixties and seventies. Prior to that the presence of a young person in college meant that he was destined for one of the learned professions. The courses offered for the B.A. were definitely pre-professional. And how could Shakespeare 'rate' at all under such a heading? If one were to be a lawyer or a statesman one would, and many actually did, make use of Shakespeare. But one picked him up, as private reading, and used him as a decoration to set off the sterner sequences of professional thinking. In fact, a young college man would already, in his course in Rhetoric, have encountered many telling Shakespearean quotations. Blair's *Rhetoric* was available in many American college courses after its publication in 1785. But Shakespeare under such circumstances is a superficial Shakespeare. It is in no sense what the modern college would understand by a 'course in Shakespeare'.

It is extremely interesting to us, now past the first third of the twentieth century, and so accustomed to the idea of using our undergraduate colleges and universities as a means chiefly of liberalizing and raising the general understanding, to see how recent such a conception is. One realizes that no matter how much talk of democracy there had been at the time of the American Revolution, the conception of the American public as a large and willing mass of workers led by a small group of specially educated professional people lingered on. It remained, too, in the American strongholds of education until new and different forces, fostered by self-reliance and native ability, pushed open the doors of American higher education.

It is very interesting, too, to see how this broader, more general conception of education cast its light into traditional darkness. There was an astonishing statement, issued in 1753, on the situation engendered by the American college as it then existed:

by far the most numerous and also the hands and strength of every government are overlooked [by the college courses then in vogue] and have nothing but this alternative left them, either to be satisfied with what small portion of the arts and sciences they can glean at private schools, or to go through a course of learning at college *for which they have neither time nor use.*

This remarkable independence and originality of thinking about education in relation to the 'general public' and its needs belonged to the Rev. William Smith who was just back from England in 1753. He had probably heard over there of the revision of the curriculum at Aberdeen in that year, under the independent judgment of William Girard. The Aberdeen programme and Smith's programme bear a striking resemblance.

Smith's schemes never got further than the pages of his theoretical pamphlet, whimsically entitled *General Idea of the College of Mirania:* 'drawn up and published at the desire of some gentlemen of N. Y. who were appointed to receive proposals relative to the establishment of a college in that Province'. To be sure, Smith's *wonderland* college (if *Mirania* stands for 'wonderland' as it should by its Latin derivation) had some liberalizing effect on later schemes. Jefferson probably was interested in it. It may have borne some fruit in the ideals of William and Mary College. But its clear-cut and logical scheme for adapting college education to the actual social conditions of this country had to wait for at least a hundred years before it was adopted.

Yet Smith's analysis of the groups in our American society already forming is astonishing as early as 1753. He sees not only the young people destined for the learned professions and statesmanship. He also sees 'those designed for the mechanic professions' (delicious phrase!). Most surprising of all, he remembers 'all the remaining people of the country' as a group who have a right to an education envisaging their needs and meeting them. If the Rev. William Smith could revisit these 'glimpses of the moon' now, he might have mixed feelings. His principles are, at last, in operation. But their effectiveness in achieving their ends he might not be so sure of. His College of Wonderland included English classics. Shakespeare is not listed among these classics. But the general argument for him as part of liberal education was already made, though it fell on deaf ears for nearly a century.

The Rev. William Smith's liberality was echoed again and again. The faculty of Amherst College in 1827 drew up a minute and presented it to the trustees. The tone of their protest against a curriculum which ignores the needs of the time, is belligerent.

In an age [it reads] of universal improvement, and in a young, free and prosperous country like ours, it is absurd to cling so tenaciously to the prescriptive forms of other centuries.

What was wanted instead of the 'prescriptive forms of other centuries' was a list of courses which might well have included Shakespeare. The Amherst faculty of 1827 wanted to see 'instruction in Modern Languages, Literature and Improvements' introduced. These would meet the educational demands of our 'young, free and prosperous country'. But the authorities could not be moved from their traditional position. To these stimulating suggestions, they merely cried 'innovation' and the Amherst faculty's minute produced no results. Yet the new American situation would ultimately be strong enough to impress its needs upon American colleges and mould them to its ambitions and deserts.

The third thing that delayed the introduction of Shakespeare was the lingering tradition that the curriculum must train the mind, and that the contents on which that mental training was built was of no importance in itself. Its sole function was to be the practice track on which the discipline of running could be learned. That the track had any value in itself, except as a means to an end, was not considered. Study as discipline, and specifically the study of classics as discipline, not as literature, this was the idea that dominated.

In protest against it undergraduates like Andrew Dickson White, who was to exercise such a liberalizing effect upon the curricula of Michigan in the fifties and sixties, left Yale without a degree in the middle fifties. They protested against the use of ancient literature as a means of grammatical drill alone. 'In English literature and language, every man was left to his own devices.' In spite of the gallant assumption that every English-speaking gentleman read the English classics, young White and his contemporaries protested. It was probably this meagre training at Yale that produced in White's new Cornell University programme of 1867 a 'hope' that 'the study of modern classics, especially those of our own language, [may have] a far more important place than they have hitherto held in our colleges'.

Yet before this liberalization had succeeded in letting down the bars for Shakespeare, he existed 'cribbed, cabin'd and confin'd', as the material on which to practise 'discipline'. He has, perhaps, only in the last ten years entirely escaped the fetter marks of this strange captivity. The courses in Rhetoric and Belles Lettres increased in number and importance. Ultimately the 'rhetoric' was abandoned and the 'belles lettres' as an English department emerged. But even in places like Harvard, this was not till sometime in the sixties. Meantime in the crannies of the worn old walls of classified rhetorical figures, Shakespearean lines spread their few scraggly and undernourished blossoms.

He also crept in as a disciplinary medium in courses in philology. For the study of words, Latin, Greek and the older forms of English literature—Anglo-Saxon and Middle English—had been used. About this time courses began to spring up which advertised that 'the English Language is studied in the same way as the Latin and Greek'. Not the most conservative could object to this. It still kept discipline rampant; it simply offered the body of Shakespeare for crucifixion in place of some Latin or Greek or early English text. *Julius Caesar* was the victim frequently selected. G. L. Craik had published a volume entitled *The English of Shakespeare, Illustrated in a Philological Commentary on his Julius Caesar*. With this volume began the printing of Shakespeare on pages which bore a line or two of text to an 'intolerable deal' of footnotes.

Craik's preface frankly abjures the devil and all his works. It disclaims any effort to 'examine or to expound the Shakespearean drama aesthetically'. The only approach will be made in strictly traditional behaviour. It will be made 'philologically' or 'with respect to language'. So Shakespeare poked an occasional flower through the bars which hemmed about American collegiate courses in the first half of the nineteenth century.

Ironically enough, he had much less difficulty in appearing in what were dubbed the 'scientific' courses. A student destined for what the Rev. William Smith had euphemistically called 'the mechanic profession' would be taking the 'scientific' course. Here, though slightly below the salt of orthodox college education, he could enjoy, all undisturbed, the plays of Shakespeare, some years before they were offered to his more fortunate 'classical' brothers. This was true both at Michigan and at Yale in the sixties.

But the steady interest in Shakespeare outside of the colleges gradually brought him within the walls of the universities themselves. James Russell Lowell, for example, had been occupied with Shakespeare all his life. He knew Shakespeare before he went to Harvard as an undergraduate. A college letter to a friend reveals him intending to buy a 'copy of a new edition of Shakespeare if he can afford it'. In 1835 he is surprised 'on looking over Shakespeare to find that I had read all his plays but two or three'. When in the early forties, Lowell began his journalistic adventures, he chose as subject for several studies the Old Dramatists. And to this subject he returned at the end of his career when he gave the Lowell Institute Lectures in the spring of 1887.

Lowell's lectures of 1855 on the English Poets were the means of injecting Shakespeare as a literary subject into the Harvard curriculum. Harvard appointed Lowell to succeed Longfellow in the Smith Professorship of Modern Languages. Of course, this chair did not include instruction in Shakespeare. But Lowell at the first opportunity, which was given by the University lectures of 1863, offered Shakespeare. His audience for the lecture was composed mostly of club women with a sprinkling of undergraduates. It was, in other words, not a part of any regular undergraduate work. But the fact remains that Lowell did lecture on Shakespeare as literature at Harvard in 1863.

Lowell has left two very interesting pronouncements on the value of the literary and aesthetic study of Shakespeare as a college subject. In a speech before the Edinburgh Philosophical Institute in 1883, he said, 'I never open my Shakespeare but what I find myself wishing that there might be professorships established for the study of his works'. He stressed the 'intellectual training' to be derived from such study. Before the Modern Language Association of America in 1889, he spoke out boldly. The old enemies were still active. The ancient classics were still fighting for a monopoly of the literature in college courses. Lowell asks, 'Is it less instructive to study the growth of modern ideas than of ancient?' College boys who 'are honestly bored by Greek and Latin' would 'take a wholesome and vivifying interest in what was nearer to their habitual modes of thought and association'. Such studies as Shakespeare are 'pastures new and not the worse for being so'. He deplores the 'purely linguistic side in the teaching' and concludes with a fair statement of his views in the century-old quarrel between ancient and modern literature as a college subject. He urges 'no invidious distinction . . . between the old and the new', but asserts that 'mental discipline' can be obtained in the study of 'new' as well as of 'old'.

The objectives which Lowell urged both in Edinburgh in 1883 and before the Modern Language Association of America in 1889 were already being put into practice. At Harvard, Lowell's young contemporary, Francis James Child, had by the seventies altered the title under which he came to Harvard in 1851. The alteration is an example of the general road by which Shakespeare travelled in American education; for Child came to Harvard as 'professor of Rhetoric, Oratory and Elocution', and that title became in the mid seventies, 'professor of English'. Child was a gifted Shakespearean. Through him, says H. W. Simon, in his valuable study on *The Reading of Shakespeare in American Schools and Colleges*, came 'the beginning of the modern teaching of literature in American colleges'. It was largely through him that 'a permanent place for the study of Shakespeare [as literature] was made in the American College curriculum'.

But Child was not the only great Shakespearean teacher. There was Hiram Corson at Cornell whom many Cornellians remember, booming great periods of Browning through his patriarchal beard from a dusky corner in the drawing room of the Andrew D. Whites at Ithaca, in the Edwardian days. Michigan, Virginia, Harvard, Columbia, Princeton, to mention only a few, were in the seventies and eighties offering Shakespeare at last without apology or without constriction of his range to philological or elocutionary ends.

What our own twentieth century education is likely to do about Shakespeare is still uncertain. Probably the method of studying him, or the complete omission of him, will follow the curves, depressions and changing prejudices of our world, exactly as they followed the needs, partialities and limitations of the nineteenth century. The genius of Shakespeare is extraordinarily sensitive to the hour and the age. Into his book, each age has peered, as into a mirror, to see its own face. The images in that mirror fade and are replaced as the decades go by. But the mirror is not discarded. There is a strange compulsion to look into it, to scrutinize this Shakespeare, no matter how cramped and dated the era may be. He responds by showing only so much of himself as is comely in the eyes of the particular world which reads him.

CHAPTER XIII

Shakespeare in the Thought of Some Nineteenth Century Figures: Emerson, Thoreau, Alcott, Whitman, Lincoln

'TELL me what you like and I will tell you what you are.' This crude saying is peculiarly applicable to the use of Shakespeare by some of the great American figures of the mid-nineteenth century. They did 'like' Shakespeare, sometimes quite inordinately and extravagantly. He is the most quoted author by both Emerson and Whitman. Yet the emphasis which each of these two great contemporaries gave Shakespeare is as different as the men themselves. For each, Shakespeare is a reflection of his peculiar and distinctive personal quality. Among the New Englanders themselves there is not such wide divergence in their images of Shakespeare as between them and Whitman. But even between the uses of Shakespeare by Emerson and Thoreau, there is just that difference which so clearly distinguishes these two friends from one another. Shakespeare is not all things to all men: he is rather the *alter ego* to each of these magnificent individualists. No one of them achieves a detached, critical estimate of him, nor wants to do so. Shakespeare becomes, in his own way, the very glass of their separate personalities.

The touching aspiration toward culture and the capacity for violence and rant were reflected in the Shakespeare of the theatre in the middle and far West. His rôle in the schools had the same highlights. Among the 'cultured' New Englanders, too, he was the object of veneration, a name to conjure with. To cite him in a lecture or an essay was to give lustre and prestige to the words and ideas that surrounded his magic name. But the specific influences of English and continental culture were, of course, more clearly seen in writers like Emerson.

Emerson had first gone to England in 1832 and had there met Coleridge and Carlyle. The effect which Shakespeare's prestige already had made upon him was given a sharper turn by this English visit. The age itself, the romantic age, was, for the mysterious reasons which determine taste in any era, building its own conception of the genius of Shakespeare. Coleridge and Hazlitt had been thundering magnificently from the lecture platforms of England, revealing to their public Shakespearean characters as the contemporary world wished to see them. Carlyle's ear was nicely attuned to the German critics. Emerson arrived just in time to canalize his nebulous American 'feeling' about Shakespeare into these critical and philosophical channels.

The conviction grew upon them all that now at last in their own century, Shakespeare was for the first time properly appreciated. Arousing 'the genius of the German nation', he evoked 'an activity which spread from the poetic into the scientific, religious and philosophical domains'. Emerson's claim for the breadth of Shakespeare's influence is, one sees, imposing. It has become, he continues, 'the paramount intellectual interest of the world'. It has reacted 'with great energy on England and America'. Emerson wrote this in the pages of the *Dial*, some half dozen or more years after his 1832 visit to England. The age saw its own reflection so luminously in Shakespeare that it came to feel that 'the passages of Shakespeare that we most prize were not quoted till within this century'. And 'all the criticism that contents us in the least, has been written . . . at least since this century came in'. The adoration of the age's own face, reflected Narcissus-like, in the pages of Shakespeare, could not go much further than this.

When Emerson returned to America he habituated the lyricism of Shakespearean praise in Europe to his own New England. He settled at Concord with his mother and found at his very door a popular platform only waiting for him to mount it and speak. The Lyceum lecture movement, an important phase of popular education in Europe, had been adapted to American use as early as 1826. The Concord Lyceum had been organized in 1829. It and the near-by Salem Lyceum were the two largest. The amount of oral harangue that the American public could listen to is comparable to the capacity of the modern radio audience. There were seven hundred and eighty-four lectures and one hundred and five debates at Concord alone in the next few years, as P. W. Stoddard points out in an unpublished study on 'The Place of the Lyceums in American Life'. Three hundred and one of these lectures were by local townsmen and ninety-eight were by Emerson alone. Compared with Thoreau's modest nineteen, this number is impressive. But Thoreau was suspicious of the real value of adult public education, especially when it was thus fluently and vocally offered. He records in his Journal that 'it is no compliment to be invited to lecture before the rich Institutes and Lyceums'. The audiences 'do not want to hear any prophets'. They prefer 'a sugar plum'. Indeed 'the little medicine they get is disguised with sugar'. Most crushing of all is his final comment that the Lyceum audiences want 'orators that will entertain them and leave them where they found them'. It sounds very like the thoughtful comment on much modern lecturing.

But Emerson, so different from Thoreau in his general attitude toward life, found the lecture his perfect medium for expression. The teeming thoughts which were recorded in his voluminous Journals (from 1820 to 1875) were expanded into lectures. These lectures were condensed into essays. They were merely a by-product of this oral transmission of ideas to his American public. This may seem to put the case too strongly. But the capacity of the American public to take in ideas and emotions through their ears rather than through their eyes was enormous. The prevalence of this rhetoric in politics, in pulpits, on the stage itself, was a mark of the era. Emerson's real vehicle of expression was the public lecture. It was immediate and congenial to the temper of our national life. And it was congenial to Emerson, too. He confesses in 1845 that some coming lectures in Boston are just the stimulus he needs. 'I find this obligation', he says, 'usually a good spur to the sides of that dull horse I have charge of.'

In the reports by eye-witnesses of Emerson in action on the lecture platform, one notices that effectiveness of personal presence and manner which made lecturers, preachers and actors simply different members of the same rhetorical guild. Another evidence of the congeniality of lecturing to Emerson and of his effectiveness in this rôle is the length of his career on the public platform. In a very interesting Appendix on the 'Chronological List of Lectures and Addresses', compiled by James E. Cabot in 1887, one sees spread out over thirty-five years (roughly from 1835 to 1869) Emerson's activities in the lecture field. They embraced a successful lecture tour in England in 1848, as well as a long triumph at home. Throughout these thirty-five years, Shakespeare is a frequent theme, both directly as the subject of lectures and indirectly as an illustration of Emerson's ideas.

How did Shakespeare fare at Emerson's hands in these famous public performances? He is 'invoked' and 'highlighted' by Emerson rather than expounded with detailed and reasoned argument. The pages of his Essays, Journals and Letters (and he left a prodigious amount of personal record) show a highly romantic and 'transcendental' appreciation of Shakespeare. His qualities are described in superlatives. He is an inexplicable phenomenon like nature or God. In his day, by his mere existence 'life was larger than before' and 'the air was fame'. In his famous essay on 'The Over Soul', Emerson asserts that the creator of *Hamlet* and *Lear* 'could utter things as good from day to day forever'. He is classed with the gods. 'When the gods come among men, they are not known. Jesus was not: Socrates and Shakespeare were not.' At eighteen, in 1822, Emerson was confiding to his Journal that in *Hamlet* 'every line is golden', and at sixty-one, in 1864, at the three-hundredth anniversary of Shakespeare's birth, he is still superlative. In 'climes beyond the solar road' they probably call this planet not Earth but Shakespeare, says Emerson. There is an elemental power about him. He 'made his Hamlet as a bird weaves its nest'. His work knows no limits but resembles 'a mirror carried through the streets, ready to render an image of every created thing'. There are scores of passages of this sort, adoring the poet, invoking him.

It was not merely a sly dig that Holmes gave Emerson when he said that he showed 'his own affinities and repulsions' and 'writes his own biography, no matter about whom or what he is talking'. Because Emerson valued Plato and Swedenborg, he imagined that Shakespeare was like them both! Emerson himself admits this position. If Shakespeare is a god to him, then this godlike estimate is the right one for him. He confesses to his Journal that he wants to know 'all possible knowledge' and 'all opinions' of Shakespeare. Yet he treasures few opinions 'beside my own'. 'And each thoughtful reader', he adds, 'has the like experience.' This is subjective and romantic. It is, however, an attitude which Emerson shared with the chief Shakespearean critics of his day on the continent and in England. It was Shakespeare according to the 'form and pressure' of the reigning romanticism.

This sort of honest rapture and generalization about Shakespeare lent itself to rhetorical expression. As such it was particularly adapted to the public platform. The American passion for self-improvement and the American taste for oratory met and merged with a romantic way of thinking in the thirties, forties and fifties. They were merged and embodied, too, in the very person of Ralph Waldo Emerson. If the modern Shakespearean critic feels impatient of Emerson's continuous rhapsody and generalization about Shakespeare, if he longs for fewer superlatives, fewer invocations of the magic name and looks in vain for specific evidence of reading the plays, he must be rebuked. To expect Emerson to run counter to his time is to expect the impossible. Rather one should delight in the fitness of Emerson's approach to Shakespeare; it exactly suited the man, the times and the public demand. It is just one more evidence of the contention which underlies this book, that Shakespeare, or some part of him, flourishes in the very crevices and idiosyncracies of each particular age and section of society on which his fecund seed falls.

In Emerson's approach to Shakespeare there are, too, the ineradicable marks of his peculiar New England inheritance. The ghost of moral opposition to Shakespeare as a part of the wicked stage still lingered in Emerson. It confirms one's estimate of the power of Puritan tradition in New England. For, all through Emerson's lifetime of devotion to Shakespeare, one finds him, at intervals, embarrassed by the thought that Shakespeare belongs to the stage and that in his plays are many lines and scenes of bawdry and license.

At the age of twenty-two, young Emerson notes in his Journal the 'indecency of the old stage'. 'Heroism, virtue and devotion' are surrounded by 'brothel associations'. In 1835 he is thanking God from the public platform that 'the English race in both hemispheres' has made 'prodigious advancement in purity of conversation and honesty of life', since the days of Shakespeare and his contemporaries. The ghost of the seventeenth century theocrats is still stalking. By 1849, when Emerson was forty-six, he was still troubled by Shakespeare's 'immoral' passages. But he comforts himself by the idea of the inclusiveness and depth of writing which presents 'the intermixture of the common and the transcendental as in Nature'. As God created a world in which good and evil are co-mingled, so Shakespeare, too, created this 'intermixture'. It is a superlative rationalization of Shakespeare's moral lapses.

Coming to the figure of Falstaff, Emerson presents Falstaff as fit for the ears of a saint. He 'is not created to excite the animal appetites, but to vent the joy of a supernal intelligence'. Further than this, in the business of transforming evil into good, not even Emerson could go! But it is not the apologies themselves but Emerson's feeling that Shakespeare *does* have immoralities and that they must be accounted for, that endears Emerson to the twentieth century eye. It makes him so clearly, in the history of America's spiritual development, a direct descendant of the early Puritan strain. Though Shakespeare has beaten down almost all the barriers of opposition, though no individual could go further in rapturous devotion, yet the ghost of opposition to him still hovers amidst Emerson's superlatives.

One discovers from the family reminiscences of Emerson's son, appended to the 1903 edition of *Representative Men*, that Emerson had no taste for or adaptation to the theatre. His son, Edward W. Emerson, records that his father had 'an intense distaste for the common amusements of society'. He felt that 'theatrical performances . . . were not for him'. Probably 'he never was inside a theatre twenty times in his life'. Yet Emerson saw Macready in *Lear* in London, in 1848. He saw Edwin Booth in Boston, though to Booth's amusement when he met Emerson afterwards in the house of a friend, Emerson 'had not once alluded to his profession or performance'. It is, too, only fair to say that there were other reasons than the Puritan opposition, for Emerson's rare attendance at the theatre and for his failure to catch its enthusiasm. He detested 'bad taste or ranting'. Even the greatest actors of his day were likely to rant.

Also Emerson's mind and responses were much more naturally directed toward the poetry and ideas of Shakespeare than to the dialogue and dramatic situations. He confessed to Edwin P. Whipple that he was a bad auditor of Shakespeare in the theatre. Instead of 'being carried away by an actor of Shakespeare . . . I am carried away by the poet'. He went further in his conversation with Whipple and elaborated his meaning. In a performance of *Hamlet* when Macready came to the line

Revisit'st thus the glimpses of the moon

Emerson confessed that 'actor, theatre, all vanished . . . the play went on but, absorbed in this one thought of the mighty master, I paid no heed to it'. Thus Shakespeare, the poet, carries all before him with Emerson as he had with Emerson's contemporary English Shakespearean critics, like Coleridge and Lamb. One remembers Lamb's argument for the superiority of Shakespeare read, to Shakespeare acted. But the old New England suspicion of play-acting was a factor in determining Emerson's attitude. As late as 1852 in his Journal, he writes that 'anything more excellent' never 'came from the human brain than the plays of Shakespeare'. He then adds 'hating only that they are plays'. Emerson not only runs with the leading critics of his time in his attitude toward Shakespeare, but he preserves that residue of peculiarly New England opinion which has its root in our Puritan origins.

Emerson's lecture on 'Shakespeare or the Poet' was first delivered to the Boston Lyceum in the winter of 1845–46. It was delivered again in England, in Manchester and in London, and was published in 1850 with other essays in the collection, *Representative Men*. In this group of essays, Shakespeare is chosen to represent the Poet. The essay is an epitome of what had been expressed fragmentarily throughout his works and in his Journals. It bears evidence of the integrity and consistency of his whole point of view.

He scorns Shakespearean Societies and researches into the actual life of Shakespeare. Even theatres and actors are rejected as coming between Shakespeare, the poet, and his reader. Emerson retells the incident of his own inattention to Macready's *Hamlet*. His platform style is at its best in this incident. 'The recitation begins', he writes, 'one golden word leaps out immortal from all this painted pedantry and sweetly torments us with invitations to its own inaccessible home.' This is in just the vein to delight the audience of the Boston Lyceum that evening at the Odeon in the winter of 1845–46. It is pure Coleridge or pure Lamb, or better, pure nineteenth century romantic criticism. But it is also excellent Puritanism, exhorting the public to neglect the playwright and to estimate the theatre and the actors at little worth, compared with the matchless power of Shakespeare the poet. Emerson sees Shakespeare as a great moral teacher, too. 'What point of morals', he cries, '. . . has he not settled?' Shakespeare belongs to America, too, for 'he drew the father of the man in America'.

Emerson had a certain amount of interest in the actual history and biography of Shakespeare and his day. In opposition to his more usual attitude that Shakespeare is a 'miracle man', he sometimes admits that his achievement depends upon human methods of working. In 1838, when he was thirty-one, he wrote in his Journal, 'We have made a miracle of Shakespeare'. He deplored the 'haze of light instead of a guiding torch' by which posterity approached him. The 'internal evidence' points to a Shakespeare, not of miracles, but of 'strong sense and of great cultivation'. He was an 'excellent Latin scholar, and of extensive and select reading'. He wrote, furthermore, 'for intelligent persons' and he 'wrote with intention'.

This is the kind of comment that the newest twentieth century Shakespearean research would favor. It is at the opposite pole from Emerson's more usual rhapsody. He returns to this point of view from time to time. 'Shakespeare seems to you miraculous', he records in his Journal much later, but his method was 'as conceivable and familiar to higher intelligence as index-making to the literary hack'. Shakespeare was 'quite too wise to undervalue letters'. In his Introduction to the brilliant new edition of *The Letters of Ralph Waldo Emerson*, Ralph L. Rusk finds in Emerson 'impressive evidence of Shakespeare scholarship'. Rusk later prints a letter from Longfellow to Emerson, commending to him a collection of books on Shakespeare by 'Mr. Ticknor [the Professor, not the bookseller]'. 'There you would find', writes Longfellow, 'everything you want, or at all events, everything that is now to be had.'

This scholarly and historical approach to Shakespeare is an indication of the liberality and flexibility of Emerson's intentions. It does not lessen its value, to say that it was not and could not be Emerson's dominant attitude toward Shakespeare.

Emerson made common cause with those educators, including Lowell, who urged the advisability of a course in Shakespeare as a suitable college subject. He advocates a course in 'appreciation' rather than in accurate literary history of Shakespeare. Both in his Journals for 1864 and in a lecture reported in *The Commonwealth* during that winter, Emerson emphasizes the idea of Shakespeare as a college study. He deplores in his Journal that Oxford and Harvard are without it. He urges it on the analogy of Boccaccio who lectured in Italy on Dante. Why should not someone in England and America lecture on our great English poet, Shakespeare? Yet what Emerson wants from this lecture for the students is 'not only *intelligence of*, but . . . *sympathy with* the thoughts of the great poets'. He concludes with this characteristic sentence, 'Let us have these warblings as well as logarithms'. Let the biographical and literary histories do what they could for Shakespeare. Emerson would read them but he preferred to these 'logarithms' the 'warblings' of the poet, himself—inexplicable, inspired.

When one turns from Emerson to his friend and younger Concord contemporary, Henry David Thoreau, and scrutinizes his attitude toward Shakespeare, one finds just those variations and shades of difference that one would expect. On his bookish side, Thoreau was nearer to the classics than to English literature. His college training and his brief teaching experience afterward led him in this direction. Yet he picked up the reverent manner toward Shakespeare which was in the air, which was almost a disease with his friend, Emerson. In *Winter*, Thoreau writes of 'the Shakespeare miracle' and uses the phrase 'transcendent genius'. In *Walden* he places Shakespeare in a list of 'altitudos' precisely as Emerson does.

But Thoreau's actual feeling about Shakespeare seems not to have been very warm and intimate. There is scarcely a significant reference to Shakespearean characters or passages throughout all his work. Actually, he preferred life to books, though he read and wrote about some books with feeling and insight. Again and again in his writing he shows his preference for man living and nature burgeoning. These are greater even than the stored-up records of man in the past. 'But after all', he writes in *Walden*, 'man is the great poet, and not Homer, nor Shakespeare.'

Because of his reverence for man as a living being, Thoreau deplores the lack of actual knowledge about Shakespeare's own life, how he lived and worked among other men. It leads him to overstate his point. 'The real fact of a poet's life would be of more value to us than any work of his art.' Here is the mirror of Thoreau's own temperament and preferences. 'Shakespeare's house!' he exclaims, 'how hollow it is! No man can conceive of Shakespeare in that house. We want . . . an actual life, to complete our Shakespeare as much as a statue wants its pedestal.' Contrast with this interest in Shakespeare as a man among men, Emerson's feeling that 'Shakespeare is a voice merely: who and what he was that sang, that sings, we know not'. And Emerson did not want to know. He enjoyed Shakespeare as a great nameless force, like God, like nature, to be adored and wondered at.

But Thoreau whose approaches to the same ideals were by distinctly different channels, whose chief business would seem to have been with life itself and how it might best be lived by Henry Thoreau, could only be content with a sense of Shakespeare living. Being a man among men was the highest art of all. 'I am not [merely] grateful because Homer and Christ and Shakespeare have lived', he cries. Any obscure living person 'all alone filling his sphere in russet suit' is equally important. 'He takes up as much room in nature as the most famous.' If Shakespeare were to compete for Thoreau's interest, he would have to come alive again and meet life's situations. The attitude toward Shakespeare is in very truth the mirror of each age's and each individual's dominant quality. To Thoreau a present dewdrop claims attention before Shakespeare.

> Tell Shakespeare to attend some leisure hour
> For now I've business with this drop of dew.

Both human nature and outdoor nature, living, come first with Thoreau.

There was another, and equally interesting reason for
Thoreau's lack of interest in Shakespeare and other figures
of English literature. It is a quality of thought which brings
him very close to Whitman, and is one of the underlying
reasons for their sympathy with one another. Thoreau,
looking at literature in relation to its social background,
suspected that English literature was 'played out'. It lacked
a quality of 'wildness' which he takes some pains to explain. 'English literature', he says, Shakespeare included,
'breathes no quite fresh and in this sense wild, strain. It is
essentially tame and civilized literature.' Then he adds a
sentence which reflects that element of anti-British feeling and aggressive Americanism which still coloured
American thought, though the War of Independence was
now three-quarters of a century away. As an antidote to
this 'tame and civilized literature' of England, 'there was
need of America'. Whitman, too, felt that there was need
of America and that Shakespeare, great as he was, could
not serve our new needs.

Yet with neither Thoreau nor Whitman is this opposition to English literature and to Shakespeare in particular
merely the petty bumptiousness of a young rebel world.
The criticism goes much deeper and has more truth. It
was immediacy and vitality and honesty that both Thoreau
and Whitman were looking for. Wherever they found it,
they gave it its due. Thoreau, though he criticizes Shakespeare as a whole, glorifies *Hamlet* because it has this essential 'wildness'. He admires 'the untamed, uncivilised, free
and wild thinking in Hamlet'. 'A truly good book', he
adds, 'is something as wildly natural and primitive, mysterious and marvellous, ambrosial and fertile, as a fungus
or a lichen.'

On the English nightingale as compared with the American thrush, Thoreau makes the same kind of comment. 'How cool and assuaging the thrush's note', he writes, 'after the fever of the day. I doubt if they have anything so richly *wild* in Europe.' Note the significant word, 'wild'. Then comes the social theory. 'So long a civilization must have banished it.' The hope and aspiration for the new America follow. 'It will only be heard in America, perchance, while our star is in the ascendant.' If Thoreau should hear the English nightingale he would not expect to find 'such unexplored wildness and fertility'. Such things belong only to the new western world, he says, picturing the thrush's note as 'reaching to sundown, inciting to emigration'.

Shakespeare, though 'invoked' by Thoreau in the best romantic jargon, does not touch him nearly. The past is less important than the living present, and single great men dead cannot compete with live men 'in russet', working and suffering. England has lost its 'wildness'. It follows that England's literature, with notable exceptions, has lost its power of speaking immediately and with noble exhortation to the new western world. Yet Thoreau has to reckon with Shakespeare. His adverse criticisms are a testimony to the effectiveness of this strange ghost from Stratford. He has became a touchstone for the fine quality of man's revolt as well as for his rhapsodies and adoration.

Bronson Alcott, another member of the Concord group, tried Shakespeare and didn't like him. Odell Shepard in his interesting study of Alcott, *Pedlar's Progress*, records that Alcott 'could make little of [the plays]'. Yet the ghost of Shakespeare's importance haunted him at intervals all his life. A trip to the West brought Alcott into touch with Henry C. Brockmeyer, a German and a student of Hegel. In the group around Brockmeyer was young Denton Snider, 'a student of Shakespeare'. But even in this atmosphere and among these interpreters, Alcott remained cold.

The reason is not far to seek. Emerson put his finger on it in a letter of July, 1836. 'Shakespeare and all works of art which require a surrender of the man to them in order to their full enjoyment, he [Alcott] suspects and disparages.' That was the point. Alcott preserved the rigidity of an earlier New England toward the seductions of all art. He refused to 'surrender'. He 'suspected' the snares and wiles of aesthetic pleasure. His spare taste in literature is revealed in the 'List of Books Bought by Me in London 1842'. It is, of course, quite innocent of Shakespeare titles. Though different in individual items, it is very like, in general taste, those books which were sent from London to Boston in the seventeenth century. As the Puritans then, so Alcott now, after the passage of a hundred and fifty years, was a reader rejoicing in the philosophical and the abstract. He, no more than the late seventeenth century Boston readers, could find room for the warm embodiment of abstract ideas in the living drama of a man like Shakespeare.

Emerson's perfect comment on the alchemy which Shakespeare wrought upon the commonplace of actuality could have meant nothing to Alcott. It was made at that famous Saturday Club celebration of the three hundredth anniversary of Shakespeare's birth in April, 1864. Shakespeare, Emerson said (or intended to say, for whether or not he read his speech is a moot question), was comparable to 'snow or moonlight or the level rays of sunrise . . . lend [ing] a momentary glory to every pump and woodpile'. Perhaps there never was a more apposite description of the Shakespearean way of metamorphosing the commonplace of life into unearthly beauty. This passage is peculiarly dear to New Englanders, because it explains Shakespeare's power in terms of essential New England. As the pump and woodpile are transmuted by moonlight or sunrise (when the chore-boy is abroad early) or by snows of a Massachusetts winter, so Shakespeare's alchemy transmutes actuality into poetry.

Alcott would not have liked Emerson's comment nor would it have helped him one whit on the way to understanding Shakespeare. Yet Emerson and the other devoted Shakespeareans could not leave Alcott alone. They kept urging him to try again or scolding him for his failures. In this same speech for Shakespeare's birthday in April, 1864, Emerson belabours Alcott for his attitude. 'Alcott thinks', says Emerson, ' "he [Shakespeare] was a rhetorician, but did not propound new thoughts". Aye, he *was* a rhetorician, as was never one before, but also had more thoughts than ever any had.' But here Emerson was wrong. Not even the most partisan twentieth century critic thinks that Shakespeare's 'thoughts', in Emerson's sense of the word, are his most notable contribution. For one who wanted 'new thoughts' and liked them 'lean', undecorated by 'rhetoric', Shakespeare was not the right reading. Alcott and others of his type would not 'surrender' to anything for 'full enjoyment'. The whole process was alien to their natures.

It is worth while to remember that certain strains in the New England temperament were proof against Shakespeare. Even Emerson balked at some phases of his art. This fact makes the enormous scope of his triumph in this alien New England all the more impressive. In New England's reservations and qualifications, one sees again how the reactions to Shakespeare among varying ages and

varying individuals furnish a touchstone for determining
their essential qualities. 'Tell me what you like' and in
very truth 'I will tell you what you are.'

Walt Whitman's interest in Shakespeare was as great as
Emerson's and in part sympathetic with it. It also had
many of Thoreau's reservations. Over and above these, it
had, at its best, an immediacy and rightness of feeling
which bear witness to Whitman's essential greatness.

It is a pity that Richard C. Harrison, who was in the
midst of a study of Walt Whitman's use of Shakespeare,
died. He presented a paper on Whitman and Shakespeare
before the Modern Language Association at Chicago, in
1925. His friends published this paper in the *Publications*
four years later, together with a compilation of passages
from Whitman which have Shakespearean references. This
compilation runs to eighteen pages and indicates in physical form the extent to which Whitman's manner of writing and actual rhythmical sense were permeated with Shakespeare. How did Shakespeare appear to Whitman? For
what did he like or dislike him? And how did he estimate
him? The answers to these questions are interesting.

Whitman all his life both read and saw a good deal of
Shakespeare. His method of reading shows how vital a
part of his life Shakespeare was. 'I would buy a cheap
second-hand book—tear out the plays I wanted—paste the
sheets carefully together—keep them with me.' The twentieth century has argued that there has been too much
reading of Shakespeare in the study, that it was never
meant to be scrutinized in an atmosphere of stillness and
consecutive thinking, amid the solemnities of high mounting rows of bookshelves and the accuracies of carefully
sorted notes. This is undoubtedly true; for Shakespeare
did not compose that way, himself, and his 'book' when

finished was out to catch the vagrant attention of a public theatre audience. But surely, if the reading of Shakespeare, off the stage, is ever suitable to the spirit of the lines, it is so in Walt Whitman's experience.

'Every week in the mild season', according to his own remembrance, he went to Coney Island, 'then a long bare unfrequented shore, which I had all to myself'. There after bathing, he would 'run up and down the hard sand, and declaim Homer and Shakespeare to the surf and sea-gulls by the hour'. To be sure, there is an element of theatricality lingering here; it is perhaps a bit of romantic attitudinizing on Whitman's part. He enjoys to the full, as an audience of one, the sense of himself thus declaiming to 'surf and seagulls'. But where may one be theatrical if not with Shakespeare? Furthermore, this was the era, as Emerson showed, when America was romantic. Whitman pictures himself reading Shakespeare in the 'right' circumstances. 'It makes such a difference', he says, '*where* [and underlines it] you read Shakespeare.'

For Whitman, of course, the 'right' place was not only country and seashore but the thick of midtown traffic. He recalls for Traubel, 'How often I spouted this [his home-bound copy of *Richard II*] on the Broadway stage-coaches in the awful din of the street'. He recalls 'stormy passages from *Julius Caesar* or *Richard*', which continued 'the whole length of Broadway on the bus'. In his walks about Washington, too, in the sixties, he would 'recite poetry, especially Shakespeare'. This sort of 'reading' of Shakespeare simply expands the stage and the audience beyond the theatre walls.

All this 'spouting' was simply an extension of experience he was having in the actual theatres of New York. 'As a boy or young man', he recalled, 'I had seen [reading them carefully the day beforehand] quite all Shakespeare's acting dramas, played wonderfully well.' Being a newspaper man, as Harrison points out, 'he had by a pressman's pass, ready access to the theatre'. According to Harrison's computation, Whitman certainly saw thirteen of Shakespeare's plays on the boards and probably several more. He saw them acted by the great artists of the time: Forrest, Hackett, Booth. This experience, continued over twenty-five years, saved Whitman from any danger of placing exclusive emphasis on Shakespeare's poetry, a practice which led Emerson often into wrong paths.

Whitman was a gifted theatregoer. His description of Booth in *Richard III* at the Bowery, in '34 or '35, shows how completely he reacted to the performance. It discloses, too, what were the accents and emphases of acting in the American theatre in the first fifty years of our national life. Whitman, on the occasion he describes, was in the pit. Booth, as the hunch-backed villain, Richard III, entered 'amidst a tempest of boisterous hand clapping'. As he walked out to the edge of the stage to deliver that fine villainous soliloquy, 'Now is the winter of our discontent', Whitman lost none of the effect. 'I can hear the clank [of his sword]', he writes, 'and feel the perfect following hush of perhaps three thousand people waiting.' In the melodramatic 'dream' scene, Whitman remembers 'the shudder' which 'went through every nervous system in the audience' and 'through mine'. He knew, too, what very few of his fellow auditors knew, that Booth's style of acting was 'inflated and stagey'. But he knew that a certain amount of 'hocum' was, and always will be, a part of the theatre. It did not keep him from perceiving beneath it a 'genius' making 'one of the grandest revelations of my life, a lesson of artistic expression'.

By the happy accident, then, which has preserved so much of Whitman's personality, so many records of his ways of living and thinking, one can be sure of his vivid sense of Shakespeare as a poet to be 'declaimed' and as a playwright whose work is essentially for the theatre. Probably to no other American did Shakespeare reach across the centuries with more of his proper emphasis and feeling.

In addition to Shakespeare's claim as a rhetorician and playwright, Whitman was also an appreciative critic of the content of Shakespeare's plays. He feels Shakespeare's 'vast and rich variety of persons and themes' and his 'wondrous delineation of each and all'. Whitman's comment on the peculiar phraseology, the elaborate, 'three-piled' figures and phrases, which Shakespeare and his age used has hardly been bettered, though Whitman got to it by sheer insight without any 'college course' in the history of Elizabethan style! Shakespeare's 'mannerisms', says Whitman, are 'like a fine, aristocratic perfume, holding a touch of musk'. Nothing better than this has been said of the elaborate and sensuous phraseology which was the vogue in Shakespeare's world. He feels apologetic in some moods, for any adverse comment. 'It seems a shame', he says, 'to pick and choose from the riches Shakespeare left us—to criticise his infinitely royal, multiform quality,—to gauge with optic glasses, the dazzle of his sunlike beams.' Not even Emerson could go further in romantic adoration.

But Whitman, more than Emerson, was aware of the pitfalls that Shakespeare could set for the unwary critic. He knew it was easy to be fulsome and extravagant. He stands sanely 'on this side idolatry' as had his great predecessors—Ben Jonson in Shakespeare's lifetime, Dryden in the seventeenth century, and the great Dr. Samuel Johnson in the late eighteenth century. In his *Conversations with Traubel*, Whitman declares that 'it's very difficult to talk about Shakespeare in a frank vein'. His greatness evokes partisanship rather than intelligent criticism, and Whitman adds 'there's always somebody about with a terrific prejudice to howl you down'.

In these years of the late 1880's, when he looked back upon the panorama of a long and full life, his conversation was constantly flavoured with Shakespearean comment. The great compulsion was still on him, though he fought against coming beneath the spell. 'Do you suppose', he said on one occasion, 'I accept the almost luny worship of Shakespeare—the cult worship, the college-chair worship? Not a bit of it—not a bit of it. I do not think Shakespeare was the all-in-all of literature.' Yet, in the next breath and in candour, he admits Shakespeare was a 'great man'. Even though he has warned himself against idolatry, he does, even in these late years, give way to it. In Shakespeare and Homer, 'you feel at once that everything you find there belongs integrally to the design—nature; speaks for nature —is nature—soil of its soil, inevitable'. This is perilously near Emerson at his most idolatrous.

Yes, Shakespeare was a 'master'. Yet, as Whitman never failed to point out, he was 'subject to severe deductions'. These reservations are the most interesting phase of his critical comment. As a propagandist,* in the finest sense of that ill-used word, working toward a different conception of the function of society in America, Whitman was bound to have reservations about Shakespeare's social point of view. Sometimes he seems to feel that America was something self-contained, with a quality essentially its

* For a comprehensive and dispassionate study of Whitman's whole social position, see *Whitman*, by Newton Arvin, Macmillan, New York, 1938.

own, not stemming from anything in Europe. On seeing a painting on 'Custer's Last Rally', he recognizes it for a 'Western, autochthonic phase of America'. There is, he thinks, 'nothing in the books like it, nothing in Homer, nothing in Shakespeare'. Furthermore, it is dear to him because it is 'all native, all our own and all a fact'.

In this comment, it is not hard for one to see that strong anti-British feeling which ran through the history of America from its beginnings. The opposition is not destructive but constructive. America's difference from Europe and her complete originality promise a new and vastly significant social future. Its sources must not be vitiated by ideas belonging to older and now defunct societies, no matter how good these ideas may have been in their own day.

When Whitman is thinking along these lines, he is afraid of Shakespeare, as he is afraid of all literature written against what he calls a 'feudal' social background. 'The great poems', he writes, 'Shakespeare included, are poisonous to the idea of the pride and dignity of the common people, the life-blood of the democracy.' The 'most distinctive poems' of the past may 'preserve and typify results offensive to the modern spirit and long past away'. 'For poetry', he argues, evolves, and therefore he sees 'the past, even the best of it, giving place and dying out'. Thus 'for our existing world, the bases on which all the grand old poems were built have become vacuums'.

He goes into the matter more specifically. Though the comedies of Shakespeare are 'exquisite' and the common characters in them 'admirably portrayed', yet Whitman believes that these 'common characters' were handled merely 'for the divertissement of the élite of the castle'. He apparently believed that Shakespeare never handled

them for their intrinsic value or regarded them sympa-
thetically. They were always, in Whitman's view, presented by Shakespeare as 'foils to the aristocracy'. If he
believed this, it followed logically that he should regard
Shakespeare's comedies as 'altogether non-acceptable to
America and Democracy'. This point of view on Shakespeare was so frequently expressed by Whitman that Harrison, in his proposed book, would have attempted to prove
that this opposition in Whitman's mind 'was an actuating
motive which lies at the base of his work'. Whether Harrison could have established his point is not certain, but
certainly, in the course of his effort, he would have laid
bare some interesting lights on Whitman.

But Whitman is much too intricate a person to allow
himself to be neatly dissected and tidily analyzed. That
he loved Shakespeare more wisely than most of his contemporaries is clear. And even his attitude toward the past,
of which Shakespeare was a part, is not simple and consistent. There is nowhere a more delicate balancing of the
constructive and destructive forces of the past than in the
1855 Preface to *Leaves of Grass*. 'America does not repel
the past', Whitman wrote in that first Preface, 'or what it
has produced under its forms or amidst other politics or
the idea of castes or the old religions.' It 'is not so impatient
as has been supposed that the slough still sticks to opinions
and manners and literature while the life that served its
requirements is passed into the new life of the new forms'.
Surely this passage shows Whitman's sense of the indestructible element in all life, whether past or present. The
passage might very justly be used to describe his attitude
toward Shakespeare.

Yet Whitman's attacks upon Shakespeare as a writer for
the aristocracy were surely wrong-headed and unin-

formed. One might well argue, however, that Whitman's was a necessary bigotry and a necessary misrepresentation. Though the specific example was wrong, the general theory which it was used to illuminate had the strength and shocking challenge which America needed. In his eagerness to evoke a great poetry, immediately derived from the greatness of a new country and a new people, he had to minimize unfairly the contribution of the past. To high-light his passionate plea for the development of truly democratic elements, he had to oppose, with untrue sharpness, the poetry of what he mistakenly fancied belonged to an aristocratic world.

Whitman did not know what staunch elements of independence and what adaptations to an English public already headed for democracy, Shakespeare exemplified in his plays. If he had known this, he would not only have liked Shakespeare (which he obviously did) but would have felt at ease and consistent in this liking. He so easily and so rightly could have applied to Shakespeare what he says later in this 1855 Preface:

The old red blood and stainless gentility of great poets will be proved by their unconstraint. A heroic person walks at his ease through and out of that custom or precedent or authority that suits him not.

This last sentence is a precise description of Shakespeare's attitude toward his age and toward the rigidities of the theatre as he found it.

That Shakespeare was deliberately falsified in Whitman's mind in order that he might more sharply defend his own ideas for the relationship of poetry to life does not diminish the stature of Whitman. It is a sublime perversity, necessary to the achievement of his great ends. But when he is not using Shakespeare as a stalking horse, he gives infinite proof of the depth and breadth of his understanding of a great poet. The opening lines of the 1855 Preface show Whitman's sensitive perception of the contribution of the past to the present. That Shakespeare could have been offered as concrete evidence of this general debt, Whitman's life-long preoccupation with his works shows. Only when he thought specifically and belligerently of the essence of America which must be kept pure and honest, which must be made vocal in our literature, did he distort and over-simplify his estimate of Shakespeare.

Abraham Lincoln's experience with Shakespeare shows, perhaps as perfectly as any single individual's life can do it, the very accents of Shakespeare as he spoke to the America of that time. Lincoln, as he himself bitterly said, had 'picked up' his education 'under the pressure of necessity'. If Shakespeare had not been a 'necessity', Lincoln would not have known him. For there was no free bestowal of cultural benefits upon Lincoln, as there is upon hundreds of thousands of American boys in the public schools of today.

He seems not to have known anything about Shakespeare till his early twenties in the New Salem days. Whether Graham, 'the neighborhood school teacher', taught him 'all manner of subjects from Shakespeare to surveying', or whether Jack Kelso, the doer of odd jobs and inveterate fisherman, mumbling passages from Shakespeare over his work, first tuned young Lincoln's ears to those cadences and heroic ideas is not important. In some such haphazard fashion, the great doors were opened, and Lincoln went inside to claim some portions of Shakespeare for his own and to return to them again and again throughout his life.

There is a rightness, amazing considering Lincoln's provincial beginnings and circumscribed existence, in the *oral* nature of his acquaintance with Shakespeare. Though he read the plays avidly, he began by 'hearing' them. He never lost the sense of their existence as rhetoric, whether on or off the stage. In his effort to meet single-handed the gigantic business of becoming educated, Lincoln discovered that 'reading aloud' was the best way of 'impressing what he read on his mind'. Shakespeare was one of the things acquired by this oral method. Necessity and the struggle against ignorance bestowed upon Lincoln a kind of Shakespeare which the school classes and lectures of a supposedly 'better' education often deny. He 'took in' the lines through his ears, as they were meant to be taken in.

This early method of 'learning' Shakespeare is no doubt responsible for the glimpses one has, throughout Lincoln's life, of his 'reading Shakespeare aloud'. This oral reading was clearly not for the entertainment of the listener but to give to Lincoln, himself, the full depth and vibrancy of the lines. 'In his most intimate circle . . . he would recite such speeches as Richard II's, beginning,

For God's sake let us sit upon the ground.'

Sometimes the oral reading was merely endured by the listeners. Thus his young secretary, John Hay, records in his diary under August 23, 1863, that 'he [Lincoln] read Shakespeare to me, the end of *Henry VI* and the beginning of *Richard III*, till my eyelids caught his considerate notice and he sent me to bed'.

At Fortress Munroe, Noah Brooks tells how Lincoln

'took up a volume of Shakespeare and read aloud'. This time it was to an aide of General Wool's who chanced to be the available audience. The selections were from *Hamlet* and *Macbeth* and from the third act of *King John*. It was just after he had lost a son. Brooks records that Lincoln closed the book and repeated from memory the lament of Constance for the son she had lost. He began with the lines

> And, father cardinal, I have heard you say
> That we shall see and know our friends in heaven:
> If that be true, I shall see my boy again.

In quoting this particular passage at this time, Lincoln shows that he, like Jefferson and Adams, read Shakespeare for those passages which spoke to him immediately in difficult corners of his life. Shakespeare was still an inspired comforter.

Lincoln made this same personal use of Shakespeare on the two-day steamer trip from City Point just before his assassination. The second day was Sunday, and Sumner, who was of the party, recalled after Lincoln's death that he had read over twice the lines beginning

> Duncan is in his grave;
> After life's fitful fever he sleeps well;
> Treason has done his worst: . . .
> . . . .   nothing
> Can touch him further.

That Lincoln could have a specific premonition of his assassination is, of course, absurd. It would be easy, after the event, for Sumner's memory to heighten the meaning of this reading from Shakespeare. Yet the occasion, like so many other occasions, was typical both of Lincoln's habit of reading Shakespeare aloud and of reading the passages for some congeniality they bore to his mood.

Lincoln also read Shakespeare to himself. Hertz reports him as reading and re-reading 'the leading plays of Shakespeare . . . in between important events and cabinet meetings'. There survives the list of books 'retained for reading and study from the Library of Congress from 1861 to 1863'. In the list appears 'Shakespeare, 12 mo., 1 vol.', taken out by Lincoln on July 23rd and returned on December 24th. The fact is there in the record that he borrowed a one-volume copy of Shakespeare and kept it from July to December.

He shared in the interest in Shakespeare which was propagated by Shakespeare Societies. When he was invited by a delegation of a literary society to attend a Shakespeare celebration, Hertz records his quoting to them as applicable to himself the line 'For am I not a man of infinite jest'. This is a misquotation of Hamlet's line on Yorick as a 'fellow of infinite jest'. Lincoln saw Shakespeare on the stage and brought to his criticism of the performances a considerable knowledge of the Shakespeare text itself and of the history of the playing versions. When the new National Theatre opened in Washington in 1863 with *Othello*, he attended a performance on October 6th. Hay records in his diary that on December 15th of the same year, the 'President took Swett, Nicolay and me to Ford's with him to see Falstaff in *Henry IV*'. Another entry at about the same time reads 'Thursday the President went to see the *Merry Wives*'.

The remarkable thing about these attendances at Shakespeare in the theatre is the critical acumen of Lincoln, his

detailed knowledge of the text, and his point of view on
the stage adaptation of the lines. At the *Henry IV* performance, for example, Hay comments that 'the President
criticised H's. [Hackett's] reading of a passage where
Hackett said "Mainly *thrust* at me", the President thinking it should read "Mainly thrust at *me*". I told the Pres.
I tho't he was wrong, that "mainly" merely meant
"strongly", "fiercely".' The passage occurs in the delec-
table scene at the Boar's Head Tavern (First *Henry IV*, II,
iv, 222 seq.) where Falstaff is regaling the Prince with tall
lies of his brave behaviour in the robbery. Certainly from
the modern point of view, Hackett and Hay have the
right reading and Lincoln is wrong. But the fact that Lincoln cavilled, that he had ideas of rendering and was interested to discuss them, shows how characteristic of the
times his Shakespearean interest was.

One remembers Hackett's work on Shakespeare's text
in articles in various English and American journals. One
recalls, too, the scholarly correspondence of John Quincy
Adams on the same subject. Shakespearean interpretation
and criticism of text were an amateur's game in those days.
One amassed a decent knowledge of it and displayed it in
correspondence, even printed correspondence, and in conversation. It was like stamp collector's lore, or golf, or
racing, or book collecting. This sort of amateur learning
is likely to attend any subject when it becomes prominent
enough. And Shakespeare, seen and read, was a veritable
national sport at this time. Lincoln's share in this sort of
thing simply shows his awareness of and response to the
Shakespearean emphases of his time.

At this same performance of First *Henry IV* by Hackett, Lincoln thought 'the dying speech of Hotspur an
unnatural and unworthy thing'. 'As who does not?' asks

young Hay in recording the incident in his diary. One must not give these chance comments on Shakespeare by Lincoln and his young secretary too much weight. But the dying speech of Hotspur certainly does not seem 'an unnatural and unworthy thing' to the twentieth century reader. Like any brave gentleman, Hotspur dies by the Prince's hand (V, IV, 77 seq.), lamenting the loss of his distinction more than the loss of his life. He then comforts himself at the moment of death, by recalling that life is at the mercy of time, and that all men and time itself 'must have a stop'.

This philosophizing about life and death, this acceptance of the littleness of man's fate in the great scheme of things, is common in the thinking of Shakespeare's world and in the speeches of his characters. What was it that offended both Lincoln and his young secretary about this idea? Perhaps there is no real significance in an answer if we could find one. Yet, is it not possible that the courageous acceptance of the negation of man's life by time and death, which was symptomatic of thinking at the end of the sixteenth century and now in the twentieth century, runs counter to the Victorian convention? For them man's life was governed by the will of God, and his death was to be accepted unquestionably as a part of that will. Certainly Hotspur's dying speech is not 'religious' as the America of 1863 would have defined 'religious'. It is bravely sceptical and submissive to the scheme of the universe. There is nothing 'Christian' about it. Perhaps it was this fact which made the speech seem to the accepted thinking of 1863 not only 'unnatural' but 'unworthy'.

Like John Quincy Adams, Lincoln did not merely criticize in private. He wrote directly to Hackett to ask him about points of Shakespearean interpretation. In a letter of August 17, 1863, he expressed his pleasure in Hackett's presentation of Falstaff. 'Some of Shakespeare's plays I have never read', he says, 'while others I have gone over perhaps as frequently as any other unprofessional reader.' *Lear, Richard III* (a favorite even in colonial times), *Henry VIII, Hamlet* and *Macbeth* are among those he has most studied. He thinks 'nothing equals *Macbeth*'. Lincoln tells Hackett that he finds the prayer of the wicked Claudius and his effort to reform, a finer speech than Hamlet's 'To be or not to be'.

Apparently Hackett published this letter from Lincoln without obtaining his permission. In any case, Lincoln wrote Hackett again in November of the same year. The letter, once printed, had evoked public comments. About these comments, Lincoln writes, he was 'not much shocked'. They are 'a fair specimen of what has occurred to me through life'. He adds, 'I have endured a great deal of ridicule without much malice; and have received a great deal of kindness, not quite free from ridicule'. He concludes with the succinct sentence, 'I am used to it'. Yet 'with malice toward none', as he was to say in his *Second Inaugural*, he apparently invited Hackett to the White House the very next month. For under date of December 13, 1863, Hay records, 'Tonight Hackett arrived and spent the evening with the President'. Young Hay is delighted at his chief's Shakespearean knowledge. He writes that 'the Tycoon' (humorous and affectionate epithet from young Hay to President Lincoln) showed 'a very intimate knowledge of those plays of Shakespeare where Falstaff figured'. He challenged Hackett on the reasons for some of his cuts.

Another reminiscence of an actor at the White House discussing with Lincoln the stage versions is recorded by

William D. Kelley, who took the actor MacDonough to call. Miss Tarbell reports it in her *Early Life*. The anecdote seems less authoritative than the Hackett visit, but it interestingly confirms this preoccupation of Lincoln with the acting versions of Shakespeare. The play of *Henry VI* (should it not be *Henry IV?*) was discussed and Colley Cibber's addition to the stage text of *Richard III*. Lincoln is represented as getting down a 'well-thumbed' volume of Shakespeare, and as reading or repeating from memory several extracts from several of the plays.

When one turns to Lincoln's speeches and writings, one finds very little direct quotation from Shakespeare. Surely if he had wished to do so, he had a store of Shakespearean passages which he might have used. But Lincoln's style was unique. In an age of rhetoric, it was spare and forceful. It could not brook even Shakespearean ornament. In one important law-case, Lincoln is reported to have used 'just enough Shakespearean padding about honour'. In the famous debate with Douglas, there is just the ghost of a reference to the 'Lay on, MacDuff' speech from *Macbeth*. In general, however, the immediacy of the occasion and the directness with which he addressed his words to it kept Lincoln's utterances free from quotation even in an era of oratory and decorative passages.

How Lincoln used *Hamlet*, though indirectly, for recruiting during the Civil War, makes an interesting story. It shows, too, the widespread knowledge in America of stock situations in *Hamlet*. A poem called 'The Oath' (humorously alluded to by Lincoln as 'The Swear'), by T. B. Read, was published in the *Cincinnati Commercial Gazette* for January 29, 1863. It was based on the scene where Hamlet is interrupted by the ghost's deep 'Swear' from beneath the stage. The poem exhorts the freemen of

282 SHAKESPEARE in America

America to fight. They are urged on by those who have
already died. The refrain of each stanza reads,

> And hark, the deep voices replying
> From graves where your fathers are lying
> *'Swear, oh, swear'*.

It is a banal affair. But Lincoln saw in it an effective recruiting document. He was present when James E. Murdock, a well-known actor, recited it in the Senate Cham-
ber. Lincoln stayed till the last 'to strenuously applaud the
noble words that urged the tardy to the defense of the
homeland'.

Thus to Lincoln, as to Emerson and Whitman and other
nineteenth century figures, Shakespeare's pages lent the
stimulation and sympathy which his own nature craved.
His rolling periods echoed majestically in an ear peculiarly
sensitive to the rhythms of exhortation. The lyric outcry
of man suffering spoke out to Lincoln amid the suffering
and confusions of his own tragic life. The rendition of the
plays in the theatre evoked from him that personal and
partisan reaction to the lines and situations which proved
that the characters of Shakespeare were often more real
than his flesh-and-blood contemporaries.

Shakespeare spoke directly to Lincoln's 'business and
bosom'. He was a substantial and constant companion, not
an artistic inheritance from the past. And so, too, he appeared, according to their various tempers and aspirations,
to the other dominant American figures of the nineteenth
century. When Thoreau turned away from Shakespeare,
or Alcott found him uncongenial, this very negation of his
influence shows positively what these men were like.
When Whitman liked him so inordinately, yet belaboured

him for being 'feudal', the contradiction is in itself an index of Whitman's complex nature. But whether adored in superlatives, or neglected with strenuous invective, or warmly welcomed as speaking immediately to one's own dilemmas and joys, Shakespeare companioned the dominant nineteenth century figures across those turbulent and changing years in America. He presented to each man the face of his own predilection and prejudice and is, looking backward, a sensitive index of the taste of that fascinating time.

CHAPTER XIV

The Flavour of Shakespearean Editing and Research in America Through the First Three-Quarters of the Nineteenth Century; The Baconian Theory—Delia Bacon and Hawthorne

W<small>HEN</small> Washington Irving published his *Sketch Book* in 1819 he included an essay on the Boar's Head Tavern, locale of the famous tavern scenes in Shakespeare's two plays on *Henry IV*. Irving's essay is a piece of gentle satire. He pictures himself in London setting off for the vicinity of the actual tavern. By interviewing blowzy old landladies and decrepit sextons he claims to have unearthed the very cup from which those deep potations of Jack Falstaff and Prince Hal may have been quaffed. He even scares up a story of the ghost of a head waiter, lineal descendant of that poor 'drawer' Francis, whose patient and bewildered 'Anon' gave Shakespeare one of his funniest scenes. Irving presents this essay as a satire upon the contemporary fashion of 'lighting up' Shakespeare's 'character or works' by 'research'. To Irving, and apparently to most American readers, the 'heavy hand of scholarship', as it fell upon the towering imaginings and creations of Shakespeare, was an abomination. He and the reading public, too, if we may judge from the American editors of Shakespeare at that time, deplored 'the common herd of editors' who 'send up mists of obscurity from their notes at the bottom of each page'.

Clearly what had happened was this. German aesthetic criticism had won our favour. It was equalled and rivalled in the rhapsody of Emerson on Shakespeare. But German scholarship had a more difficult time in securing a foothold. America had for two centuries been kept from feeling at ease in the Zion of Shakespeare's pages. And now that the moral strictures were beginning to be relaxed, Americans insisted upon enjoying him without scholarly restrictions. It was only when he became a substitute for the mental and linguistic discipline of the classics in the colleges after the Civil War, that the scalpel of scientific scholarship began its long and painful period of vivisection upon the living body of his works.

The history of American editions of Shakespeare, then, in the first two-thirds of the nineteenth century, is the history of reading editions for the intelligent layman. The first American edition, printed and sold by Bioren and Madan in Philadelphia in 1795–96, blazons its British authority on the title-page. It is 'corrected' from the latest and best London editions. It is 'embellished with a striking likeness from the collection of his Grace, the Duke of Chandos'. But it also has American emphasis. The 'Preface by the American * Editors' shows clearly the requirements of their public which they bore in mind. The years 1795–96 still belonged to the eighteenth century, and the business of assuring the reader that Shakespeare's plays are documents in moral teaching was still urgent. The 'American Editor' assures the public that they will gather the best lessons in morality here; for 'the fools

* Mr. Henry N. Paul of Philadelphia, whose invaluable unpublished volume on American Editions of Shakespeare is in the Folger Shakespeare Library in Washington, thinks that Joseph Hopkinson of Philadelphia may have been the author of this Preface. I am indebted to Mr. Paul's volume for several points in this chapter.

of Shakespeare are always despised and his villains always hated'.

The editors, furthermore, do not 'send up a mist of obscurity' from notes, a practice which Washington Irving would have deplored. There are no notes except one by Dr. Johnson at the end of each play. The Preface commends this freedom from scholarly apparatus. 'An American reader', it maintains, 'is seldom disposed to wander through the wilderness of verbal criticism.' Then follows a figure of comparison fitting to our new world with its great open spaces. 'An immense tract of excellent land', the editors write, 'uncultivated and even unexplored, presents an object more interesting to every mind than those ingenious literary trifles that in Europe are able to command so much attention.' Here is not only a stricture on meticulous scholarship but the self-assertive tone of the new republic, raising itself arrogantly above the tastes of a 'played-out' Europe.

At about this time there apparently developed a public who after attending Shakespeare in the theatre wished to read the script of plays they had seen. Single plays, in a series called 'West's Boston Theatre', began to be issued in Boston. *Hamlet* in 12mo, running to seventy pages, was the first in the series in 1794. It bore on its title-page 'as performed at the Theatre in Boston'. *Twelfth Night* and other separate plays followed. This argues a reading public for Shakespeare that was distinctly theatre-minded and cared not a whit for those editions which furnished, in addition to the lines of the play, a 'wilderness of verbal criticism'. New York had a series of the same kind, starting in 1804. D. Longworth was the publisher. *Richard III*, as altered by Cibber and played at the New York Theatre, was the first play in the series. Others followed.

They were poorly printed on cheap paper. Sometimes a sheaf of them was bound together and sold. They were also issued separately. They remind one, afar off, of those cheap little paper-covered quartos of Shakespeare's plays which, by hook or by crook, appeared in his own lifetime to delight the general public then but to confound the editors and bibliographers ever since.

In a somewhat more 'genteel' class, though still designed for the general reader, was the Boston Edition by Munroe and Francis, issued in 1802, '03 and '04. The edition came out originally to subscribers. This meant that the publishers knew a section of the public that were sure purchasers. They were issued in sixteen paper-covered parts. Each part, as was advertised on the cover, would contain two or three plays with Dr. Johnson's notes. The price to subscribers was thirty-eight cents a part, and there was stipulation for 'payment on delivery'. They came out monthly or oftener. There is something lighthearted about these arrangements. Like magazines, or the famous 'Dickens in parts', the plays of Shakespeare, in monthly paper-covered 'installments', were set down at one's door like other kinds of light and diverting reading. One had presumably one's thirty-eight cents ready on the hall table to be handed over when the delivery boy knocked. All the ponderosity of a classic is left outside in this publishing venture. Probably never since Shakespeare's own day had his plays been so gaily handled.

There was a 'come-on' for the reader, too. If he secured eight new subscribers, he was entitled to a ninth 'part' free of charge. Not even the modern book-of-the-month clubs could do better than this. The whole venture is tremendously jolly, in contrast to those de luxe editions, those elegant, crested tall copies, which looked down with hauteur from the shelves of ducal libraries in the preceding centuries. The First Folio of 1623 had started the bad practice of publishing Shakespeare learnedly and expensively. It took the new America in the early years of its independence to restore him to the literature of inexpensive entertainment, where he began.

Munroe and Francis issued a second edition in 1807. The publishers aimed this enterprise at the undergraduates in various colleges. One remembers that there were no courses in Shakespeare, as such, in American colleges in 1807. This interest of the American undergraduate was, therefore, purely literary and personal. He still belonged to the category of 'general reader', so far as Shakespeare was concerned. College undergraduates were buying him for their private reading in their leisure hours. In the list of subscribers in one volume, Paul records that one-half of the students of Harvard, or ninety-nine out of about one hundred and seventy-five, appear. Brown has twenty-eight names; Union has seventeen and Dartmouth seven. 'Yale', says Mr. Paul, 'I am sorry to say is conspicuous by its absence from the list.' The edition of at least fifteen hundred copies takes, in the opinion of Paul, 'a preeminence over all other American editions so far as regards the awakening of an interest in Shakespeare's works'. Whether in monthly paper-covered 'parts', with 'payment on delivery', or in editions for the leisure hours of American undergraduates, Shakespeare still belonged to an honest and pleasurable reading tradition. The shades of the prison house had not yet begun to close about him.

The 'family circle' was also a mark to be hit by American publishers of Shakespeare. America did one edition of the Bowdler Shakespeare. It was printed in both Philadelphia and New York in 1849 and promised the omission of all parts 'which cannot with propriety be read aloud in a family'. In the same year appeared Howe's *Shakespearean Reader*, brought out by Appleton in New York. It was a collection of the 'most approved' portions. It was 'prepared expressly for the use of classes and the *family reading circle*'. Howe, as a Professor of Elocution in Columbia, could be trusted to know the most rhetorical bits for oral rendition. This *Reader* went through several editions. In 1863, it still advertised that the material was 'carefully expurgated' and still had the 'family reading circle' in mind. Plays in their entirety have no place here. Rhetoric and emotion in brief bursts were what was wanted. Yet, even in this truncated form, and subject to the most delicate proprieties of a 'mixed group', Shakespeare still belongs to the 'general reader'.

The dominant names among American editors in the first two-thirds of the nineteenth century belong to men who, in their editorial work, reflect the tastes and demands of a 'general reader'.* The editorial policy and critical point of view of such men as Henry N. Hudson, Dr. William J. Rolfe, G. C. Verplanck, Richard Grant White, different though their editions are in scope, yet show certain common characteristics in their attitude toward Shakespeare's readers in America.

The career of Hudson is clearly the closest to American popular taste. Hudson is a figure about whom legends easily cluster. That he walked to college and then took his shoes off during the day on campus so that there might be less wear and tear on shoe-leather; or that a New

---

* For the newest definitive work on American editions and related critical problems, the reader is referred to Dr. Alfred Westfall's *Shakespearean Criticism in America*, which is promised from the press of H. W. Wilson Co., New York. The author regrets that the manuscript of *Shakespeare in America* goes to press before the appearance of Dr. Westfall's book.

England school teacher, teaching in Kentucky, first
opened his eyes to the beauties of Shakespeare, after he
had graduated from Middlebury; these are the kinds of
legends which attached themselves to him. On the other
hand, in a lifetime of earning his living by purveying
Shakespeare to the American public, in the form of popular lectures and editions and finally as Professor of Shakespeare at Boston University, the quality of Hudson's best
Shakespearean criticism was so good that it still, in these
carping days, is commended. Robert K. Root in his estimate of Hudson says that 'his analysis of Shakespeare's
characters still retains a significant value'.

Hudson illustrates the Janus-like quality of Shakespearean appreciation in nineteenth century America. His early
lectures (printed in two volumes in 1848) were full of
rhapsody and full of emphasis upon the 'moral' value of
Shakespeare. They have little or no real critical value. Yet
this very man, by the broad field of influence which he
created in his lectures, by his 'Harvard Shakespeare' of
1870–73, by his 'School Shakespeare' which printed entire
plays each in a separate volume, rendered an incalculable
service to American culture. It is interesting, by the way,
to see how far in advance of the schools and colleges the
general American reader was as an 'appreciator' of Shakespeare. Hudson's school and college editions come only
in the seventies but his lectures for the general public were
flourishing in the forties and were worth putting into a
volume as early as 1848. He could risk a 'general' edition
of Shakespeare as early as 1851.

To be sure there was always a 'parson' quality in Hudson's exposition of Shakespeare. He was, after all, an editor
of church papers, a chaplain in the Civil War. It was right

and natural that he should be fundamentally concerned with the moral effect of things upon society. Even as late as 1872, Hudson's book on *Shakespeare, His Life, Art and Characters* combined the rhapsodic mood of Coleridge and Schlegel with the morality which sugared Shakespeare so nicely for his middle-class American public.

In a section headed 'Moral Spirit', Hudson does his best to reconcile art and morality. Of Shakespeare's men he feels that 'the good they do, in doing it, pays itself . . . the mere consciousness of rectitude suffices them'. And as for Shakespeare's women 'here it is that the moral element of the Beautiful has its fullest and fairest expression'. This does not mean very much but it sounds 'noble'. Hudson says something really significant about Shakespeare's moral value when he declares that 'next to the Christian religion, humanity has no other so precious inheritance as Shakespeare's'. We, today, do not like the way this is said; we dissent from its exaggeration. Yet in different terminology, it is still the actuating motive for our relentless preoccupation with the lines of these three-hundred-year-old plays. The essence of life and the secrets and confusions of human action seem to be caught there and preserved for our scrutiny, whatever century we live in.

W. J. Rolfe carried on the same dissemination of Shakespearean texts in separate volumes for each play. His edition for schools, first appearing in 1870, with its brick-red cover and red edges, has come to be the symbol of Shakespeare in the minds of a whole generation. Rolfe had less originality and 'flare' as a popularizer than Hudson, but his editions were substantial and the notes were honestly helpful to the amateur. His world was the world of the preparatory school. It was both natural and appropriate that he should publish a book on *Shakespeare the Boy*, in 1896. It 'describes and illustrates a boy's life in the time of Shakespeare'.

Verplanck, Professor of the Evidences of Christianity at the General Theological Seminary of New York, brought out between 1844 and 1847 a three-volume Shakespeare under the imprint of Harper. Verplanck was a man of wide interests. He was a member of the State Legislature and a writer on topics of public concern. He made no fanfare about 'new findings' in his Shakespeare. Yet he approached the problems of Shakespeare's art without too much awe and with the application of sound common sense. The result is a highly readable set of prefaces to the individual plays. Verplanck's edition was one more acknowledgement of the rights of the 'general reader', though this time the reader was assumed to have a well supplied pocketbook which could afford an 'elegant' publication in three substantial volumes.

With the publication of Richard Grant White's edition in twelve volumes, between 1857 and 1866, something new came into the conception of 'editing' Shakespeare. White, nobly educated and inheriting the finest traditions, still put the 'general reader' first in his designs for the edition. It is a venture 'intended for all classes of readers', he says. Notes are to assist the reader not to bemuse and bewilder him. 'A note', says White, 'thrust between a poet and his reader which is not required for the full comprehension of the poet's meaning is always an offense.' Then with humour and nice sense of proportion, he declares that 'an editor, like a physician or a lawyer, is a necessary evil'. America should be proud of producing a Shakespearean editor with such a constructive sense of his function. This is the 'amateur' tradition at its very finest.

Yet as the best amateurishness is bound to take into itself the skill and knowledge of the professional, so White contributed something very definite to the history of Shakespearean scholarship. He had become a good deal of an authority on the text of the First Folio, had been 'one of the first to detect the spuriousness of J. P. Collier's forgeries', had written learnedly and accurately about scholarly problems in a volume published in 1854, under the title of *Shakespeare's Scholar*.

When he came to the preparation of a text for his big edition, in the interests of honesty, of getting back to what Shakespeare wrote, instead of presenting what centuries of light-hearted editors thought he should have written, White turned again to the First Folio, as a version representing honestly the Elizabethan text. He 'renovated' his text, purged it from the errors of the eighteenth century editors and established a sensible textual policy which has been pursued, though with changes in emphasis as our knowledge of the Elizabethan book world has changed, right down to the present day. White's edition textually is not as distinguished as the great Clark and Wright Shakespeare which was going forward in England at the same time. But it works from the same general premises and is in its own right distinguished for its clear-headedness and independence.

James Russell Lowell, then editor of the new *Atlantic Monthly*, wrote a long review of White's Shakespeare, which appeared in two different issues of the *Atlantic* for the year 1859. His review highlights this new attempt of White's to get back to the lines of the plays as Shakespeare wrote them. His venom against the eighteenth century 'emendors' is, of course, partly the romantic nineteenth century's fury at the temerity of the preceding century in matters Shakespearean. For the eighteenth century had not only presumed to criticize Shakespeare adversely, it had rewritten and improved him. This, to the nineteenth century, was treason.

Accurate textual scholarship, in other words, began as an act of worship of Shakespeare as he was, unclouded by the temerity of 'emendors' who would improve him. Lowell, in reviewing White's edition, deplores Shakespeare's earlier 'most inadequate editors'. Beating himself to a fury, Lowell continues, 'as his own Falstaff was the cause of wit, so he has been the cause of the foolishness that was in other men'. Lowell glories in White's effort to purge Shakespeare's text of these impertinent emendations. 'We should be grateful' to White who 'scrape[s] away these barnacles from the brave old hull'. By way of reverence for Shakespeare as he was and by way of a wish to deliver him 'in his habit as he lived' to the general reader in America, White instituted a sound scholarly method in textual criticism. This is how scholarship should exist, in the service of art and honest interpretation. It should, however learned and specialized, have as its ultimate goal the fine elucidation and interpretation of art for the layman.

Lowell's qualifications for the perfect Shakespearean editor, which he lays down in the course of this review of White, call for a combination of accuracy and imagination. Lowell would endow this ideal editor with 'thorough glossological knowledge' and a knowledge of 'Elizabethan metrical practice'. Next he must respect his great original; he must have 'such a conviction of the supremacy of his author as always to prefer him to any theory of his own'. If this is nineteenth century 'idolatry' of Shakespeare, it is also sound scholarly practice. It substitutes for what one fancies Shakespeare *should* have written, a deference to what he *did* write, as it was reproduced in the editions of his own lifetime.

Then Lowell asks that the editor have enough of the creative quality in him to be able to perceive the high reaches of Shakespeare's own imagination and leave them inviolate. He calls for 'enough logical acuteness of mind and metaphysical training to enable him to follow recondite processes of thought' or, as he puts it more generally, 'familiarity with the working of the imaginative faculty in general, and of its particular operation in the mind of Shakespeare'. This is a very large order indeed. It practically demands for the editor a grain of that precious radium with which Shakespeare is so luminous. Yet the great editors have all had this quality, combined with their accuracy and thorough knowledge of details. It is romanticism tempered with reason and shows how very good as a critic Lowell, at his best, could be.

When we come to Horace Howard Furness and his son, we are in a later period of American development. The genius of Furness, to whom the world owes the inception of the modern Variorum Shakespeare, is felt right up to the present moment. The venture which he started in 1871 (having already done a 'Variorum' of *Hamlet* in his undergraduate days) and which his son Horace Howard Furness, Jr., continued, is now being carried on toward completion under the impetus of the Folger Shakespeare Library in Washington and its able director, Joseph Q. Adams. But Furness belongs to the last third of the nineteenth century. The age was more complex; the experience that lay behind it had contributed its knowledge; the emphases are less clearly discerned, less able to reveal the advances and retreats of our national 'coming of age'.

As a facet of America's romantic idolatry of Shakespeare in the first half of the nineteenth century, no story is more revealing or more touching than Delia Bacon's. Her Shakespearean researches were the *reductio ad absurdum* of Shakespearean idolatry. She had read and lectured on Shakespeare and taught him in a series of brave adventures to earn her living in New England. Though born in a log cabin in Ohio, during a futile attempt of her Connecticut father to 'go west' and enlarge life and opportunity, she belonged to the ancient tribe of Connecticut Bacons.

Her too much brooding on the greatness of Shakespeare convinced her that the plays were too great to be written by a country boy from Stratford, 'Lord Leicester's groom', as she persistently called him. It was the ultimate in wreaths of laurel to crown his greatness. He was so great that his genius must be lodged in a more noble frame than the Stratford butcher's son's. And thus she hit upon the elegant person of Lord Francis Bacon, himself. And not on him alone but on several others, including Ralegh and Spenser. It was as if so much genius would overflow a single frame and spend its superfluity upon a whole group of Elizabethan personages.

Hawthorne, our consul at Liverpool during Miss Bacon's years of research in England, understood this aberration of hers for what it was. The Preface which he wrote for her book, *The Philosophy of the Plays of Shakespeare Unfolded*, was against his belief. But it was meant to comfort and support her brave and mad contentions. If the book failed, he wrote, 'her failure will be more honorable than most people's triumphs; since it must fling upon the old tombstone at Stratford-on-Avon, the noblest tributary wreath that has ever lain there'.

The whole story of Delia Bacon's effort is a pathetic distortion of this idolatry of Shakespeare. When she set off for England in May, 1853, to prosecute 'on the ground itself' her proofs that Shakespeare's plays were the work of a literary coterie who 'produced plays in order to set forth a liberal political philosophy which they could not present openly', America's best intellectually were at her service. She was financed by Butler. Emerson wrote Carlyle to do what he could for her. *Putnam's Magazine*, then the most prominent periodical, negotiated with her for articles. Philips, Sampson and Company, Boston publishers, gave her an advance on her future book and corresponded with Emerson about it, as if he were her unofficial American agent.

In England, the Carlyles gave her hospitality and comfort long after they were convinced that she was mentally unbalanced and that her project had no value. Grote, the great historian of Greece, came into it. Some touch of authentic nobility and cultivated taste in this shy New England woman, combined with the magic of Shakespeare's name, was just what was calculated to engage the attention of the mid-nineteenth century literary world on both sides of the Atlantic. How decently and delicately they all behaved toward her, as if there were something precious in the very process of research on this romantic chimaera. 'A very delicate, indeed painfully shy lady', writes Carlyle to Edward Everett, 'though of evident worth, talent and liked in the house.' This from the booming bear of Chelsea is recognition indeed.

Delia Bacon's relationship with Hawthorne in this affair is revelatory of the essential quality of them both. Caught up into the frame of a misguided, crazy search for 'high' origins for these great plays are the thumb nail portraits of two New England exotics. They were both shy, both haunted by the past, both aware with an awareness which comes only when life is slightly out of balance. They both understood the appeal of withdrawal from life.

Yet on another side, they had the New England trimness and spare decorousness of daily habit. In Hawthorne's story of his encounter with Miss Bacon in London (in an essay 'Recollections of a Gifted Woman', in *Our Old Home*), one sees this unique quality of sympathy for one very special sort of New Englander by another. 'Her conversation', he says, 'was remarkably suggestive, alluring forth one's ideas and fantasies from the shy place where they haunt.' It is the perfect comment on them, both for what it says and for its way of saying it. Both of them possessed 'fantasies' which only some secret sympathy could lure forth from 'the shy places where they haunt'.

Hawthorne's account of Miss Bacon's stay at Stratford and her plans for opening Shakespeare's grave is full of those 'haunted' touches which they both loved. 'She took a humble lodging', he writes, 'and began to haunt the church like a ghost.' The opening was planned for 'after nightfall'. She went thither 'with a dark lantern, which could but twinkle like a glow worm through the volume of obscurity'. It is in Hawthorne's very vein. Yet there was a more essential phase of understanding between Miss Bacon and Hawthorne than this, one less spectacular, more sound. Her quest for the origins of those remarkable plays was, barring her insane extremes, a sound romantic approach. And Hawthorne understood this. 'Whatever you seek' in Shakespeare, he maintains, 'you will surely discover'. And then he adds, 'Shakespeare has surface beneath surface . . . adapted to the plummet line of every reader'. No better or truer romantic criticism can be found than this. Although Miss Bacon overdid it, because her poor brain lost its balance, yet Hawthorne knew that her ravings had a modicum of rightness. 'The immortal poet,' he concludes, 'may have met her on the threshold [of eternity] and led her in . . . thanking her (yet with a smile of gentle humor . . . at the thought of certain mistaken speculations) for having interpreted him to mankind so well.'

And this is a good utterance on which to leave the record of American editorship and scholarship in the first two-thirds of the nineteenth century. It had 'certain mistaken speculations' at which from this distance we may smile with 'gentle humor'. But it had certain robust common sense, too. The editors never forgot that the general reader was the ultimate consumer and that the business of scholarship was to elucidate Shakespeare and not to obscure him.

CHAPTER XV

Shakespeare Marches On

SHAKESPEARE in America in the last third of the nineteenth
century is less picturesque than in the earlier decades. Life
became more elaborate. Riches accumulated. Railroads and
factories and the Republican Party began to have their
effect. Social and economic life became complex, even
sophisticated after its own fashion. Yet the old emphases
are still clearly discernible. They echoed and reechoed
down through these more complacent times.

Shakespeare, as he was played in the thirties and forties
in the frontier theatre, furnished Mark Twain with incidents for *Huckleberry Finn*. The 'Duke' and the 'King'
whom Huck befriends and takes on his river-raft include,
among ways of making their daily bread, the playing of
the balcony scene from *Romeo and Juliet* and the sword
fight from *Richard III*. The playbills in their bulging
carpet-bags are caricatures of the actual playbills. 'Garrick the Younger of Drury Lane London' is still a drawing
card. They propose to perform in a 'little one-horse town,
in a big bend' in 'Arkansaw'. They advertise one night
only 'on account of imperative European engagements'.
They rehearse the Hamlet soliloquy in the traditional
style; in 'a noble attitude, with one leg shoved forwards
and his arms stretched away up . . . he begins to rip and
rave and grit his teeth'. Everything as it really was in the
River Shakespeare of the 1830's is here. But it is recorded
by a successful author, who utilizes his youthful memories

as a Mississippi River pilot to entertain the effete East of
1884 at the very height of the 'Gilded Age'.

The wheel has come full circle. Pioneering has become
parlor entertainment. The roguery and toughness of frontier days have been translated into heroic legend. Mark
Twain, whose very pen-name came from the 'call of the
leadsman, on river boats when a depth of two fathoms was
sounded', scrambles his Shakespearean lines in the best
burlesque manner. The Hamlet 'soliloquy', a page long,
rejoices in such sequences as

> Ope not thy ponderous and marble jaws

from *Romeo and Juliet*, placed next to

> But get thee to a nunnery—go!

from *Hamlet*. It has the same kind of humour that Shakespeare's travesties had in the mining camps of the late
fifties. This liberty with royalty, this twisting of the lion's
tail, tacitly admits the royalty and leonine greatness behind the prank. But it marks a new stage in American cultural development. The old crudities are now recollected
in the tranquillity of a more settled and more affluent
world.

The America of the seventies felt its pioneer origins
strongly. When the J. Q. A. Ward statue of Shakespeare
was dedicated in Central Park, New York City, in the
spring of 1872, Bayard Taylor wrote a poem on the occasion. It is a very indifferent poem, but it shows how
clearly they knew that Shakespeare had companioned the
frontier phases of American development:

He [Shakespeare] came, a household ghost we could not
   ban,
He sat on winter nights by cabin fires.

As late as 1909, Professor Samuel Eliot of Smith College still found Shakespeare a magical source of entertainment to the cowpunchers of south central Arizona. He would recite passages, especially from *Macbeth*, around the camp-fire in the desert with the stark mountains of the horizon as a back-drop. For his courtesy and his pains, the cow-punchers named him 'Bill Shakespeare'.

The attempt to assign Shakespeare's plays to Bacon still persisted. It is paradoxical that America, founded on belief in the common man, should have been so loth to grant creative genius to a common man of Stratford and should instead try to substitute a gentleman of birth, education and title like Francis Bacon. It was the same paradox which has haunted our 'democracy' throughout its whole career. No one loves 'pomp and circumstance' so much as those who have never had it. Nineteenth century America did dearly love a Lord. The publication in 1888 of *The Great Cryptogram* by Ignatius Donnelly was a brave attempt to prove 'by an ingenious cipher that Bacon wrote Shakespeare'.

This Ignatius Donnelly was a person of flamboyant episodes. He must have thought that he could reckon on the 'spectacular' nature of *The Great Cryptogram* to sell it. He was a first generation American, son of an Irish physician. He chose, in turn, all the spectacular ways that America then offered of getting up in the world. He 'read law'. He went West in the 'boom' and crashed in the panic of 1857. He won a seat in Congress. When he was defeated in 1877, he turned to writing and lecturing as the next best way of selling himself to the American public. There was enough general interest in Shakespeare to make a book on him a good gamble. Ignatius Donnelly took the chance. That he failed, is no argument against the popu-

HENRY CLAY FOLGER, donor of the Folger Shakespeare Library in Washington, D. C., greatest modern monument to the genius of Shakespeare.

larity of Shakespearean topics with the American reader.

The social position and importance of the Shakespearean actor continued. Actors still, as in Hackett's day, invaded the realms of Shakespearean scholarship and their conclusions were treated with respect. Edwin Booth, in 1877–78, under the title of *The Prompt Books,* published his stage arrangements of fifteen of Shakespeare's plays with notes, stage-business, and comment on interpretation. These were given serious consideration by Furness in making his Variorum edition.

Emerson's passionate Shakespearean enthusiasm of the fifties reaches down through Henry Clay Folger to the greatest modern monument to the genius of Shakespeare. It is the Folger Shakespeare Library, given by the Folgers to the nation in 1932 and housed in an exquisite building in Washington. Dr. Joseph Q. Adams, the distinguished director of that Library, has written a history of Folger's collection, published for the trustees of Amherst College in 1933. Adams records Folger's enthusiasm when, as a senior at Amherst, he heard Emerson lecture there. The subject of the lecture was not Shakespeare; but Folger, inspired by this great personality, began to read Emerson. He discovered a printed version of his address on Shakespeare for the Saturday Club of Boston in 1864. 'Emerson's glowing eulogy of Shakespeare as the world's outstanding genius fired young Folger's imagination and sent him at once to a thorough study.' Adams recounts Folger's purchase of Routledge's 'Handy-Volume' edition in thirteen volumes. This was the beginning of an interest which, pursued with skill and the liberal expenditure of a fortune throughout his lifetime, has made Henry Clay Folger's Shakespearean collection the most valuable in the world. The continuation of purchases for the Library under the judgement and finesse of Dr. Adams is keeping the Folger Library well in the lead of all Shakespearean collections. Emerson's Shakespearean enthusiasm has, through Henry Clay Folger, borne glorious, tangible fruits.

Shakespeare in the schools and colleges reached a peak of importance at the end of the nineteenth century. His prestige on the stage was greater than ever. The productions grew more and more elaborate. The same elements of acting persisted, though they were handled with more sophistication. English stars were still a social attraction. Performances like Sir Herbert Tree's *Henry VIII*, in which a portion of Westminster Abbey was elaborately reproduced, marked the peak of physical and material homage to Shakespeare. The productions cost outrageously but the audiences, who came in white kid gloves, needed not one effort of their imagination to perceive what the play was about. It was all there before them in stained glass and stucco columns, in velvet and gold lace. They had only to pay extravagantly at the box office and sit passively through the performance. This state of affairs suited the temper of the times. 'Business', everywhere rampant, scooped up the theatre as one more sure outlet for its shrewd game of getting rich out of the American public.

The turn of the century marked something new. In 1906 President Neilson of Smith College, then Professor of English at Harvard, brought out his one-volume 'Cambridge Shakespeare'. A new historical sense, the combination of scientific textual study with literary judgment, went into the making of Neilson's text. It became 'the most scholarly one-volume American edition'. The same text, issued in a play to a volume, under the title of the

Tudor Shakespeare, followed. The editor chosen by Dr. Neilson for each volume was a scholar of distinction. As a group they represented a wide range of America geographically. They were, as A. H. Thorndike pointed out to a British audience in 1927, an evidence 'of cooperative enterprises [on Shakespeare] far more extensive than any which have yet been undertaken'. The Neilson text, still preeminently sound and sensitive, is now in the process of revision for a new edition by Dr. Neilson, assisted by Professor Charles J. Hill.

On the stage, too, after the twentieth century came in and especially since the Great War, Shakespeare has offered something new. Literalness in costume and setting are banished. No producer cares to have Shakespeare's lines carpeted and cushioned to reproduce the palaces and battlefields of which he wrote. We are, for the moment, through with photographic reproduction. The result in Shakespeare has been, not only the bravado of the 'modern dress' performances but the deliberate 'jumbling' of centuries. English Gielgud's *Hamlet* presented a play of one century in a costume and setting of a hundred years later. Orson Welles' *Julius Caesar* was played against the bricks and radiator pipes of the actual backstage walls. Two ways of thinking, distinctly characteristic of our present world, are responsible for these changes. The first is a keener sense of the Shakespearean age. We know now and act upon the knowledge that Shakespeare's plays were produced with a minimum of scenery and stage illusion. If they were written to be played that way, they should still be played that way. We perceive, too, that the poetry and perception in Shakespeare's lines must not be smothered by literal setting. Those lines were cunningly devised to evoke from the audience a contributing share toward the realization of the situation. *Papier-maché* and rhinestones must not interfere with the joint imaginative venture.

So our own time looks at Shakespeare and sees its own reflection in his pages. Probably the twentieth century Shakespeare is no more 'right' than Garrick's or Kean's, or than the ranting versions of our growing frontier. We cannot be expected to believe this, for we suffer from the blindness of being in the midst of our own time. We are sure that our predilections are not predilections but the ultimate verities. Yet when the history of Shakespeare in America is carried on after another hundred years, some one will be pointing to Gielgud and Orson Welles and Maurice Evans and seeing in the emphases of their productions the characteristic limitations and foibles which made up the spirit of our age.

Ben Jonson wrote more truly than he knew when he described Shakespeare as 'not for an Age but for all time'. He will survive each separate time, inviolate and indestructible. But he yields, too, to the manipulation, the 'form and pressure' of each succeeding era, and, in the process, turns himself into the most delicate barometer of social and cultural history.

Index

Abbott Academy, Andover, 234
Abbott, Jacob, 235
Adams, Abigail, 91, 92-94
Adams, John, 85; quotes *Macbeth*, 86; quotes *Merry Wives*, 86-88; quotes *Troilus and Cressida*, 89-90; visits Stratford, 90-91
Adams, John Quincy, 149-150, 160, 164-167, 193, 234, 278, 279
Adams, Joseph Quincy, 238, 295, 303-304
Alcott, Bronson, 263-266, 282
Amherst College, 242-243
Aristotle, 8, 127
Arvin, Newton, 270
Astor, John Jacob, 140, 209

Bacon, Delia, 296, 299
Bacon, Francis, 296, 302
Bailey, Ebenezer, 235
Ball, Samuel, books in library of, 29
Bancroft, George, 193
Beecher, Henry Ward, 191-193, 200
Berkeley, Edmund, 30, 221
Blair, Hugh, 224-225, 240
Booth, Edwin, 212, 256, 303
Booth, Junius Brutus, 153, 193, 210, 211, 212, 268
Boston University, 290
Boswell, James, 172
Bowdler, Thomas, 288-289
Bradford, William, 14
Brewster, William, 15
Brockmeyer, H. C., 263
Brooks, Van Wyck, 192-193
Brown University, 239, 288
Bruce, Philip A., 28
Buchanan, McKean, 214
Burgoyne, Gen. John, 119-120
Byrd, William, probable owner of a Shakespeare Folio, 31-32
Byron, Lord, 152

Cabot, James E., 252.
Caldwell, James H., 201, 202
Carlyle, Thomas, 250, 297
'Carter, King', library of, 30, 32
Channing, William Ellery, on Juliet, 157-158
Chapman, Caroline, 203, 211, 212
Chapman, William, Jr., 203, 211, 212
Chapman, William, Sr., 202-203, 204
Chauncy, Elnathan, 20
Child, Francis James, 246-247
Chiswell, Richard, 22-23
Cibber, Colley, 67, 70
Colcord, Lincoln, 6
Coleridge, Samuel Taylor, 127, 143, 149, 158, 164, 250, 257
Collier, J. P., 293
Columbia University, 224, 247, 289
Conkling, Roscoe, 216
Cooper, Thomas A., 148-149, 150, 180, 185
Cornell University, 243, 247
Corson, Hiram, 247
Cotton, John, 19, 20
Cotton, Seaborn, 20-21
Craik, G. L., 244
Cushman, Charlotte, 169

Dana, Richard Henry, *Two Years Before the Mast*, 6-7
Dartmouth College, 239, 288
Davenant, Sir William, 30
Dennie, Joseph, 128
Dickinson, John, 102-103
Donnelly, Ignatius, 302
Douglass, David, 40-42, 44-45, 60-63, 77-79, 82, 83
Drake, Dr. Daniel, 194
Duff, Mary Ann, 153
Dunlap, William, 63, 115, 128
Dunster, Pres. Henry, 220-221
Dunton, John, 22

307

310   INDEX

119, 151, 153, 157, 159, 170, 171,
172, 176, 180, 187, 189-190, 200,
201, 211, 213, 268, 275, 280, 281,
286, 300
Romeo and Juliet, 51, 61, 69, 76-77,
78, 79, 83, 147, 149, 157, 169, 170,
172, 184, 187, 190, 198, 300-301
Taming of the Shrew, altered by
Garrick to *Katherine and Petru-
chio*, 67, 79, 117, 118, 155, 179,
180
Tempest, 67, 82, 83, 104, 105
Troilus and Cressida, 89-90, 97
Twelfth Night, 286
Venus and Adonis, 20
Winter's Tale, 67
Shepard, Odell, 263-264
Sheridan, Richard Brinsley, 227
Sheridan, Thomas, 227
Siddons, Mrs., 93-94, 156
Simon, H. W., 219, 247
Smith, Sol, 177, 186-188, 190, 195,
197, 200-201
Smith, Rev. William, 241-242, 245
Spencer, Hazelton, 39
Spicer, Capt. Arthur, *Macbeth* in li-
brary of, 29-30
Stagg, Charles and Mary, 46
Stoddard, P. W., 251
Sumner, Charles, 237

Tarbell, Ida, 281
Taylor, Bayard, 301
Theatres, American, described: Alabama (Mobile), 179; California
(San Francisco), 208, 209, 210-
213; Georgia, 177; Illinois (Chicago), 182; Kentucky, 178; Louisiana (New Orleans), 183-184;
Massachusetts (Boston), 139,
141; Missouri (St. Louis), 183-
184; New York, 58-59, 61-62, 63-
64, 114-119, 139-140, 142, 153;
North Carolina (Greenville),
186; Ohio (Cincinnati), 180-181;
Pennsylvania (Philadelphia), 40-
41, 60, 62-63, 139-141, 152-153;
(Pittsburgh), 181-182; South Carolina (Charleston), 170; Texas
(Houston) 189-190; Virginia
(Williamsburg), 54-55

Thomas, Isaiah, 108-109
Thoreau, Henry David, 249, 251-
252, 260-263, 266, 282
Thorndike, Ashley, 203-204, 305
Ticknor, George, 259
Tilden, S. J., 216
Traubel, Horace, 267
Tree, Ellen, 190
Tree, Sir Herbert Beerbohm, 304
Trollope, Mrs., 137
Trumbull, John, 101
Twain, Mark, 300

Union College, 239, 288
Upton, Robert, 57, 72
Usher, John, 22-23

Vail, H. H., 230-231
Verplanck, G. C., 289, 292
Virginia, University of, 247
Voltaire, 145

Walker, John, 234
Ward, J. Q. A., 301
Washington, George, 99, 103, 170;
owns a Shakespeare, 104; quotes
Tempest, 104; witnesses *Hamlet*,
Tempest, 105; Shakespearean pri-
vate theatricals, 106
Webster, Daniel, 153, 156, 192
Welles, Orson, 305
Wemyss, Francis Courtney, 181-182
Westfall, Dr. Alfred, 289
White, Andrew Dickson, 243, 247
White, Richard Grant, 131, 289, 292-
294
Whipple, Edwin P., 256-257
Whitman, Walt, 131, 249, 262, 266-
274, 282
William and Mary College, 241
Willis, Eola, 48
Willoughby, E. E., 25, 29-30
Wilson, J. Dover, 166
Winsor, Justin, 25
Winthrop, John, 14
Wood, W. B., and Warren, Wm.,
171
Wormeley, Col. Ralph, books in li-
brary of, 28
Wright, L. B., 30
Wright, T. G., 21

Yale College, 221, 224, 243, 288